THE TIMES
GUIDE TO EASTERN EUROPE

The contributors

Keith Sword, the general editor, is Research Fellow at the School of Slavonic and East European Studies (SSEES), University of London, with a special interest in Poland and Polish-Soviet relations.

This book includes contributions from

Dr Jonathan Aves, SSEES, University of London
Mr Marko Bojcun
Professor Richard Crampton, Rutherford College, University of Kent
Mr Denis Deletant, SSEES, University of London
Mr Jim Dingley, SSEES, University of London
Mr Anton Logoreci
Dr Martin McCauley, SSEES, University of London
Mr Stevan Pavlowitch, University of Southampton
Mr George Schöpflin, SSEES, University of London
Ms Kersti Uibo

Publisher's note

As this book goes to press, after one of the most remarkable years in modern European history, the publishers would like to express their appreciation to all the contributors for their extraordinary energy, judgement and enthusiasm in this project. Against a constantly shifting background of political change, this book attempts to present a considered assessment of the history and development of the nations of central and eastern Europe from the end of World War II up to June 1990. What has already happened may be recorded as history. What may happen in the immediate future, as many of these nations begin a new era in their histories, is impossible to predict. But whatever may occur can only be understood in the broader historical and social context which this book seeks to provide.

It should be noted that any opinions expressed in this book are those of the editor and the contributors.

The publishers would also like to thank Professor Norman Davies, of SSEES, Mr George Brock, Foreign Editor of *The Times*, Mr Charles Wilson, former Editor, and Mr Simon Jenkins, Editor of *The Times* for their support, advice and encouragement.

THE ✦ TIMES
GUIDE TO EASTERN EUROPE

THE CHANGING FACE OF THE WARSAW PACT
A Comprehensive Handbook
EDITED by KEITH SWORD

TIMES BOOKS

First published by Times Books,
16 Golden Square
London W1R 4BN

© Times Books, London 1990
British Library Cataloguing in Publication Data
The Times Guide to Eastern Europe: the changing face of the Warsaw Pact.
1. Warsaw Pact countries, history
I. Sword, Keith
909.09717

ISBN 0-7230-0348-3

Typeset by
Rowland Phototypesetting Limited,
Bury St Edmunds, Suffolk

Printed in Great Britain by
Richard Clay Limited,
Bungay, Suffolk

CONTENTS

INTRODUCTION   7

PART 1: EASTERN EUROPE

1 ALBANIA:
Continuing Stalin's legacy   36

2 BULGARIA:
Cautious reform and emerging nationalism   43

3 CZECHOSLOVAKIA:
The velvet revolution   53

4 THE GERMAN DEMOCRATIC REPUBLIC (EAST GERMANY):
The people's revolution   71

5 HUNGARY:
From Kádárism to democracy   92

6 POLAND:
A step-by-step revolution   109

7 ROMANIA:
A reign of terror – then ethnic unrest   125

8 YUGOSLAVIA:
First and (almost) last to change   144

PART 2: THE SOVIET UNION

9 AN OVERVIEW:
From dogmatism to uncertainty   167

10 RUSSIA:
The elder brother   182

11 THE BALTIC STATES:
Struggles for sovereignty   194

12 BYELORUSSIA:
Change on the way – but not yet   214

13 UKRAINE:
The issue of national self-determination   224

14 MOLDAVIA:

Reform and reunion   237

APPENDICES

1: The Warsaw Pact, 1955   244
2: Charter of the Council for Mutual Economic Assistance (COMECON), 1959   246
3: Postwar Summit meetings   247
4: The Helsinki Conference, 1973–75   248
5: Economic statistics   251
6: Eastern Europe after the First World War   252
7: European economic and defensive blocs   254
8: Nations and languages of Eastern Europe   255
9: Nationalities in the USSR   256
10: Pollution in Europe   257
11: 1990 election results   258
12: Useful addresses   260

INDEX   262

INTRODUCTION

The 1989 revolutions

The momentous changes that swept across the Communist states of the Soviet bloc during the latter half of 1989 have altered the political map of Europe. By throwing off the shackles of Communist rule in Poland, Hungary, Czechoslovakia, East Germany, Romania and Bulgaria the peoples of east-central Europe removed an artificial division of the continent which had existed for over a generation. The world was treated to the sight of the most potent symbol of this division – the Berlin Wall – being breached and then dismantled, amid emotional scenes.

The revolutions represented a drive for the kind of freedoms which we in the West take for granted but were previously denied to those under Communist rule in these states: the right to freedom of expression and association; to participate in and influence the political process; to a culture and mass media free from political control; to feel that their state is sovereign and free of the daily outside pressures and influences that had come from Moscow; to a decent standard of living (comparable to that enjoyed by their Western European cousins); and to clean air and water, to avert the ecological calamity which threatens in many areas.

The magnitude and the unexpectedness of the political earthquake are difficult to capture in words, although journalists have been vying with one another in reaching for hyperbole. 1989 has already been compared with the two other years in this century when the political face of Europe was radically altered – 1918 and 1945. The similarities are limited, though. The changes in both 1918 and 1945 came about as the result of world wars, at a time when the exhausted world was looking towards long periods of peace and recovery. They were also the result of conferences of the Great Powers at Versailles (1919) and Yalta and Potsdam (1945).

The events of 1989, by contrast, were not precipitated by major conflict, nor were they imposed by decree. They were the result of an irresistible pressure for reform and change on the part of people who had for too long endured the drabness, stifling restrictions, arbitrariness, untruths and economic shortages of Communist rule. The irony did not escape journalists and commentators that the six-month period of change and upheaval was preceded in July 1989 by the bicentenary celebrations of the French Revolution. Future historians may indeed, as *The Times* leader writer suggested at the end of the year, prefer to compare the events of 1989 with the storming of the Bastille, or perhaps with 'the Springtime of Nations' – the revolutions which swept Europe in 1848.

The upheavals were not restricted to Communist regimes outside Soviet borders. Within the Soviet Union we have also seen the growing momentum of support for democracy, local autonomy and even secession from the Soviet Union. The Baltic States – Estonia, Latvia and Lithuania – have been the most outspoken, protesting loudly against their forced incorporation into the Union during the Stalinist years. (We should not forget that 1989 also marked the 50th anniversary of the Hitler–Stalin Pact which led soon afterwards to the Soviet takeover of the Baltic states.) Similar voices calling for an end to one-party rule and greater self-determination have been raised in Transcaucasia, Ukraine and Georgia.

The aim of this book is to review the changes that have taken place in recent months in Eastern Europe, to explain both how Communist rule was introduced or imposed and how the structures of Communist rule have been, or are being, dismantled.

The geography of Eastern Europe

For the purposes of this book 'Eastern Europe' is taken as being the large area which lies east of a line from Lübeck to Trieste and is bordered by the Ural and Caucasus Mountains. We include, therefore, those central and southern European states which came under Soviet influence at the end of World War II, and also the European republics of the Soviet Union. This may lead to some confusion. We all suffer from the peculiar optical illusion that decades of Cold War have fostered. Accordingly, the expression 'Eastern Europe' has commonly been used to refer to the arc of Soviet satellite states established after World War II between the Baltic and the Black Sea. (Yugoslavia and Albania, which were never subject to Moscow, are sometimes referred to as being in 'Eastern Europe', more often as belonging to the Balkan region or 'southern Europe'.) It refers to what should, in a purely geographical sense, be central Europe. Prague, often during the interwar years taken as being at the heart of Europe, is almost equidistant from Madrid and Moscow. (Though it should not be forgotten that the Urals are almost 900 miles further east than Moscow.) Many people forget that Vienna is further east than Prague or Zagreb, that Athens is further east than Warsaw, Budapest and Belgrade. The terms 'central Europe' and 'east-central Europe' are increasingly used as attention is directed to the political events between the Soviet border and the states of the European Community.

The Ural Mountains are commonly taken by geographers as marking the Europe's eastern perimeter, but some readers may feel that this is a somewhat artificial boundary in political terms. After all, even if the USSR is on the point of breaking up into its constituent parts as many observers are predicting, the Russian Federative Republic stretches far beyond the Urals – indeed to Vladivostok. There is some validity in such objections, and this book discusses the Russian Republic as a whole. Yet what are the alternatives? Drawing a line at the present Soviet frontier and excluding all present Soviet territory from 'Europe' does not allow for the prospect that the Baltic states, Ukraine and Byelorussia may eventually find themselves freed from Moscow rule. Conversely, to have included all Soviet territory within the scope of this book would have been too great an undertaking, although we have attempted to locate events in the western republics within the wider context of all-Union structures. As it is, Transcaucasia and the Soviet Muslim Republics are discussed only in passing.

The region we are referring to as eastern Europe covers an area of 5.5 million square kilometres and contains some 330 million inhabitants. However, there are great differences between the various states and republics. Poland is the most populous state outside the Soviet frontier with a population of 37 million, which contrasts with Albania's 3 million. Within the Soviet frontier differences are even more pronounced; the Ukrainian SSR has 52 million inhabitants, compared with tiny Estonia's 1.5 million. In spatial terms, Poland is ten times the size of Albania, and more than twice the size of Czechoslovakia or Hungary. But the neighbouring Ukrainian Republic, apart from dwarfing the Baltic States in size, is more than twice the area of Poland.

The differences in ethnic and religious terms are also marked. While many of the minority problems that plagued the region in the interwar period have disappeared, most still have a residue of minorities. Few are as homogeneous in ethnic and religious terms as Poland; but at the other extreme there is Yugoslavia, with its ethnic complex jigsaw of Albanians, Serbs, Croats, Slovenes, Macedonians and others. In religion, too, there is a diversity. The Poles, Lithuanians, Byelorussians, Czechs and Hungarians are predominantly Roman Catholic; Latvia and Estonia are mainly Protestant, although a considerable number are found in Czechoslovakia; Bulgaria, Romania and Ukraine are mainly Orthodox, while Yugoslavia and Albania are mixed.

The dawning of the Communist age

The world's first successful Communist revolution took place in Russia in 1917. The Bolsheviks' 'October Revolution' came as something of a surprise even to most Marxists, since Russia was a relatively backward country economically. Marx had always believed that revolution would occur first in the industrially advanced states. It was the industrial working class – the proletariat – which he thought would be the vanguard of social upheaval and change. During the early days the success of the Bolshevik faction led by Lenin was by no means a foregone conclusion. Indeed, at one time the Bolsheviks believed that only a Communist revolution in the West could guarantee the success of their movement. But similar attempts at this time to create soviet regimes – that of Bela Kun in Hungary or the Soviet Republic declared in Bavaria in 1919 – were shortlived. At home, the

'Reds' faced strong opposition and had to fight a lengthy and bloody civil war before emerging triumphant.

As they consolidated their revolutionary success the Bolsheviks grew in confidence and believed, far from seeking help from the West, that revolution could be exported to the rest of Europe – on the bayonets of the Red Army. Drawn into a war with the resurgent Polish state, Soviet forces were able to reach the approaches to Warsaw in 1920 before being driven back and routed by the Polish army. This defeat persuaded the Bolshevik leadership to concentrate on consolidating their power nearer to home. Although the Bolsheviks were heirs to the vast, multinational empire of the Tsars, it took them several years to reconquer and reabsorb a number of the outlying republics which had tasted independence and had developed along nationalist lines. Soviet Russia became transformed into the USSR (Union of Soviet Socialist Republics) only following acceptance of the 1923 Constitution.

Communist Russia was treated with suspicion by the international community and remained isolated during the early years of its existence (although further Communist states in Central Asia or the Far East, such as the Mongolian People's Republic, were established under Soviet protection). Russia had not been a party to the Versailles treaty, although the 27 signatories included the unlikely names of Honduras and Liberia. The USSR ceased to be an international leper in the late 1920s, when Western states began to give the USSR grudging recognition. In the meantime, however, Soviet Russia had found common cause with Germany – which felt similarly ostracized following its defeat in World War I and believed that it had been unfairly punished at the Versailles Conference. German–Soviet co-operation in the military–industrial sphere was extensive during the 1920s and was suspended only when Hitler came to power.

For a number of years the Nazis' open hostility towards Communism made co-operation impossible. Then, in a remarkable reversal of policy (which dismayed his Italian and Japanese allies), Hitler agreed to a new understanding with the Soviet leader, Stalin. The Nazi–Soviet Non-Aggression Pact of August 1939 resulted from the Soviet leader's belief, on the one hand, that the Western powers (Britain and France) were not serious about opposing Hitler's expansionist aims. They were offering Moscow nothing except the prospect of becoming engaged in a costly war. Stalin considered that rather than oppose Hitler, it would be better to go along with him, especially as Hitler was making extremely attractive offers of territorial gains. The Nazi–Soviet Non-Aggression Pact was, in fact, a misnomer; it was a blueprint for aggression, but against weaker third states. Following Hitler's attack on Poland and the outbreak of war, a new division of Europe into 'spheres of influence' took place. It brought the Soviet Union during 1939–40 half of Poland, the Baltic states, and some parts of eastern Romania.

When in the summer of 1941 Hitler turned his armies east to attack his former ally, the Soviet Union was plunged unexpectedly into a desperate struggle for survival. The earlier alliance with Hitler was expunged from the national memory as all resources were mobilized for the defeat of Nazism. Soviet war casualties were huge (over 20 million dead) and the country suffered enormous material losses during what came to be known as the 'Great Patriotic War'. Immediately Hitler attacked, the Soviet leadership found itself allied with Nazi Germany's existing enemies, notably Britain and, subsequently, the USA. The wartime alliance of the Big Three Powers was born.

The Great Power Conferences

The postwar division of Europe can be traced back to the Great Power conferences (particularly those at Teheran in November 1943 and at Yalta, in the Crimea, in February 1945) which took place in the closing stages of the war. The Western Allies in the anti-Nazi coalition were eager to pave the way for a postwar world in which there would be an end to rivalry or squabbling about borders. Western policymakers realized after the Soviet victories of Kursk and Stalingrad that the defeat of Germany was inevitable. They saw, moreover, that the Red Army would liberate most areas of east-central Europe from German occupation. Faced with this inevitability, Churchill and Roosevelt attempted to meet with Stalin at an early stage to agree on the principles of postwar reconstruction.

The crucial role that the Red Army was playing on the eastern front (engaging two thirds of the German Army), and the security concerns of the Soviet regime (attacked from the west for the second time within twenty years) were in the forefront of people's minds. The Americans wanted (at Yalta) to engage the Soviets in the war against Japan. There was also a desire on the part of the USA and Britain to ensure that Stalin, who had been drawn out of his isolation and had made a favourable impression on Churchill and Roosevelt, remain a partner and take a full role in the ordering of the postwar world. Consequently, there was a readiness to make concessions to Stalin and smooth over any points of conflict.

In late October 1944 Churchill had put to Stalin the famous 'percentages agreement' concerning the relative influence of the Great Powers in south-central European countries expected to be liberated by the Red Army's advance. The Soviets were to have a 90% interest in Romania, 75% in Bulgaria and 50% in Hungary and Yugoslavia. In return, the British were ceded a 90% interest in Greece. Significantly, Stalin kept his word on Greece, even though it had a strong Communist movement. (Indeed, once this movement was defeated, thousands of Greek Communists sought refuge, and eventually settled, in the new 'people's democracies' of central Europe.)

At Teheran Churchill made the proposal to Stalin that Poland should be moved bodily westward, forfeiting almost half of its prewar territory and losing major centres of Polish culture such as Wilno (Vilnius) and Lwow. In return, Poland would be compensated at Germany's expense. Stalin accepted this proposal. But he also seized the Baltic states (to the disquiet of the Western allies, who refused to recognize their absorption into the Soviet Union), Bessarabia and northern Bukowina from Romania, and part of Czechoslovakia. In fact, Stalin reclaimed nearly all the territory he had occupied during 1939 and 1940 as a result of his Pact with Hitler. Two results flowed from this. The first was that Poland, having lost almost half its territory in the east, was compensated in the west at the expense of Germany. A large strip of territory from the Baltic coast to Silesia became Polish, including towns such as Stettin (Szczecin) and Breslau (Wrocław). Millions of German inhabitants were expelled to make way for Poles being 'repatriated' from the Soviet-occupied eastern regions of the country. The second was that after 1945 the Soviet Union had a common border with Hungary and Czechoslovakia. This was to have considerable significance in 1956 and 1968.

At Yalta the Declaration on Liberated Europe which was drafted by American officials and signed by the Big Three was couched in fairly elastic language, but it did include the undertaking that the Polish authorities would hold 'free and unfettered elections' once hostilities had ceased and a civilian administration had been restored to the country. (The assumption was that the exiled governments which had taken refuge in London and other centres would be free to return and head temporary administrations.) In retrospect, it may seem surprising that Stalin, whose experience of holding democratic elections was limited and whose track record abysmal, should have been trusted with such a task. The 'plebiscite' carried out in Soviet-occupied Poland during October 1939 had been a travesty. The 'elections' in the Baltic States during the summer of 1940 were similarly fraudulent. These abuses of power had been brought to the attention of Western politicians and policymakers. Might not, then, provision have been made for international supervision of the elections, as happened in Greece? The answer seems to be that Western politicians did not want to risk Stalin's wrath by suggesting such a course.

It is doubtful, though, whether the Western allies fully understood what Stalin conceived by the term 'influence'. Stalin's comments from his wartime conversations with the Yugoslav Communist Milovan Djilas have often been quoted, but were not known at the time. (Stalin said that this war was not like past wars; in this war whoever occupies a territory imposes his own system.) In the beginning there was little to arouse the fears of Western politicians, although Churchill had been alerted by the Soviets' cynical failure to support the Warsaw Rising. When, in the late summer of 1944, the Red Army were approaching Warsaw an insurrection had been launched by the underground Polish Home Army. The hope of pro-London Poles was that they would be able to liberate their capital and welcome the Soviets as masters in their own house. But the Red Army halted on the eastern bank of the Vistula, and watched as the Germans slowly extinguished the last remnants of resistance. In some sixty days of fighting, a quarter of a million Poles died.

The takeover of east-central Europe

The Communist takeover of east-central Europe between 1944 and 1948 – the imposition of one-party rule – took place by stages. The first was that of military occupation by the Red Army. With the Soviet forces stalled outside Warsaw in the summer of 1944 the offensive moved to the south. Bucharest fell on 31 August 1944. On 5 September Moscow declared war on Bulgaria and the Red Army crossed the Danube. On 19 October Soviet troops were established in Debrecen in eastern Hungary. Only in January 1945 was Warsaw eventually taken, and Soviet troops crossed into Czechoslovakia in March of the same year. The Soviets were sufficiently subtle not to install Communist regimes at the outset. But everywhere (except Yugoslavia, where Tito's partisans took control, and Albania, which was beyond the reach of Soviet units) the Red Army was able to install 'its' people in the local administration and to eliminate (for 'collaboration' or any other charge which could be trumped up) potential opponents.

The second stage of the takeover was marked by the establishment of provisional coalition governments, with the participation of both Communist and non-Communist representatives. The aim of these 'national fronts' or 'popular fronts' was, in all cases, the same: to create administrations which contained members of the prewar parties, including those who had returned from exile, and by so doing to allay Western suspicions. The Communists had, at best, marginal influence in most of these states before the war and were given a role which, in importance, far exceeded their support. They were helped by the outlawing, agreed in the Yalta accords, of parties which were 'fascist' or had 'collaborated' with the Germans. Thus, in Poland the right-wing National Democratic Party, one of the strongest before the war, was not allowed a part in government. Similarly, in Czechoslovakia, the Agrarian Party, which had commanded widespread support before 1938, was excluded because of the collaboration of some of its members.

The third stage involved propaganda and terror. In all cases the Communists took control of key ministries such as Justice, Internal Affairs or Security, and Defence. This put them in an ideal position to use the NKVD-trained security and intelligence forces to break the back of democratic opposition and cloak their actions in legality. Many members of resistance groups which had fought the Germans but were not Communist controlled were arrested (in Poland thousands were deported to the Soviet Union). Skilled use was also made of propaganda. This – especially using posters and slogans – had developed as an art form since the earliest days of the Revolution, and had proved very effective, especially among the poorer, less-educated sections of the population. The Communists habitually made lavish promises, whether or not they were able to carry them out. At the same time, they poured abuse on the enemies of 'progress'. As Communist control of the mass media grew, the population became increasingly subject to the Party's line on all matters. Communist ideological censorship was more severe than that imposed during the German occupation.

The fourth stage involved 'salami tactics' to undermine their enemies, by subversion, intrigue and bribery. Communist support varied widely (from 17% in Hungary to 38% in Czechoslovakia), but in all cases they were in a minority in government. They overcame this obstacle by a number of means. In some cases an opposition party could be divided, by turning its leaders against one another. Some were invited to amalgamate or be absorbed. Others faced competition from a bogus rival party which bore a similar name and policies. They watched helpless as their confused supporters were drawn away. In the case of yet others, their leaders and officials were denounced or arrested. By such means the Communists managed to weaken and destroy many of their opponents.

The fifth stage involved the elections themselves. Although the 1946 elections in Czechoslovakia were fairly conducted, those in Poland and Hungary during 1947 were not. In the case of Poland, Stalin was probably convinced that the Poles were such irreconcilable enemies, there was little point in beating about the bush. The final stage involved the further settling of accounts with political opponents once political power had been consolidated.

In asking why the Communists were successful we have to recognize a number of characteristics, in addition to skilful use of propaganda and terror, mentioned above. They were, on the whole, better organized than their democratic opponents. During this period the Party apparatus was highly centralized and extremely disciplined. Many activists had been indoctrinated in the Soviet Union and had a firm grasp of Stalinist methods of seizing power and maintaining control. They planned to take power, and were not merely content to participate in the democratic process. They did not trust improvization or anything so quixotic as a free election. They were ruthless and unscrupulous in the methods they used to achieve their aims. Also, they were prepared to hide or camouflage their real aims from the electorate. All in all, they were playing the political game to a different set of rules from their opponents, who were, in any case, often divided among themselves.

Far from coming out of his shell, as Western policymakers had hoped he would do, Stalin was creating a further barrier – or 'cordon sanitaire' – behind which to hide. Indeed, if, between the wars and as a result of the Versailles settlement, the newly independent stages of central Europe had provided the West with a protective barrier against the contagion of Bolshevism, after World War II, they gave the USSR a security shield behind which it could recover and arm itself.

Hopes that the 'Big Three' alliance would last beyond the war were disappointed. As senior Foreign Office official Sir Frank Roberts observed with some humour, the British and the Americans thought that if only they treated Stalin like a member of the 'club' he might possibly start behaving like one – by joining the United Nations and playing a responsible part in the postwar structure. 'But Stalin did not want to be a member of that club. He much preferred to be the Director General of his own club, which was quite a different club, and which he would not have had us in either.'

The onset of the Cold War

Historians are divided about when the Cold War actually began. Some choose March 1946, when Churchill attempted to draw the world's (and particularly the American public's) attention to what was happening in east-central Europe. Churchill had been awarded an honorary degree by a small American liberal arts college at Fulton, Missouri. His acceptance speech, delivered in the presence of President Truman, echoed around the world. An 'iron curtain', said Churchill, had descended across Europe from Stettin in the Baltic to Trieste in the Adriatic. Behind it the Communist parties which were previously very small had 'been raised to a pre-eminence and power far beyond their numbers' and were seeking everywhere to obtain totalitarian control. They constituted 'a growing challenge and peril to civilization'.

Churchill, who had been in opposition since the July 1945 General Election, went on to say that he did not believe that Soviet Russia wanted war. What it desired was the fruits of war and the indefinite expansion of its power and doctrines. The West could not close its eyes to the danger, he maintained; there was a need for a 'special relationship' between the USA and Britain to counter the threat of Communist expansion. Churchill had used the term 'iron curtain' before. As early as August 1945 he had mentioned it in a parliamentary speech, when referring to the expulsions of Germans from Poland. But after the Fulton address the term entered into popular usage and became part of the vocabulary of the Cold War.

In fact it was not until 1947 that the pattern of events in east-central Europe became clearer, first with faked elections in Poland and Hungary and then with a campaign of terror against opposition politicians (directed particularly against peasant leaders in Hungary, Bulgaria, Romania and Poland). The year also saw the creation of the Communist Information Bureau, the 'Cominform'. By the end of 1947 the division of Europe was clearer. The Communists were no longer hiding behind coalition governments, but had in most states taken absolute control, had outlawed the opposition and were hounding them.

The West began to respond to Churchill's warnings about Communist expansion during 1947. In March of that year the American President outlined what came to be known as the *Truman Doctrine*. The USA would not abandon those states which sought to avoid coming under Communist domination. Washington would help such countries to retain their freedom and independence. This policy of 'containing' Communist expansion was later superseded under the Eisenhower administration by a more aggressive design to 'roll back' Communism.

The European Recovery Programme, or *Marshall Plan* (named after the US Secretary of State, George Marshall), was also brought to life during 1947. This was a move to extend economic aid to rebuild Europe's war-shattered economies, a condition being that the Europeans agreed to economic co-operation ($12 billion dollars was sent to Europe between 1947 and 1951). The Soviet government abruptly rejected such help, but the Polish and Czech governments at first welcomed the Plan. Only after Soviet pressure was exerted did they, too, withdraw from it. By the time the first Marshall Plan conference began in Paris on 9 July, with the participation of fourteen nations, Romania, Yugoslavia and Finland had also withdrawn.

The Soviet response was the *Zhdanov Doctrine*. A. A. Zhdanov was an associate of Stalin's who expounded his theory of the 'two camps' to delegates at the founding session of the Cominform in Polish Silesia in September 1947. According to Zhdanov's vision, the world was divided into opposing camps – the 'imperialist', 'anti-democratic' camp (headed by the USA) and the 'socialist', 'anti-imperialist', 'democratic' camp led by the USSR. The speech was couched in extremely aggressive terminology, and was intended to provide a justification for the sovietization of east-central Europe.

If 1947 marked the rupture of the wartime alliance, it is 1948 which is usually taken as marking the onset of the Cold War. This is partly because of the 1948 Berlin blockade and airlift, when the superpowers confronted each other directly, no longer via proxies, and the confrontation threatened to develop into something more than verbal sparring.

Following the defeat of Nazi Germany, Germany had been divided into four occupation zones, to be administered by the victorious Allied powers: the USA, Britain, France and the Soviet Union. (Poles often claim that although they fought from the first day of the war to the last, they were not rewarded with a share in the occupation. But Poland, the Allies could argue, got more than mere supervision of German territory, it 'swallowed' its area of Germany.) The Soviet zone accounted for only one-third of postwar Germany, but it included the prewar capital, Berlin. The Allies had agreed at the Potsdam Conference (July 1945) that they would create a unitary but disarmed German state, and that Berlin would remain under four-power control – itself divided into zones. When moves to fuse the Western zones were eventually taken in 1947, and currency reform was effected in the West without Soviet agreement or participation, the scene was set for a showdown. The Soviets retaliated in June 1948 by cutting

Western road and rail traffic in the 'corridors' which crossed Soviet-occupied territory to the capital. By severing the West's links with its zones of the German capital the Soviets hoped to starve the inhabitants into submission – or at least force the West into a humiliating climbdown. They were foiled by a massive airlift of supplies along the air corridor into Berlin – which had not been blocked – and Stalin eventually (in May 1949) backed down.

This huge operation demonstrated the West's determination not to be prised out its foothold in Berlin, but, more importantly, it showed Stalin that he could no longer expect to get his own way quite as easily as he had during the wartime alliance. Subsequently, the demarcation line with the Eastern, Soviet, zone became virtually a state border. (The German Democratic Republic – East Germany – became *de jure* an independent state from 1949, with its own parliament and decision to frame a constitution. In 1955 it joined the Warsaw Pact.)

In February 1948 Czechoslovakia became the last of the states on the Soviet western border to fall to the Communists. By contrast with Poland, the Communist takeover occurred without any Soviet troops present on Czechoslovak soil (though they returned with a vengeance in 1968). However, Czechoslovakia had what Poland lacked, a strong basis of Communist support. Coincidentally, at the same time that Communist rule was being consolidated in Czechoslovakia, to the south Tito was declaring his independence of Moscow and arousing Stalin's fury. This caused the first split in the Soviet bloc, and reaffirmed Stalin's fears that freedom to follow the national 'deviationist' line would make for untrustworthy, unreliable partners. Hostility grew between the two Communist parties. Consideration was given by Moscow to military intervention, but in the end the USSR reluctantly allowed Tito to go his own way.

The consolidation of Communist rule

The twin blows to Stalin's ambitions that occurred during 1948 (defeat in the Berlin confrontation and Tito's defection) were added to by the signing of the Atlantic Pact in Washington during July. These events served only to increase Stalin's paranoia, and moves began to consolidate Communist rule in the satellite states and to weld them into a political bloc. In the economic sphere, industrialization was pushed forward and central planning bodies set up. Tighter censorship was imposed, and a greater cultural and artistic conformity demanded. Increasing pressure was exerted on the Church. In December 1948 the Hungarian Roman Catholic primate, Cardinal Mindszenty, was arrested and later imprisoned. The Polish primate, Cardinal Wyszyński, met the same fate in 1950. Church property was confiscated and church charitable organizations wound up or taken over by the state. Actions of this nature prompted the Pope to issue a declaration that members of the Communist Party and its sympathizers would be excommunicated.

The use of secret police to eliminate political opponents was soon directed inwards towards the ranks of the Party itself. In June 1949 the Hungarian Interior and Foreign Affairs minister, Laszlo Rajk, was arrested, together with seventeen other people. He was accused to having had contact with American intelligence before the war, of being a Gestapo agent during the war, and of having spied for Yugoslavia since the war – a colourful and damning inventory of misdemeanours. He was sentenced to death along with two of his 'co-conspirators'. The Rajk affair set the tone for a series of Party purges over the next few years. (The next took place in Bulgaria during December 1949 and ended with the hanging of former deputy premier, Trajcho Kostov.) The lesson ostensibly being taught was one of constant vigilance against the enemies of socialism. But the real message was one of absolute conformity; that deviation from Moscow's line would not be tolerated.

Czechoslovakia managed to avoid such extreme measures for rather longer than its neighbours, but eventually had to submit to Moscow's prompting. This country was an important piece in the jigsaw, one of the most highly industrial regions in the Eastern bloc, and had to be secured for socialism. When the purges did come they were ruthless and extensive. Almost 10,000 people were in prison for political offences in the Czech lands alone at the end of 1950, and more than 16,000 arrested over the next two years by the state security forces. In the four years to the end of 1952 almost 200 people were executed. The best-known victim of these purges was Rudolf Slánský, Party general secretary, who was arrested and put on trial along with thirteen other people for 'Trotskyist, Titoist, Zionist, bourgeois-nationalist treason'. (The anti-semitic character of these trials has been seen by some historians as a legacy of Moscow's failure to transform the infant state of Israel into a left-wing, pro-Moscow outpost in the Mediterranean.) At the end of 1952 Slánský and ten other people received the death sentence.

In January 1949 the Communist world's trade organization, the *Commission for Mutual Economic Aid* – known as Comecon or CMEA – was called into being in Moscow. Six nations (the USSR, Poland, Czechoslovakia, Romania, Hungary and Bulgaria) took part in its early meetings, although Albania joined later in the same year. The forming of Comecon was regarded by most observers as the Soviet answer to the Marshall Plan. While violently hostile to the Americans' initiative, the Soviets had not hitherto been able to respond with any positive moves of their own. Although Soviet-bloc spokesmen denied that this was the case, the communiqué which announced Comecon explicitly stated that 'broader economic co-operation between the peoples of the people's democracies and the Soviet Union' was being planned, because 'these countries do not consider it possible to subordinate themselves to the dictates of the Marshall Plan, as this plan infringes on the sovereignty of countries and the interests of their national economies'.

The aims of Comecon, as outlined in the communiqué, were to 'exchange economic experience', to extend technical aid and encourage trade between the member states. Its stated political aims were to 'strengthen the unity and solidarity of members' and encourage co-operation 'in the interest of the building of socialism and communism'. The initial setting up of Comecon seems to have been more for propaganda purposes than for anything else. The Organization remained virtually inactive until 1954, when its Secretariat was created, and only in December 1959 – more than ten years after the announcement of its formation – was the Charter of the Organization signed in Sofia. Gradually, more began to be achieved in co-ordinating five-year national economic plans, in encouraging specialization and co-operation of production (particularly in chemicals and engineering). But much of this co-ordination was done on a bilateral basis. Although Comecon was created as an organization of equals, one was more equal than others; the Organization was dominated by the Soviet Union. Soviet personnel took most of the top positions, and the secretariats were eventually concentrated in Moscow. In the early days, at least, the Organization served Soviet economic, as well as political, interests.

The fusing of the Soviet bloc nations in a military alliance did not take place until 1955, when the *Warsaw Treaty Organization* (better known as the *Warsaw Pact*) was created. As with Comecon, its creation was largely a response to events in the West; the creation of West European Union in the previous year and the inclusion of the newly created German Federal Republic in the North Atlantic Alliance, which the Treaty saw as 'increasing the danger of a new war and creating a threat to the security of peace-loving states . . .'. The Treaty provided for consultation on military and defence matters and for assistance to be offered to a member state in the event of an armed attack. It specified 'armed attack in Europe', and therefore, by implication, did not oblige any intervention by Eastern bloc countries should the Soviet Union become embroiled in a conflict in Central Asia or the Far East. (Perhaps ignorant of this or else sceptical that it would be observed, many citizens of the Warsaw Pact states were nervous during the Afghanistan conflict about the possibility of 'allied contingents' being sent to fight the mujahaddin.)

Western analysts have suggested that the formation of the Warsaw Pact was an early Soviet gambit to bring about the dismantling of NATO and the withdrawal of American troops from Europe – on a *quid pro quo* basis. Indeed, the proposal to liquidate both organizations – NATO and the Warsaw Pact – which has been revived recently by Gorbachev was first made at the 1955 Geneva summit meeting.

The Pact had a useful effect, from the Soviet viewpoint, of 'locking in' the member states to Moscow. The prospect of a rearmed Germany so soon after the war, and before memories of the ravages of Nazi occupation had subsided, was frightening to Germany's neighbours in east-central

Europe, who had suffered so terribly at its hands in the past. It was put to excellent propaganda use by Moscow, which was then able to represent itself as defending the true interests and freedom of these peoples. This was effective with the Poles, especially, who, despite a traditional suspicion of the Russians, feared that growing German economic strength and military power would be accompanied by attempts to reclaim their eastern territories acquired by Poland in 1945. True, East Germany had signed a treaty with Poland in 1950 confirming the inviolability of the new border. West German opinion had remained hostile and felt that the Communists did not have the right to sign in the name of the German nation.

In addition to the USSR, seven countries signed the Warsaw Treaty – Poland, Czechoslovakia, East Germany, Hungary, Romania, Bulgaria and Albania. Yugoslavia never became a member following the split with Moscow in 1948; indeed, it signed the Balkan Pact with Greece and Turkey during 1954. But some of those that did join showed a great deal of unease with the Pact. During the course of the 1956 Hungarian uprising the government of Imre Nagy stated its intention to leave the Organization. Naturally, with the suppression of the Rising, such moves were foiled. Romania too was early in adopting a cautious attitude to the Treaty, although it avoided a complete break. From 1962 onwards it allowed no Warsaw Pact troops on its soil for 'joint manoeuvres'. Albania withdrew from the Organization in 1968, shortly after the invasion of Czechoslovakia. Since it is completely surrounded on the land side by Yugoslav and Greek territory, the Albanian regime presumably felt safe from the intervention of Warsaw Pact tanks!

Soviet justifications for the creation of the Eastern bloc pacts – that they were reacting to developments in the West – ignore the reasons why the Cold War began; the aggressive methods undertaken by Moscow, especially during the Stalinist period, to enforce Communist rule on its Western neighbours.

The nature of Communist rule

The regimes which came into power in east-central Europe after 1945 called themselves 'people's republics' or 'socialist democracies'. In fact they were neither socialist in the accepted Western sense of the word nor were they democracies, since they did not allow for free choice in competitive elections. Nor were the regimes in any way the choice of the people. Misuse of such terms and misinformation about the true nature of conditions obtaining under Communist rule have been characteristic of Communist regimes.

The emerging Communist states did have a number of things in common. The first is that they were all buttressed by an official ideology – Marxism or Marxism–Leninism. This had three important elements which adherents found attractive: it provided a 'scientific' interpretation of history in class terms; it explained that the victory of the proletariat and the triumph of Communist rule was logical and inevitable; finally, it presented a vision of a more egalitarian society, with the elimination of poverty and exploitation. The concept of 'building socialism', the society of tomorrow, was portrayed as a thoroughly worthy and progressive exercise. Social engineering on a wide scale was used to further the interests of the workers (for example, preferential selection for university education for their children).

Marxism provided the moral and theoretical justification for Communist Party rule in the name of the working classes. Once this foundation stone of Party rule had been set in place any challenge to the arrangement – even from within the working class itself – could be branded 'reactionary' or 'counter-revolutionary'. The Communists' claims to be bringing social justice and an end to extremes of wealth and poverty were powerful moral arguments, and beguiled sections of the electorate in many of the states concerned, not to mention more credulous groups in the West. Increasingly, as corruption, abuses of power and stark inequalities under Communist rule became evident the ideological underpinning became frayed and then completely discredited.

The second characteristic was the introduction of single-party rule. Although other parties were tolerated throughout the period, these were 'fellow-travelling' parties which were completely subservient to the Communists. Party control was extended outwards and downwards by means of the *nomenklatura*, Party nominees selected for key posts in all areas of public life – from the economy and local government to the media and the diplomatic service. It was also an invaluable source of political patronage. Over a period of time the Communist Party tended to develop into an elite caste. Indeed, the Polish former dissident, Adam Michnik, compared the division between Party and people to the apartheid system in South Africa. The Party, he suggested, was the white community. Privileges such as special shops, better housing and jobs, and easier foreign travel existed for members. This, however, had a deleterious long-term effect on Party morale and discipline. It attracted careerists, those who were not ideologically motivated but merely wished to share the benefits of Party membership.

The economic systems introduced into east-central Europe were modelled on the Soviet type; that is, the market relationship between consumer and producer was largely removed. As large areas of the economy were drawn into public ownership a large bureaucracy came into being to cope with economic management. Consumer wants or demands became largely an irrelevance, as the state increasingly determined what should be produced, allocated the necessary resources and set targets. Typically, this meant large investment in the extractive industries, in engineering and heavy industry at the cost of living standards. Heavy and wasteful use of labour, raw materials and energy produced early results, but by the 1970s (if not earlier), the Communist economies were looking decidedly unwieldy. Central planning meant lack of initiative and innovation. The incentives which in the West led to the development of new ideas and entrepreneurship were missing, since not only was the profit motive distrusted but the road to advancement was blocked by Party appointees.

The result all too frequently was empty shops and queues for basic necessities. Stalin's successor, Nikita Khrushchev, once boasted during a visit to the USA that the Soviet economy would be turned to service the needs of its consumers and would outstrip the West, but no significant improvement in the supply of consumer items took place.

The Polish attempt to reverse the downward trend under Edward Gierek's regime in the 1970s involved the large-scale import of Western technology and investment. The rush for growth failed because the structures which would have enabled it to work were not in place. The whole system needed reform, as has been belatedly realized.

Communist economic systems almost everywhere failed in terms of the efficiency and the standards of living achieved under the successful market economies. It is true that in their early stages they took steps towards a more egalitarian system by attempting to eliminate most traces of absolute poverty; true also that massive state subsidies kept prices artificially low. But the end result was negative, and could be seen at its worst in Poland and the Soviet Union. Currencies which were not convertible and had little purchasing value led to a black market in dollars. The empty shops, queues and absence of much-sought Western consumer items has resulted in black market trade, speculation and hoarding. The government 'bought off' elite groups of workers by allocating them a greater flow of resources together with higher pay, special shops and other privileges.

The fourth characteristic that the postwar Communist regimes shared was elimination of civil society. 'Civil society' is a term used by historians and political scientists to describe the change that took place when societies emerged from the feudal era. Using the term in this context draws an interesting parallel between the tendency of both feudal and Communist systems to exert control over all aspects of an individual's life. In a totalitarian society, as Václav Havel has argued, the state aims not only to control all areas of political and economic life, it is suspicious of all forms of social organization which do not come under its aegis – be they angling clubs or scouting groups. It reduces and atomizes society, and at the extreme treats its subject people as prisoners or slaves, denying them the right to independent thought, action, association.

Fifthly, Communists everywhere worked to achieve a monopoly on the supply of news and information to the public. At the outset, this helped them to gain and consolidate power. In later years, it aided in concealing the shortcomings of their policies. The Party-controlled censorship became an important part of the power structure, creating a further bureacracy with well-paid posts for the *nomenklatura*. The censors' painstaking attention to detail can be illustrated by reference to the Black Book of the Polish Censor, an instruction manual smuggled out to Sweden in 1977 and since published in the West. The importance the regimes attached to preserving this news monopoly can be deduced by the persistence with which they jammed Western radio stations such as the BBC, Voice of America, and Radio Free Europe. The London assassination of .nalist, Georgi Markov (widely attributed to the Bulgarian secret police), and the death sentence passed by the Polish Government *in absentia* on RFE head, Zdzisław Najder (in May 1983), are further evidence of the damage done to the domestic propaganda efforts of the Communists.

Further characteristics which the regimes shared were their lack of legitimacy and accountability. The power they wielded had been achieved illegally and retained by force, or the threat of force. They did not rule with the authority and legitimation that comes with political consensus. The absence of democratic procedures meant that mistakes could be concealed or, at the very worst, a member of the *nomenklatura* could be replaced by another Party nominee. True, at the top, where the buck stopped, some degree of accountability was evident, as indeed it had to be. Once other scapegoats had been exhausted, government or Party leaders (in Communist systems there is little difference between them; the same people often fill posts in both the government and the Party's Politburo) could be replaced when popular discontent reached the level of demonstrations and strikes. But the Party monolith remained in place. 'Change' meant a shuffling of the leadership pack and the ritual, token sacrifice of a disgraced member.

How the web began to unravel

What were the factors which led to the break-up of Soviet hegemony over east-central Europe? Much has been written about the 'changing of the guard' in the Kremlin, of the passing away of the gerontocracy which had maintained a hold on power for so long. Certainly the new Party leader, Mikhail Gorbachev, who came to power in 1985, represented a new generation – one for whom the days of the Red Army's triumphs during World War II were scarcely more than a childhood memory. But from his early policy statements there was little to suggest that we would see the far-reaching transformation which has occurred, both in East–West relations and in those between Moscow and its central European satellites.

It seems clear that the radical change in policy leading to the Soviet disengagement from central Europe was not just a spontaneous process. Influences of an almost irresistible nature on the Kremlin leadership forced a reassessment of traditional policies and relationships. These influences or pressures came from three areas; pressure for change from within central Europe itself, pressures due to developments in Moscow's relationship with the West, and domestic Soviet policy considerations.

The nations of east-central Europe did not submit happily to Communist rule and became increasingly turbulent over the four postwar decades. Protests and unrest were apparent from an early stage. The first major upheaval of any consequence occurred in East Germany in June 1953 – shortly following the death of Stalin. Strikes and demonstrations broke out throughout the country and were put down savagely by police, who shot at demonstrators in Berlin. In 1956 came the Polish October – this following Khrushchev's denunciation of Stalin at the Soviet Party's Twentieth Congress. Mass strikes and demonstrations occurred in Poznań, following which workers stormed the headquarters of the Party and the security police. Over fifty people were killed in putting the unrest down, but it had the effect of returning Władysław Gomułka to power. The Polish events were followed by the Rising in Hungary, during which Nagy declared not only Hungary's withdrawal from the Warsaw Pact but also the introduction of a multi-party system. This revolt against the twin principles of Communist one-party rule and alliance with Moscow was put down by Soviet tanks.

Strikes and demonstrations were not the only means by which subject peoples, deprived of recourse to the ballot box, could make their dissatisfaction known. Many took the chance to vote with their feet, despite the bureaucratic and financial restrictions on travel abroad. Large numbers of East Germans were able to abandon Communism in this way, by travelling to Berlin and passing over to the Western sectors of the city. By the end of the 1950s this route had become so popular it was becoming an embarrassment to the Communist authorities – an estimated 20,000 people a month were flooding across. On the night of 12/13 August 1961, barbed wire was put up along the boundary between Soviet and Western sectors, to be replaced within days by a more substantial structure – the Berlin Wall.

The Wall became a symbol of the postwar division of Europe – and of Communist repression. It illustrated in stark form the lost freedoms of the people who lived behind it. Many Germans were henceforth cut off from their families and friends across the border, and only in the 1970s did the restrictions on cross-border contacts ease. The flood of refugees was reduced to a trickle – those brave, hardy, and sometimes ingenious souls, who were prepared to risk death in challenging the Wall's defences. The erection of the Wall and the storm of international protest which resulted detracted somewhat from the propaganda value of Yuri Gagarin's first manned space flight, which took place during the same year.

A mere seven years later, the Czechoslovak Communist Party made a courageous attempt to reform the system from within. Without going quite as far as Nagy had gone in Hungary – there were no plans to abolish one-party rule – the Prague leadership under Dubček hoped to make state socialism more tolerable, to give it a 'human face'. The intervention by Warsaw Pact troops and tanks was a further disastrous move in political terms for the Kremlin. It harmed East–West relations, increased Warsaw

Pact members' suspicion of the Organization, and undermined Moscow's standing with previously sympathetic leftist groups in the West.

No sooner had the Prague Spring been nipped in the bud, then unrest broke out again, this time along Poland's Baltic coast. Strikes and demonstrations resulted in repressive police action and the shooting of dozens of workers. Popular discontent led to a change of leadership – Gomułka was replaced by Edward Gierek. The 'recurrent crises' which afflicted the Communist regime in Poland struck more tellingly ten years later, though, when Gierek himself fell from power. The rise of the Solidarity trade union under Lech Wałęsa's leadership proved the most serious threat to Soviet control of the region, and the most difficult to put down, precisely because it clearly had such huge public support (10 million members).

The introduction of martial law in December 1981 removed the need for Soviet tanks to intervene directly, but it presented the world with the unlikely spectacle of 'proletarian rule' being maintained following a military coup – a coup directed, moreover, against the very industrial working class whose interests the Party was supposed to be representing! The vision of Poland, the largest of Moscow's central European satellites, being ruled during the 1980s by a South American-style military junta forced the Soviet leadership to rethink its policy in the region. The line of states that had been acquired by Stalin in the 1940s to provide a 'cordon sanitaire' and a zone of stability had itself become unstable – and therefore a liability. Furthermore, the trade costs of maintaining the defensive cordon had become prohibitive. Moscow was selling its partners valuable supplies of oil below world prices in return for poor-quality manufactured goods.

Developments in East–West relations were also important in influencing Soviet policy towards Central Europe. One of the early moves to defuse tensions was the reorientation of West German foreign policy towards rapprochement with Eastern Europe. This 'Ostpolitik' was set in motion as early as 1966 under Chancellor Kurt Kiesinger, but flourished under his successor, Willy Brandt, with whom it is now chiefly associated. It resulted in the signing in Warsaw (in 1970) of a treaty by which the Federal Republic recognized Poland's western borders, removing fears of German revanchism. (Similar treaties were later signed with Czechoslovakia, Bulgaria, Hungary and East Germany.) Earlier, a visit by Brandt to Moscow had resulted in the signing of a Treaty on the mutual renunciation of force in relations between states. This led to closer ties with Moscow and helped convince the Soviet leadership that Germany was no longer a threat in military terms.

Brandt's Ostpolitik led to the process of East–West détente in the 1970s. It paved the way for a thaw in relations between East Germany and the Federal Republic, but, more significantly, led to the Helsinki Conference on Security and Co-operation in Europe (CSCE). An important aspect of the Helsinki talks was that for the first time all the European states (with the exception of Albania) and the North Americans participated as equals. There had been no general peace treaty at the end of World War II – only the Great Power conferences which had 'imposed' the postwar settlement. Some influential Western voices were critical of the subjection of central Europe to Moscow rule and even called for the Yalta accords to be revised. So the main aim of the Soviet side, which was the instigator of the Helsinki talks, was to secure general recognition of Europe's postwar frontiers. Indeed, it was a desperate attempt to guarantee the stability of the existing structures, given the growing threat to security, not so much from the West's military or economic power but from within Eastern Europe itself, from the inherent instability of the Soviet satellites.

The Helsinki talks were divided into three 'baskets': confidence-building measures of a mainly military kind, economic co-operation, and the third 'basket' on security and human rights. The Soviets were persuaded to recognize that international security was not just something that could be determined by governments sitting around a table. They were shown that the causes of insecurity were inherent in the Soviet system. The security of states was inextricably linked with the security of individuals. In order to encourage security and stability it was necessary to foster internal order – an order which could only be guaranteed by reference to human rights. Soviet policymakers were forced to recognize that the stifling of the aspirations of its citizens was a greater threat to stability than NATO tanks.

By signing the Helsinki Final Act, Moscow acknowledged the linkage between co-operation in other spheres and the observance of certain standards in the treatment of its citizens. It had effectively forfeited (though was slow in realizing it) the excuse that human rights violations were 'an internal matter', and was henceforth denied recourse to the argument that principles of non-intervention in the domestic affairs of a sovereign state should apply. The determination of the West to monitor human rights abuses gave the impetus to indigenous dissident groups to carry out their own monitoring process. Groups came into existence both in central Europe (KOR in Poland, Charter 77 in Czechoslovakia) and in the USSR. The Helsinki talks revealed the need for continuing East–West dialogue, and so the Helsinki process was born. A series of meetings took place such as those on disarmament at Madrid (1983), Stockholm (1984–6), and Vienna (1986–9).

In the USA, however, right-wing critics of détente saw it as a form of appeasement and, unwilling to treat the Soviets as an equal, rejected the concept of military balance or parity with the USSR. The Soviet invasion of Afghanistan led to the collapse of détente and the return to a Cold War atmosphere in the last years of the Brezhnev period. This, in turn, resulted in a renewal of the arms race. In President Ronald Reagan the Kremlin found a leader who was firm and prepared to confront the Soviet leadership. He was ready to increase US military spending, and forcefully backed the 'Star Wars' programme (to develop a satellite-borne umbrella of laser weapons to counter Soviet ballistic missiles). Soviet attempts to drive a wedge between the Americans and their European allies (for example, the campaign to prevent dispersal in Europe of Cruise missiles) failed.

If increased military spending was creating imbalance for the US budget, it was making the economic pips squeak in Moscow, which was banned from receiving advanced technology and found it almost impossible to increase the burden of military spending. (Western experts estimate that the USSR was spending twice as much proportionately to maintain its position in the arms race as the USA.) The war in Afghanistan constituted a further drain on the resources and the international standing of the Soviet Union. Further east, the Chinese Communists had introduced limited economic reforms and were achieving impressive 9% annual growth rates throughout the decade. Not only was Japan now an economic superpower, but the nations of the Pacific Rim, with their market economies, were making commendable efforts to emulate it. It was against this background that the Soviet leadership looked to the West, saw the impressive moves towards economic and political union made by the West European states and their prosperity, and realized that greater hope for stability lay in courting, rather than confronting, their West European neighbours.

From this the principles that have characterized Soviet policy in the closing years of the decade developed; liberalization at home, rejection of the arms race and rapprochement with the West, enunciation of the concept of the 'Common European home', and, in regard to the central European satellites, rejection of the Brezhnev Doctrine in favour of the so-called 'Sinatra Doctrine' ('let them do it their way').

How and why change came

In both Hungary and Poland change began earlier and was altogether more gradual and less dramatic than elsewhere. In Hungary the ousting of Kádár as early as May 1988 signalled the beginning of a more open political discussion between Party and opposition elements. The elevation of reform-minded Imre Pozsgay to the Politburo forced the pace of reform from within the Party. In the early months of 1989 the Party made repeated concessions to an opposition movement headed by the Democratic Forum, until the way was eventually cleared for a multi-party democracy. The Hungarian Party reshaped itself in preparation for elections in the spring of 1990. In Poland, too, the first concrete moves took place in the autumn of 1988, with attempts by the Jaruzelski regime to reach an accommodation with the Solidarity opposition. Solidarity representatives were invited to round-table talks, which took place in the spring of 1989. These led to the 'partly free' elections in June and to the appointment of the first non-Communist premier of a Warsaw Pact state.

During this period the eyes of analysts were repeatedly turned to

Moscow. How far would the Soviet leadership permit the liberalization in their vassal states to go? Could it be taken as far as real democracy and possible divorce from Moscow? In the central European capitals the message had been received early that the Soviets were prepared for a liberalization and a loosening of ties. Gorbachev made his views clear during two key speeches in July 1989 – one to the Council of Europe in Strasbourg and the other at the Warsaw Pact summit in Bucharest. In Bucharest, the Soviet leader stressed to his allies his rejection of the Brezhnev Doctrine; there was no set model for the building of socialism. Each Communist party had the right to pursue its own strategy in line with national conditions. Henceforth, he hoped there would be 'unity in diversity' – a looser, more pluralistic alliance of equals.

At Strasbourg, Gorbachev signalled his desire to 'consign to the archives the postulates of the Cold War, when Europe was regarded as an arena of confrontation'. In a final break with the doctrine of interventionism, he stated,

> The affiliation of the states of Europe to different social systems is a reality, and the recognition of that historical state of affairs, respect for the sovereign right of every people to choose a social system as it sees fit, is a vital prerequisite for the normal European process. The social and political orders of one country or another changed in the past and may change in the future as well. However, that is exclusively the affair of the peoples themselves, a matter for their choice. Any interference in internal affairs, any attempts to limit the sovereignty of states, both of friends and allies, no matter whose it is, is impermissible.

While Gorbachev gave the green light to change it is unlikely that even he realized how rapidly change would come.

In August and September of 1989 (28 years after the erection of the Berlin Wall) waves of East Germans began once more to exercise their choice of political order. East German 'tourists' flooded to the West via Hungary, Czechoslovakia and the West German embassy in Poland. This outflow – heading, of course, for the Federal Republic – was an acute embarrassment for the state, which had perhaps the most successful economy in the socialist bloc. Not least embarrassing was the fact that its neighbours and allies (no doubt with an eye on relations with the Federal Republic) were not prepared to lift a finger to stop the migrants. The refugee exodus was followed by mass demonstrations in East German cities against the leadership, which led in October to the resignation of Party leader, Erich Honecker, in favour of a younger colleague, Egon Krenz. The reforms which Krenz introduced brought no relief for the leadership. The demonstrations continued, the ultimate goal now, it was clear, being the complete removal of the Communists from power. On 7

November the government resigned, to be followed a day later by the whole Politburo. On 9 November the Berlin Wall was breached by the authorities, by which time some 200,000 East Germans (1% of the population) had left the country. Krenz himself was eventually forced to resign in early December, after only 49 days in office.

On the day after the Berlin Wall was breached, Bulgarian leader Todor Zhivkov was toppled by Party colleagues. The 78-year-old leader had been the longest serving in central Europe (he had come to power seven years before the Berlin Wall was erected in 1961). Zhivkov precipitated his own downfall when his despotic policies to 'Bulgarianize' the country's Muslim community resulted in a mass exodus across the Turkish border. This, in turn, had led to severe problems for the Bulgarian economy, and to Zhivkov's replacement by Petur Mladenov.

Within days, the Czechoslovak regime capitulated. Hitherto defiant and resolute in its determination to retain socialist policies, the Prague leadership overreacted to student demonstrations in the capital on 17 November. The police violence (now widely believed to have been instigated by a faction inside the secret police apparat, and not the leadership) caused outrage and led to further demonstrations, which grew in support and spread to other towns. The Party's hold on power was loosened by the end of the month and was finally shaken off completely in early December.

Finally, the dramatic and bloody events in Romania erupted in the days before Christmas 1989. The rule of the Romanian leader Nicolae Ceauşescu – labelled the 'Balkan Caligula' in a *Times* leader – had been harsh, even by Communist standards. He had treated the country as his personal fiefdom and ruled with his family like a true despot. The arrest of a Hungarian pastor in Timişoara provoked demonstrations which were put down by the security forces with great bloodshed. The protests moved to the nation's capital and gathered strength when the army refused to shoot at demonstrators. Ceauşescu's attempt to flee failed, and he was executed with his wife after a summary trial.

What came as the greatest surprise to onlookers was the speed with which the old structures of power collapsed. Their frailty surprised even those opposition elements responsible for their downfall. The movement for change and reform seemed to gather its own irresistible momentum. Once it began, and not without justification, observers began to refer to the 'domino theory' working in reverse. (The 'domino theory' was formulated during the 1960s to account for the predicted collapse of neighbouring states in South-east Asia to Communist rule.)

Why did the regimes collapse so quickly in central Europe? It is difficult to generalize. But we can say first, that the states that fell to Communism after World War II, while having far from lengthy traditions of democracy, lacked the almost unbroken tradition of absolutism that the Russians had inherited from Tsarist rule. In their philosophical, religious, cultural and political traditions they identified more closely with the West. We can also refer to the collapse of belief in Marxist ideology (and therefore in the future it promised), the economic failures, the removal of the threat of force (both domestic and external). The Soviet policy of greater openness – *glasnost* – also had an effect. It encouraged re-examination of the past and a questioning of Party legitimacy. Finally, there was the 'behaviourist' policy adopted by the West. The system of financial rewards or incentives offered as aid but linked to progress in liberalization.

In the aftermath of revolutions

Whereas the second half of 1989 saw the toppling of Communist regimes in much of central Europe, in the first half of 1990 there was a consolidation of the reforms that had been set in motion. The interim governments that had been formed immediately set about the task of removing the 'left luggage' of Communist rule. First to go were the most obvious legacies – street names, statues, emblems, and other icons. Also jettisoned was the out-moded and discredited terminology of state socialism. The term 'People's Republic' was abandoned and many states reverted to their prewar titles, becoming once again simple republics. Other steps were to take a more gradual course; the weeding out of the Party *nomenklatura*, the winding up or reforming of the security police, the removal of censorship, the seizure of Party assets and property and, importantly, moves towards free elections and economic reform. Work has also begun on some of the new constitutions which will serve the peoples of central Europe during the post-Communist era.

The most significant events to take place in the first half of 1990 were the elections in East Germany, Hungary, Romania, Czechoslovakia and Bulgaria – the first democratic, multi-party elections to be held in the region for more than four decades. In Yugoslavia elections were also held in the northern republics of Croatia and Slovenia. (Poland, a notable absentee from the list, held local elections during May, but is unlikely to have a further general election before its new Constitution is ready in the spring of 1991.) The elections did not pass without surprises. In East Germany they brought the unexpected victory of the conservative alliance led by the CDU over the Social Democrats. In Romania and Bulgaria, they provided controversial, but convincing victories for former Communists. (Indeed, even in Czechoslovakia, where Civic Forum won resoundingly, the Communists fared better than expected with 13% of the vote.) One major test of the latter new democracies will be the readiness of opposition forces to come to terms with the results of the elections – monitored in both cases by international observers. Another will be the degree of commitment on the part of the new leaders to democratic forms and how determined they are not to slip back into an authoritarian style of rule.

One feature common to all the states emerging from the dark night of Communism is the way in which the ghosts of the past have come back to haunt the new leaders. Once the euphoria of unseating the Communists had faded, the thoughts of some began to turn to revealing, possibly with retribution in mind, those who had collaborated with the previous regime, or had acted as informers. Smear tactics – accusing political rivals of complicity with the Communists – were used in more than one election campaign. Many accusations have also been made about the clandestine destruction of secret police files. Some crucial decisions lie ahead about whether the files that remain should be kept under lock and key, or destroyed, or released into the public domain.

On the economic front there have been moves throughout the region to end central planning and introduce market mechanisms to slash spending on the defence, armaments and security forces. Steps are being taken to remove state subsidies, to privatize state-owned concerns and to encourage foreign investment. Many states are making efforts to balance budgets and strengthen currencies in anticipation of full convertibility. During the period of upheaval, and later, as democratic rule was being consolidated, promises of aid arrived thick and fast from governments in the West (including the Japanese) and international organizations. In the USA an initial offering of $145 million in aid to Poland and Hungary in July 1989 rapidly expanded into a Senate Bill promising aid of $2.75 billion to seven central European states by the end of 1992. The European Community agreed to the formation of a new European Bank for Economic Reconstruction – to be located in London – which will channel Community development funds to east and central Europe. In early June, following pressure from exporters and from Western governments, COCOM restrictions on the export of advanced technology goods to the Soviet Union and central Europe were relaxed.

Western firms have been quick to see the possibilities of these emerging economies – and of the sizeable potential market they represent. The result, as controls have been lifted, has been the establishment of scores of 'joint ventures' between Western firms and partners in central Europe. It is by no means certain though that east-central Europe will prove to be the dynamic, thrusting economic force that Japan was in the 1960s and 1970s and the countries of the Pacific Rim have proved to be in the 1980s. Economic forecasts for the region vary widely from 'gloomy' (a report by the UN Economic Commission for Europe published in April 1990) to those which foresee a possible boom (Economic Commission). The reality is likely to be considerably more complex, with significant divergences in economic performance between individual states. East Germany, with the rapid moves being made towards political and economic union with the Federal Republic in the course of 1990, is widely tipped to prosper, despite the many problems that reunification entails. Hungary and Czechoslovakia too have attracted considerable interest from investors. If there is a question mark over Poland, it is because of uncertainty as to whether the drastic medicine which the Solidarity-led government administered in January 1990 will take effect in revitalizing the economy. There is further doubt about the average Pole's readiness to tolerate indefinitely the austerity these measures have brought. Political stability, of course, is a major factor in determining where foreign investment will be directed. But there is the further problem in all the new democracies of changing attitudes to work and developing the skills necessary to run a market economy. It will not be easy to develop an entrepreneurial culture rapidly in societies where private trade has been frowned on for decades as 'speculation'.

The collapse of Communist rule in central Europe has also led to questioning about the future of the bloc alliances. Since the Soviet bloc treaties (Comecon and the Warsaw Pact) were formed primarily not as an association of equals, but to bind the satellite states to Moscow, the Kremlin's 'unleashing' of its former subjects has reduced the need for them. Steps have been taken to reform Comecon with Poland, Czechoslovakia and Hungary eager for change. Bilateral trade between the member states will now be conducted in hard currencies, rather than the dubious 'convertible rouble'. The ultimate goal of many of the states is membership of the European Community – and a number have been accorded associate status – but full membership will remain unpracticable until their economies have recovered sufficiently to enable them to compete on equal terms. Several of the newly independent states have already joined, or are applying for membership of, organizations such as the IMF and OECD.

There remain considerable doubts about the future of the Warsaw Pact – indeed, doubts as to whether it has any future at all. As progress is made towards German reunification it is clear that the Pact has lost one member – East Germany. Hungary too has made plain its desire to leave, determined it seems to carry out a step first declared in 1956. Throughout central Europe steps are being taken to reduce the burden of military expenditure which Warsaw Pact membership entailed, and to remove Soviet garrisons. Faced with the imminent collapse of the organization, the Soviet leadership was forced to commit itself to a radical overhaul at a Pact summit in June 1990. Henceforth the Warsaw Treaty Organization will become a political body, rather than a military alliance. It will also be more democratic than in the past, and less secretive.

German reunification has occupied the thoughts of policymakers of both East and West during 1990. Concern in Western Europe that this new 80 million strong superstate will dominate the European Community economically have been matched in the east by concern about the military and strategic ramifications of the merger. A series of 'four plus two' talks (the victorious wartime allies – the USA, the USSR, Britain and France – with representatives from both Germanies) set in motion in May aimed to iron out the problems arising from unification, but no agreement had been reached by the time of the Washington summit in June. At the time of writing there is some doubt as to whether Moscow will agree to the greater, united Germany remaining in NATO, or will agree to withdraw its troops from the former territory of the GDR without some guarantee that the area remain demilitarized – or that some ceiling is placed upon German military growth.

The question remains, as Europe begins to grow in confidence and to assert itself, as to what the future role of the superpowers in Europe will be. Indeed, will they have a role? In both Washington and Moscow claims are made that their involvement must continue. Gorbachev stated un-equivocally during his speech to the Council of Europe in July 1989: 'The USSR and the USA are a natural part of the European international political structure. And their participation in its evolution is not only justified, but also historically conditioned. Any other approach is unacceptable. . . .' This view was immediately challenged by former French president Giscard d'Estaing, and with the passing of time the claim seems even less well grounded. The Soviet leadership is plagued by seemingly intractable economic problems, and harried by increasingly shrill calls from its constit-uent republics for independence. Moscow no longer has the time or the resources for a significant level of strategic involvement, and for the time being has only a minor economic role. With the passing of the Soviet military threat, the rationale for maintaining the costly American involve-ment in Europe must also come into question.

The power vacuum which has resulted from the withdrawal of Moscow's *diktat* from central Europe has already caused alarm in some quarters as both nationalist tensions and old territorial claims have begun to resurface. A proposal from (among others) Czechoslovak President Václav Havel, that a pan-European Security system replace both NATO and the Warsaw Pact, has received considerable support. This and other security considerations will be discussed at a 35-nation Helsinki-style summit proposed for the autumn of 1990, most probably to take place in Paris. Some see the prospective summit in epoch-making terms – as a twentieth-century equivalent of the Congress of Vienna. They are surely correct. If the architecture for a secure, post-Cold War Europe can be drawn up, it is likely to last well into the next century.

The future political character of central Europe is, as yet, unclear. It will take years, perhaps decades, for democratic political systems to take root and develop into sturdy growths. Post-Versailles Europe showed how fragile a plant democracy can be, and how little time it can have in which to grow. In the meantime there is the distinct possibility that once the euphoria has died down and the citizens of central Europe have grown used to their new freedoms and their market economies, they may feel that there is still something missing: the 'Western' quality of life that they had expected to enjoy after Communism.

Mrs Thatcher has been among those who have declared the defeat of the socialist system and, implicitly, saluted the victory of the West. But this victory is far from complete, and will only be achieved when stability is assured in central Europe. Central Europe has in the past been a source of instability and conflict – it has sucked others into its problems. We must hope that if and when, as seems inevitable, we are joined together in some wider Common European Home, the postwar stability of Western Europe is not put at risk.

Part 1
Eastern Europe

1 ALBANIA

Continuing Stalin's legacy

After the dramatic collapse of Communist rule in central and eastern Europe in 1989 Albania was the last truly Stalinist bastion left on the Continent. In that great turmoil the country lost four hardline allies and valuable trading partners with the disintegration of the Communist regimes of East Germany, Czechoslovakia, Bulgaria and Romania. To understand why Albania was able to provide apparently strong enough resistance against such revolutionary tides one has to take a brief glance at its history, particularly that of World War II and of the Communist rule established at the end of 1944.

The rise of Enver Hoxha

Albania gained its independence in 1912, the last colony of the Ottoman Empire to do so. But true independence proved short-lived. Its territory was overrun by several foreign armies during World War I. The Albanian state only came into being in 1920. It lasted until 1939, when fascist Italy invaded its territory and annexed it to Mussolini's empire.

The 1920–39 period, fraught with great political, economic and international difficulties, was dominated by Ahmet Zogu, a wily politician who served as cabinet minister, prime minister and president of the republic. In 1928 he was finally proclaimed King Zog. Under his authoritarian rule the country became gradually entangled, politically and economically, with Mussolini's fascist regime. This policy finally led to the Italian invasion of 1939 and the end of national independence as well as Zog's rule.

Between 1939 and 1943 Italy established a harsh military dictatorship in Albania, which became a base for the Italian invasion of Greece in 1940. Very gradually a resistance movement against foreign occupation began to emerge. When the Communist Party was founded in Albania at the end of 1941 it set up its own resistance group. Two right-wing resistance bodies also appeared on the scene: the National Front (*Balli Kombëtar*) and a pro-Zog royalist organization. The resistance movement became really active when the German army invaded Albania after Italy's defeat in 1943. Fighting against Nazi occupation soon gave rise to conflict and tension between the left-wing and right-wing groups. Broadly speaking, the Communists were more willing than the two other groups to fight against the Germans whenever an opportunity arose, regardless of the severe reprisals the occupying forces might inflict on the civilian population.

The man who became the dominating figure of the Communist resist-

ALBANIA

Official name	The People's Socialist Republic of Albania
Area	28,750 sq. km (11,100 sq. miles)
Population	3,140,000 (1988) (annual growth rate 2%)
Capital	Tirana (Tiranë)
Language	Albanian (Gheg, Tosk)
Religion	Made illegal in 1967. Muslim, Roman Catholic and Greek Orthodox minorities
Currency	lek

ance movement almost from the beginning was the party leader Enver
Hoxha (1908–85). Hoxha rose from a boiling crucible made up of several
explosive ingredients: the daily travail of poorly armed and badly organized guerrilla units fighting against well-equipped and highly trained
occupying armies; a nationalist determination to prevent the more powerful Yugoslav resistance movement from interfering unduly in Albanian
domestic affairs; constant bickerings with mainly right-wing British liaison
officers operating in Albania during the war years; and the civil war of
1943–4. Hoxha emerged from this blood-stained period as a very ambitious, ruthless, cunning and fanatical Communist guerrilla leader and
politician. He also managed to combine very dogmatic Communist beliefs
with fierce nationalism.

After pursuing the retreating Nazi armies from Albania and defeating
their right-wing rivals the Communists set up their own government,
under Hoxha's leadership, in November 1944. Unlike the Yugoslav Communists, their Albanian counterparts had no direct links with Moscow
during the war. This state of affairs continued in the early post-war years,
when the Albanian regime was in effect a Yugoslav satellite. But Tito and
his colleagues soon discovered that their desire to make Albania part of the
Yugoslav federation was strongly opposed by Hoxha himself. They consequently tried hard to replace him with a more pliant leader. But Hoxha
employed all his Machiavellian deviousness to thwart Yugoslav efforts to
topple him, and in fact succeeded in doing so.

Hoxha came to display the same ruthlessness in his determination to
create a one-party state. All opposition – political, economic, social and
cultural – was crushed with the utmost brutality. The only group towards
whom he showed any wariness or consideration during the early years
was the peasants, who made up the great majority of the population. He
first introduced a mild agrarian reform in order to win their support. But
later, when he had consolidated his own position in the party and the
country, he embarked upon a fierce campaign of full collectivization of
agriculture.

The Yugoslav ambition to annex Albania created a split within the
Albanian party between a pro-Yugoslav and an anti-Yugoslav faction. The
situation was aggravated by the fact that the leader of the pro-Yugoslav
faction, Koci Xoxe, was appointed Minister of the Interior, thus in control
of the secret police (*Sigurimi*) and all other security forces.

The 1948 schism between Stalin and Tito suddenly gave Hoxha an
opportunity to achieve three main political ambitions: to escape once and
for all from Yugoslavia's tight clutches; to eliminate pro-Tito opponents
who had made life difficult for him for several years; and to establish his
first direct links with Moscow. From 1948 onwards he was to embrace
Stalinism with unparalleled eagerness and fervour. One could say that he
became one of the Soviet dictator's most natural and consistent disciples.
Hoxha visited Stalin in Moscow on several occasions, when he discovered,

to his delight, that there was great affinity between them. Although the Albanian leader had been a natural proto-Stalinist most of his life, the close alliance and friendship with Stalin served to confirm and reinforce all his innate domineering and bloodthirsty propensities. Both believed in absolute personal power, which was justified (and disguised) by a very flexible ideology which could be manipulated to suit all possible situations. Like Stalin, Hoxha was utterly determined to destroy all opponents, real or imaginary, and remove every obstacle his orders and policies encountered. Hence under his rule every trace of natural justice, of freedom of thought and expression, as these terms are understood in the civilized world, was wiped out in his country, just as it had been in the Soviet Union under Stalin. Towards the end of his life Hoxha wrote a sycophantic book (*With Stalin*, 1979) in which he poured out all his effusive devotion and nauseating sentimental feelings towards his powerful headmaster and ally.

After the break with Yugoslavia, the Albanian leader set in motion a series of party purges which, in one form or another, went on for most of his career. Koci Xoxe, the Interior Minister, and several other politicians and officials were tried and executed as pro-Yugoslav traitors in 1949. During the next few years a large number of people were expelled from the Party. Most of them were accused of being 'enemies of the people'. Some were executed after secret trials. The purges affected several institutions, including the Party's central committee, the government, and the People's Assembly (parliament).

The rift with Belgrade left the Albanian economy in a very poor state. In order to stave off disaster and the possible collapse of the isolated regime the Soviet Union and its allies rushed food and other essential supplies to the country. This urgent aid operation marked the beginning of a long-term programme of economic and industrial aid which continued until 1961, and in which the Soviet Union and other Communist countries, particularly Czechoslovakia and East Germany, took part. Experts in various fields were sent to Albania, and many Albanians received their training in the Soviet Union and other parts of Eastern Europe. The Albanian *Sigurimi* also established close links with the KGB in Moscow, as did the Albanian armed forces with their counterparts in the Soviet bloc.

The death of Stalin

Stalin's death in 1953 and the emergence of Nikita Khrushchev as party leader in Moscow were a severe blow to Hoxha. Not only did he lose a powerful friend and like-minded teacher, he suddenly passed under the control of a highly volatile and unpredictable political leader who held dangerous reformist ideas. Hoxha's first shock came in 1955, when Khrushchev decided to bring about a reconciliation between Moscow and Yugoslavia, whose relations had remained frozen since 1948. The Albanian leader was asked to bring to an end his regime's long hostility towards Yugoslavia and establish normal relations with it. Although he made a few superficial friendly gestures towards his neighbour, Hoxha was at heart opposed to any genuine reconciliation, and he remained so mainly because he feared Tito's reformist ideas. Yugoslav attempts to overthrow him a few years earlier also played a part in his decision not to give in to Khrushchev's demands.

Another greater shock was Khrushchev's denunciation of Stalin in his 'secret speech' of 1956. Hoxha saw this as an attack not only against the policies of his regime but also against his own personal position in the Party and government. The Soviet leader's efforts to persuade Hoxha to reform his rule and give up some of his Stalinist policies also proved ineffective. As a result, tension between Moscow and Albania steadily grew from 1955 to 1961, when the final break occurred. So did Hoxha's anti-Soviet, anti-Yugoslav and anti-Western paranoia. The first signs of trouble in the Soviet–Albanian alliance appeared in 1960, when Hoxha sided with China in the early stages of the Soviet–Chinese ideological dispute. Matters came to a head at the international conference of 81 Communist parties held in Moscow in November 1960, where the Albanian leader openly defied Moscow by supporting China's cause. A year later Moscow broke off diplomatic relations with Albania and stopped all economic, industrial and military aid.

The Chinese quickly came to the rescue of their small ally in Europe with a package of economic help. They undertook to build 25 industrial plants in Albania with the assistance of Chinese technicians. But relations between the two countries faced great difficulties from the beginning because of their immense difference in size and the huge cultural and political chasm that divided them. Nevertheless, Mao's 'Cultural Revolution' did have one profound impact on Hoxha: it led him to make all religious practices illegal in 1967. However, serious strains between the two countries arose when the Chinese government opened up to the USA and Yugoslavia in the early 1970s. Hoxha rejected China's advice that his government should do the same. The alliance finally came to an end in 1978, when Peking stopped all economic and military aid and withdrew its experts. As a result, not only was Albania left completely isolated, it was also deprived of all the foreign aid it so desperately needed.

Economic and industrial decline

The end of the alliance with China marked the beginning of a period of steady economic and industrial decline. Factories and industrial plants built in the 1950s with Soviet bloc aid became outdated and derelict. Shortage of new machinery and equipment led to the widespread use of manual labour in collective farms. The situation was aggravated by a highly centralized bureaucratic system and inefficient management. At the same time, incessant official propaganda exhorted people to increase production and to rely more than ever on their own efforts and on national resources.

1985 was an important watershed for all Communist countries of Europe but especially for Albania. In March, Mikhail Gorbachev became Soviet Communist leader. In April, Enver Hoxha died at the age of 76, after having ruled the country almost like his private fief for over 40 years. He was succeeded by Ramiz Alia, a member of the Politburo who had served for several years as Hoxha's principal deputy.

Alia made it plain from the beginning that he would pursue Hoxha's policies with the same tenacity and vigour that his predecessor had displayed throughout his career. In fact, official propaganda glorifying Hoxha, in one form or another, has continued ever since. On the other hand, Alia and his colleagues began to show greater readiness to admit serious economic, industrial and cultural failures than ever before. It was disclosed, for instance, that oil, gas, chromium and copper production had declined. Serious failures were also reported in agriculture, particularly in maize production and dairy farming and in the system of distribution. Another significant admission was that young people were bored and alienated by the mediocre cultural level of newspapers, books and entertainment that were on offer.

Gorbachev's coming to power in Moscow frightened the Albanian leadership. A fierce press campaign was soon mounted against the whole gamut of the Soviet leader's *glasnost* and *perestroika* policies. These were said to be 'revisionist', capitalist and counter-revolutionary in character. Time and again it was stressed that although Albania faced grave economic, social, industrial and cultural problems, it would avoid Soviet-type reforms. It would only introduce such changes as were appropriate to its own needs and conditions. Radical reforms were clearly seen as a dangerous threat to the Communist Party's monopoly of power.

Cautious reforms

Nevertheless, the post-Hoxha leadership has proposed a number of very cautious economic and political changes designed to prevent any possible domestic turmoil as well as improve the ugly Stalinist image it has abroad. There are plans to introduce wage and price incentives in order to stimulate production in all fields, particularly in the oil and chromium industries. Agricultural enterprises will be allowed to sell farm and livestock products at competitive prices.

The *nomenklatura* system is to be abolished. The only criteria governing many appointments will henceforth be what is officially called 'loyalty to socialism' and professional qualifications. The right of legal defence and of appeal is to be introduced in court cases. The Ministry of Justice, dismantled some years earlier, is to be reinstated.

In foreign affairs, there have been a few signs that the regime wants to expand its diplomatic and trade links with Western countries. In 1986 it established diplomatic relations with Spain. Two years later it did so with Canada. A rather more significant step was taken when it exchanged ambassadors with West Germany in 1987. In addition to concluding an agreement to exchange scientists, specialists and scholars, the Bonn government, which had shown an interest in the country's chromium industry, made Albania a gift of DM26 million.

In the hope of preventing the Albanian regime from being overtaken by the kind of disaster that had overwhelmed the Communist regimes of Eastern and Central Europe in 1989, Ramiz Alia, speaking at the end of January 1990, urged Party members to forge the closest possible links with the people. This was to be done not through a multi-party system but by making the utmost use of such existing Communist institutions as the Democratic Front (a political mass organization), the youth and women's associations, and the trade unions.

Other changes concerning human rights were announced in May, just before the Secretary-General of the United Nations, Javier Pérez de Cuéllar, visited the country. The number of capital offences is reduced from 34 to 11, but the death penalty still applies to stealing state property, economic sabotage, spying, terrorism and murder. For the first time in postwar history, Albanian citizens wishing to travel abroad will be able to apply for passports.

Although there is great discontent, frustration as well as fear throughout the country, there has been only one recent occasion when these feelings have been expressed in public. In January 1990 the Yugoslav official news agency reported that, according to four people who had recently escaped from Albania, there had been two fairly large anti-government demonstrations (on 11 and 14 January) in the northern town of Shkodër. Those taking part had tried to pull down a large statue of Stalin in the centre of the town, but were prevented from doing so by the police, who used tear gas and truncheons (*Tanjug*, 25 January 1990). The Yugoslav report was later confirmed by Sue Lloyd-Roberts, an Independent Television News correspondent, in a programme on Albania (Channel 4 Television News, 14 March 1990). A group of young Albanians who were interviewed by her in Shkodër (their backs turned to the camera) said that demonstrations had in fact taken place.

How long can the Albanian Stalinist regime survive as the last heap of stones left over from the wreckage of the Communist edifice of Eastern and Central Europe? Albania suffers from one great disability when compared to some of the other countries of the region. Because of its short interlude of national independence, wedged in between centuries of Ottoman despotism and 45 years of Stalinist dictatorship, the country had hardly been in a position to cultivate the kind of democratic traditions that exist in, say, Czechoslovakia or Poland. This legacy tends to help any hardline politicians determined enough to cling to power regardless of the consequences. So the current political and economic stagnation could continue for some time to come.

2 BULGARIA
Cautious reform and emerging nationalism

The modern Bulgarian state was created by the Treaty of Berlin in July 1878. Its internal affairs were soon the preserve of corrupt politicians dominated by Prince Ferdinand. In external politics its chief desire was to secure control of Macedonia, whose Slav inhabitants the Bulgarians regarded as their co-nationals, but before 1914 their only gain was the small area of Pirin Macedonia.

It was the desire to possess Macedonia which determined Bulgaria's alignment with Germany in World War I. Defeat in that war meant the discrediting of the established political parties, and a struggle therefore took place between the nation's two major radical forces: the Communists and the Bulgarian Agrarian National Union (BANU). The former's origin could be traced back to the early 1890s while the latter were essentially a product of the agrarian crisis which affected the country at the turn of the century. The Agrarians proved victorious, but their radicalism and their willingness to compromise with the Yugoslavs, who controlled Macedonia, created many enemies. In 1923 the Agrarians were deposed and their leader, Alexander Stamboliiski, murdered.

There followed over a decade of instability, which ended on 19 May 1934 with a *coup d'état* staged by army officers and discontented elements from the intelligentsia. They did not last long. After they had succeeded in containing disruptive Macedonian elements they were elbowed aside by King Boris and his advisors. The King's major preoccupation was with foreign affairs. By the end of 1938 Bulgaria was the only European power defeated in 1918 not to have recovered some of its lost territory, a condition which was a strong impulse towards alignment with the revisionist powers, primarily Germany. By 1941 the pressures to join Germany were irresistible, but although Bulgaria joined the Axis it would not commit itself to war against the Soviet Union, nor would Boris agree to the deportation of Bulgarian Jews.

Boris died in somewhat mysterious circumstances in August 1943, by which time Bulgaria was anxious to escape from the conflict. In this it failed. The Soviet attack which so many Bulgarians had feared materialized in September 1944 and was aided by the small partisan units of the Fatherland Front, an opposition group consisting of Communists, Agrarians, supporters of the 1934 coup, and a number of left-wing 'bourgeois' parties.

On 9 September 1944 the Fatherland Front formed a government.

BULGARIA

Official name	The People's Republic of Bulgaria
Area	110,910 sq. km (42,810 sq. miles)
Population	8,973,600 (1988) (annual growth rate 0.2%)
Capital	Sofia (Sofiya)
Language	Bulgarian, up to 10% Turkish
Religion	Eastern (Bulgarian) Orthodox, 10% Muslim
Currency	lev

During the following three years the Communists systematically under-mined their coalition partners, the major confrontation coming in 1947 when the Agrarian leader, Nikola Petkov, was arrested and executed after a grotesque show trial. Within a year all real opposition to Communist domination had been broken; what was left of the Agrarians capitulated to the Communists and became junior partners in the nominal Communist–Agrarian coalition which was to rule the country for over 40 years.

The first years of Communist rule saw industrialization, collectiviz-ation, and the general sovietization of Bulgaria. After Stalin's death changes took place which brought to prominence Todor Zhivkov, who was to lead the Bulgarian Communist Party (BCP) from 1954 to 1989.

Pressure for change

Zhivkov's position began to weaken in the early 1980s. Unsavoury inci-dents such as alleged Bulgarian involvement in the attempted murder of the Pope in 1981 tarnished Zhivkov's image while at home the regime failed to fulfil all its promises with regard to increasing living standards. To improve economic performance a series of reforms were initiated. These did little more than tinker with the administration of the economy, thus causing further dislocation. To retrieve credibility, Zhivkov hauled out the chauvinist drum. He decided to go down in history as the man who united all Bulgarians into one, homogeneous, socialist nation. More crudely put, he decreed that the Turks, who formed around 10% of the population, must be assimilated. To this end, Turks were required to adopt Slav names, broadcasts and publications in Turkish ceased, and it was made illegal to speak Turkish in the streets.

Many Bulgarians were revolted by such policies. To mitigate oppo-sition, Zhivkov extended his 'reforms' from the economic to the political sector. The doctrines of 'self-management' and pluralism were widely debated and even incorporated into seemingly advanced legislation such as the Labour Code of 1986. In the summer of 1987 Zhivkov delighted the reform-minded with the so-called 'July concept', which promised liberaliz-ation, pluralization and many of the other attractions which were now on offer in other East European states. At the end of 1987 the Bulgarian reformists made full use of these new-found freedoms.

The city of Rousé had for some years been suffering from periodic poisoning by emissions from a metallurgical plant across the Danube in Romania. An exhibition staged in Rousé at the end of 1987 showed that the incidence of lung disease in the city had risen from 969 per 100,000 in 1975 to 17,386 per 100,000 in 1985. There was a huge national outcry. An unnerved Zhivkov began to backtrack. The Party newspaper, *Rabot-nichesko Delo*, dilated upon the distinction between positive and negative *glasnost*, and in the summer Zhivkov sacked one of the Party's leading reformists, Choudomir Alexandrov.

In previous years Zhivkov's opponents would have been cowed by such menaces but now, with the Soviet Union a bastion of reform rather than reaction, they were not to be intimidated. By the beginning of 1989 a number of opposition groups had been formed, including The Discussion Club for the Support of Perestroika and Glasnost (later changed to Democracy), the Independent Association for the Defence of Human Rights, the independent trade union, *Podkrepa* (Support), the environmental organization Ecoglasnost, and the Committee for the Defence of Religious Rights. Government attempts to bludgeon these groups into quietude were totally ineffective, and by the spring of 1989 it was clear that a major political confrontation between government and opposition in Bulgaria was imminent.

The first serious clash came over the Turkish issue. A number of the new political groups sympathized with the Turks and their determination to resist assimilation. In late May 1989, immediately before the opening of the Paris Conference on Security and Co-operation in Europe, a handful of leading Turkish protesters began staging hunger strikes. These led to clashes with the police and to the expulsion of a number of Turkish activists who immediately appeared as honoured guests at the CSCE conference. Zhivkov now made worse of a bad job. He challenged the Turkish government to open their borders and allow Bulgaria's Muslims a free choice between their socialist homeland and Turkey. The Turks called his bluff, and by late August over 300,000 Bulgarian Turks had fled to Turkey, which was forced once more to close its frontiers.

The uneasy calm produced by the closing of the borders lasted until October, when Sofia was the venue for a meeting of the EcoForum, another Helsinki follow-up conference. The growing Bulgarian ecological movement, headed by Ecoglasnost, staged a number of demonstrations, one of which, on 26 October, was disrupted by the police in full view of the international press. Public frustration increased, as did the anger of many leading BCP officials. By early November an anti-Zhivkov cabal had formed and, once the support of the military had been assured, the plotters moved, deposing the dictator and his closest supporters during a Central Committee plenum on 10 November. Zhivkov was arrested soon after on charges of corruption.

End of an era

The removal of Zhivkov inevitably marked the end of an era. The collapse of the old regime in Bulgaria, however, was the result of a palace coup, not a popular revolution. 'People power' had not been totally absent but it was as much, if not more, the result than the cause of the end of the *ancien régime*, with the largest demonstrations taking place in December and January rather than October and November. For that reason, the non-Communist opposition forces are much less confident of the permanence of their gains than the equivalent groups in other East European states.

Zhivkov was replaced as Party leader and head of state by his foreign minister, Petur Mladenov. Mladenov moved rapidly to consolidate his position, and by early December had replaced all the remaining Zhivkovites in the Politburo and had reduced their strength in the Central Committee. The new leadership pledged itself to end the abuse of personal liberties, to allow free, multi-party elections at the earliest feasible opportunity, and to inaugurate a massive economic restructuring which would abolish the 'administrative-command' system and allow much greater play to market forces. Political relaxation was immediately apparent. Within days of Zhivkov's fall, old parties were being reborn and new ones founded. Most prominent among the former were the Social Democrats, and the Nikola Petkov Agrarians, a revived version of those Agrarians who had refused to compromise with the BCP in the 1940s. The new groups included a Green Party. On 14 November the more prominent of the opposition groups achieved a loose form of unity in the Union of Democratic Forces (UDF), which by March 1990 had fifteen constituent elements.

The Turkish issue

Before further progress towards structural political change could be made, the new leadership and the opposition alike were faced with the possible threat of counter-revolution. The issue on which the reactionary forces chose to make their stand was that of the Turkish minority.

Mladenov, as foreign secretary, had been all too aware of how much damage Zhivkov's assimilationist policies had done to Bulgaria's international reputation. Given the crushing need for foreign aid, such policies had to be disavowed. This was done by a government decree of 29 December 1989. It produced a furious reaction. In Kurdjali, Haskovo and other areas with mixed populations the Bulgarians were loud in their protests. Demonstrations were organized, strikes were staged and on Sunday 7 January 1990 coachloads of protesters descended on Sofia to besiege the *Subranie* (National Assembly) with complaints that so important a change could not be enacted without a referendum. The Turkish issue had indubitably roused many passions, but there can be little doubt that the protests were exploited, if not instigated, by BCP officials, particularly those middle-ranking full-time Party employees who stood to lose position, power and privilege as a result of the reforms.

The demonstrations of 7 January may well prove to be the turning point of the Bulgarian revolution. Those demonstrations were raucous and threatening, yet the new leaders were undaunted, not least because in the following week Mladenov was to travel to Kuwait to hold discussions with the Turkish foreign minister. Concessions to the chauvinists would have wrecked these talks and, with them, realistic hopes of loans from the Arab world. The week after the nationalist protests there were even larger demonstrations, this time sponsored by the UDF but condoned by the

BCP, and now demanding that full liberty be granted to all Bulgarian citizens irrespective of ethnic identity or religion. The authorities responded by setting up a Social Council on which 65 organizations covering a wide variety of interests were represented. The Council was to investigate the ethnic question and to recommend appropriate legislation to the *Subranie*. On 17 January, acting on the Council's recommendations, the Assembly adopted a bill allowing all Bulgarians to choose freely the names which they wished to bear, and removing any discrimination based upon religion or race. As a *douceur* to the nationalists, the bill also stated that only the Bulgarian flag could be raised in the country, that Bulgarian was the only official language, and that no political parties based purely on religious affiliation would be allowed. The latter was a great disappointment to many Muslims.

From BCP to BSP

It was significant that the session of the *Subranie* which endorsed this bill also modified Article One of the 1971 constitution, the article which enshrined the leading role of the Communist Party. The resolution of the Turkish problem played some part in this. If the confrontation of early January seemed to have drawn the teeth of the nationalist dragon, it had also shown that the government and the major opposition groups did have some common objectives. This was a reassuring discovery, because contact between the two sides had, until then, been fitful and hardly fruitful. There was clear need for dialogue, but the opposition was wary of being trapped, and would do nothing without reassurance that the BCP was prepared to abandon its leading role. The BCP leadership had given many such assurances, not least in a self-flagellating Central Committee plenum on 11–13 December 1989, when a total restructuring of Party and state was promised. There had also been some moves to dismantle the Party's primary organizations in educational institutions, the armed forces and the media. But there had been no legislation, and this problem had been partially responsible for slowing down moves towards the round-table talks which both sides had wanted. The deadlock was not resolved until early January, and full talks did not begin until 18 January, the day after the *Subranie* had legislated to end the BCP's leading role.

The UDF was not entirely satisfied with the bill of 17 January. It repealed only clauses two and three of Article One, those which designated the BCP as the leading force in society and the state, and which allotted to it and its BANU allies the task of constructing an advanced socialist society. Clause one remained intact. It stated that Bulgaria was 'a socialist state of the working people of the town and the countryside, led by the working class', a wording which left many non-socialists feeling distinctly uneasy.

The BCP had, however, sacrificed some of its privileges, and it now set about preparing itself for the electoral contest that was to come in the early summer. Soon after the fall of Zhivkov it had been agreed that the next party congress should convene earlier than its scheduled date of late 1991. In fact the 14th Extraordinary Congress met from 31 January to 2 February 1990. It was the most turbulent and radical congress in living memory. First, Mladenov announced that he would no longer serve as head of party and head of state, relinquishing the former post to Alexandur Lilov. The party congress also agreed that prime minister Georgi Atanasov should be replaced by Mladenov's close confidant, Andrei Loukanov. Much more surprising, however, was the decision to abolish the Central Committee and the Politburo which were replaced by a Supreme Party Council and a Praesidium. The new structure was intended to be more democratic and to encourage greater participation by the mass of party members. It was also intended, no doubt with the forthcoming elections in mind, to mark a determined shift away from old practices and old personalities, and in the latter regard at least it must be accounted a success, for no more than 10% of those elected to the Supreme Council had been members of the previous Central Committee. Furthermore, the Supreme Council included representatives of the various factional groups which had by now become visible in the BCP, including the Democratic Forum, the Movement for Democratic Socialism, the Road to Europe Platform, and the Alternative Socialist Organization. On 3 April the BCP renamed itself the Bulgarian Socialist Party (BSP). Its newspaper, *Rabotnichesko Delo*, was henceforth to appear as *Duma*.

The January–February restructuring of the BCP was followed by the formation of a new government. Ironically, shortly after the BCP had renounced its leading role, Bulgaria was to have its first purely Communist administration. The reason for this lay in the dynamics of opposition politics. The emergence of the Nikola Petkov Agrarians had alarmed the official BANU leaders, whose previous co-operation with the BCP was denounced as collaboration by the Petkovists. The 'official Agrarians', leaping at the chance to disassociate themselves from the Communists and to initiate talks with the Petkovists for union, refused to re-enter the government. The BCP leadership, meanwhile, was clearly hoping that the UDF and other opposition parties might join in a government of national unity to guide the country through to the general elections which were soon, because of opposition pressure, put back from May to June. The opposition, however, were not prepared to co-operate. They insisted that they would not be part of any government which had to rely for its support on a *Subranie* elected under the old conditions. Nor were they happy to join with the Communists while so little had been done to dismantle the *nomenklatura* and to limit the powers of the secret police. Furthermore, the opposition, learning from the experience of the 'official Agrarians', feared that cohabitation with the Communists now would appear as collaborationism in the electoral battle which lay ahead.

The elections of June 1990

The timing of the electoral contest and the conditions under which it was to be conducted had been the subject of protracted and intense debate in the round table. Early in April it was agreed that polling should take place on 10 and 17 June 1990 for a Grand National or Constituent Assembly. The assembly would consist of 400 delegates, half elected by a simple majority and half by the list system. There was to be a 4% minimum threshold for party representation. After drawing up the new constitution the assembly would itself decide whether to continue in session as a legislative body or to dissolve itself and make way for a successor parliament elected under the new system.

Before these details had been agreed the BCP/BSP had been considerably embarrassed and damaged by public revelation of conditions in labour camps in the early 1960s, revelations which implicated at least one member of the party's Supreme Council. Nevertheless, the party continued to enjoy a large number of electoral advantages. It was one of the oldest and most entrenched of all the East European Communist Parties. Bulgaria had a long tradition of political clientism in which the masses, particularly in the countryside, voted for those already in power. Shed of the incubus of the Zhivkov clique the Party could claim that it was capable of the regeneration of which the nation was so greatly in need. The Party also benefited from the traditions of discipline and unity upon which much of its previous strength was founded.

The opposition presented a very different picture. The UDF included a number of prominent and able intellectuals, among them Petur Beron of Ecoglasnost, Konstantin Trenchev of *Podkrepa*, Father Hristofor Subev of the Committee for the Defence of Religious Rights, and the UDF chairman, Zheliu Zhelev. But none of these figures commanded universal support among the opposition. There was no Bulgarian Wałęsa or Havel. Nor were the opposition groups firmly united, agreeing on little more than that they wished to see the end of Communist rule. A conference in Plovdiv in March 1990 produced declarations of solidarity, but they were not easily secured nor particularly convincing, the more so when shortly after the conference one group, the Independent Association for the Defence of Human Rights, conducted a purge of its leadership.

There were also differences in policy. Some of the UDF's constituent groups wished to see the elections delayed until November 1990 to give them time to prepare for the contest, others were happy to go to the polls in June. There was no unanimity on the extent to which market forces should be allowed to determine the economy, nor on how far private property should be restored. Moreover, the opposition lacked proper facilities for fighting a sustained election campaign. Neither the UDF nor its constituent organizations were wealthy. They lacked access to the media and to basic equipment such as photocopiers, fax machines and telephones. Many of them lacked even office space and staff, especially outside Sofia.

Inevitably the national question also played a part in the election campaign. Chauvinist groups were vociferous in their condemnation of the mainly Turkish and Muslim Rights and Freedom Movement which did surprisingly well at the polls, and one organization, Ilinden, was banned because it advocated the cession of part of south-west Bulgaria to Yugoslavia. In addition to these tensions there were some irregularities at the polls, particularly in the second round of voting, but neither the nationalists' passions nor the infringements of the electoral law seem to have made any real difference to the final outcome. The BSP remains in office but it lacks the two-thirds majority needed to enforce constitutional changes. Opposition groups are reluctant to join the former Communists in coalition and a second general election is therefore likely within the next two years.

An economy 'on the verge of cardiac arrest'

The economy had been one of the issues at stake in the election. It remains a question of fundamental importance. The need for radical change is great, and one of the first results of the overthrow of Zhivkov was that the deceptive, self-congratulatory economic statistics of the old regime were replaced by more honest and more sobering figures. On 11 December 1989 Mladenov told a Central Committee plenum that the Bulgarian economy was 'on the verge of cardiac arrest'. Production in some commodities was lower than in 1980, inflationary pressures were intensifying, up to half of the production plant in the country was old-fashioned and worn out, agricultural production had declined so sharply that food was being imported, and the foreign debt, previously calculated at around $4 billion, was in reality over $10 billion; $8 billion was thought to be the critical limit.

The economy suffered further as a result of the changes of late 1989. Increased freedom meant a rash of strikes which drove December's monthly industrial production figures down to a level of 12.7%, lower than those for 1988. Nor was inflation helped by widespread increases in pensions and wages. In some cases inflationary pressures were boosted by the government's capitulation to strikers. In January 1990 miners were awarded a 50% wage increase, a six-hour working day, and retirement at 45. There was no indication of any corresponding increase in productivity.

A further economic difficulty arises over environmental issues. Bulgaria has very little in the way of natural fossil fuels and atomic energy is therefore an attractive alternative, the plant at Kozlodui already producing about a fifth of the country's energy needs. The ecological lobby, however, is growing in strength, and in February 1990 succeeded in halting construction of a reactor at Belene, an area said to be in an earthquake zone. Nor is nuclear energy the only ecological issue. Massive pollution is produced by the metallurgical complex at Kremikovtsi, outside Sofia, and at many other industrial sites, largely because existing regulations are disregarded and the equipment is antiquated. Remedying these ills is both necessary and widely desired, but it will also be very expensive.

The Party's answer to the economic crisis was to increase investment in agriculture and consumer industries, to cut subsidies and other wasteful aspects of the internal budget, and to allow greater play to market forces. The last inevitably means another twist to the inflationary spiral, and already shortages have driven up prices of newly deregulated items such as vegetables. The more reform-minded Communists, particularly those on the Road to Europe Platform, seek salvation in closer links with non-socialist economies, especially those of the European Community. Others fear the inevitable social consequences of rapid and extensive deregulation, though few would contest that decentralization is necessary, that private production, particularly in agriculture, should be stimulated, and that the necessary liberalization of property laws must be enacted.

3 CZECHOSLOVAKIA
The velvet revolution

The modern Czechoslovak state emerged in 1918 out of the ruins of the Austro-Hungarian empire. The new republic was composed of two contrasting regions. In the west were the Czech lands – Bohemia and Moravia – with their large areas of flat plain, which had seen considerable industrial development under Habsburg rule. The Czech people, after almost 300 years of Austrian rule, were more advanced in economic, political and cultural terms than their Slovak neighbours to the east. Slovakia, a region of largely mountainous, forested terrain, had been dominated for centuries by Hungary. It had little industry and its mainly peasant population depended upon agriculture for their livelihood. While the growth of industrialization in the western regions had led to the rise of a Czech urban middle class, in Slovakia the towns were mainly peopled by Germans and Jews.

Czechoslovakia under Masaryk
Tomáš Garrigue Masaryk, a prime mover in the drive for Czechoslovak statehood, became the country's first president and remained its leader for most of the interwar period. A Slovak from Moravia, Masaryk was of humble origins, but had risen to become Professor of Philosophy at Prague University. He was a firm believer in unity between the Czech and Slovak people, since only by the creation of an alliance or federation of the two peoples, he felt, could a state be formed which would be strong enough to survive. He also believed in unity on cultural grounds (although the Czech and Slovak languages have differences, they are closely related and mutually comprehensible offshoots of the west Slavonic group of languages).

Until its loss of sovereignty in 1938–9, Czechoslovakia was unique in east-central Europe in retaining the democratic system of government with which it had been endowed in 1918. Its success in this respect and the relative political stability it enjoyed compared with its neighbours can be attributed to several factors. First, it was prosperous and most sections of society benefited from this prosperity. Land reforms did much to satisfy the peasants' craving for land, while financial reforms helped to avoid the kind of uncontrolled inflation which undermined political stability elsewhere in the region. Second, for most of the interwar period the country was governed by a coalition of five parties, the Pětka, members of which had developed the habit of working together while representing

CZECHOSLOVAKIA

Official name	The Czech and Slovak Federative Republic
Area	127,870 sq. km (49,360 sq. miles)
Population	15,620,000 (1988) (annual growth rate 0.3%)
Capital	Prague (Praha)
Language	Czech, Slovak
Religion	65% Roman Catholic, 4.5% Protestant (Czechoslovak Church)
Currency	koruna (Kcs)

Czech affairs in the Austrian parliament. Third, the Czechoslovak constitution, based on the French model, provided for a strong executive, and in the person of Masaryk, a president was elected who was widely respected and who contributed personally to the political stability of the federation.

This is not to say that the country did not have problems. The sense of grievance felt by the Slovak minority mounted, as earlier promises of :tical autonomy continued to be ignored. More of a problem in the western border regions (the Sudety uplands) was the 3 million German population, which became increasingly restive with the growth of Nazism across the border. The effects of the Depression were severe in Czechoslovakia, and as they set back the country's prosperity, so there was a corresponding growth of radicalism and militancy among both Slovaks and Sudeten Germans.

Munich and after

The year 1935 marked a watershed in Czechoslovak politics. In November the 'President Liberator' Tomáš Masaryk stood down as president and was replaced by a disciple and colleague, Eduard Beneš. Earlier, in May, the pro-Nazi National Front Party had captured 62% of German votes in the election. This rejection of a future with their Slav neighbours in favour of a resurgent German imperialism was an ominous sign for Prague politicians. They made efforts to strengthen diplomatic links with France and the Soviet Union, but proved impotent to stem the tide of National Socialism. In March 1938 Hitler staged his *Anschluss* – the annexation of Austria – and in September of the same year came the tragi-farce of Chamberlain's meeting with Hitler at Munich. The attempt to buy peace was made at Czechoslovakia's expense. The Prague government was persuaded not to resist Germany but to cede the Sudety region with its German population to the Reich. Independence and democracy were sacrificed without a shot being fired. As George Kennan, then a young diplomat, wrote: 'A remarkable little people . . . found themselves standing out in lonely bitterness against what they felt to be an unjust and unsympathetic Europe.' As a direct result of Munich, Czechoslovakia was dismembered. The Sudety region was immediately incorporated into the Reich. But in the following year Hitler annexed the remainder of the country. An independent Slovak state was declared and a German 'Protectorate' of Bohemia and Moravia created. In the east an area of the Carpathian foothills and its mainly Ruthenian population was ceded to Hungary, while Poland took a small piece of disputed territory around Těšin (Cieszyń).

German rule in Czechoslovakia was by no means as harsh or destructive as in neighbouring Poland. The most dramatic event was the assassination of Reinhard Heydrich by members of the Czech resistance movement, an operation which resulted in reprisal executions and the massacre of the male population of the village of Lidice. In the summer of

1944 a rising took place in Slovakia which took the Germans several weeks to put down. Throughout the war an exile government in London, under the presidency of Beneš, maintained the continuity of the Czechoslovak state.

The greater part of Czechoslovakia was liberated by the Red Army. Although American forces entered the country, and Patton's troops were at one point closer to Prague than the Soviets (they liberated Pilsen), they were ordered to withdraw. While some historians have seen this withdrawal as a further abandonment of Czechoslovakia by her Western allies, in fact Soviet troops also withdrew within six months. There were no foreign troops in the country by the time of the first postwar election. In the wake of the Red Army came both Czechoslovak Communists who had found refuge in Moscow during the war years and members of the 'London' camp – headed by Beneš – who had reached an understanding with the Communists in Moscow. Beneš had become convinced that Czechoslovakia could not rely on the support of the Western democracies; the country needed friendly relations with the Soviet Union. He was hopeful that Czechoslovakia, situated in the centre of Europe and with its traditions of humanism and democracy, could act as a 'bridge' between East and West. As the Polish historian M. K. Dziewanowski has written, though, Stalin was not seeking 'bridges' in central Europe but rather 'bridgeheads'.

On crossing the border and reaching Košice, Beneš appointed a provisional government which included six Communist ministers as well as a number of 'fellow-travellers'. The programme outlined by the new government reflected the Moscow Agreement. It provided for free elections, nationalization and land reform, the outlawing of fascist organizations, and for preventing the renewal of political parties which 'had transgressed so gravely against the interests of the nation and the Republic' during the war. This included the Agrarian Party, the largest in Czechoslovakia before the war, and the Slovak Populist Party, both of which were banned. A further measure was the immediate expulsion of the German population from the Sudety region. Here, as in Poland, the Communists ensured that they controlled the redistribution of land vacated by the Germans. This valuable form of political patronage helped them to build support and party membership. Border changes were small but significant. The Soviet Union, having seized Polish and Romanian territory, proceeded to take the small area of Carpathian Ruthenia, following a 'plebiscite'. By contrast with its prewar situation, Czechoslovakia now had a common border with the Soviet Union.

The postwar elections

The elections foreseen under the Moscow Agreement took place on 16 May 1946, and their results provide us with one of the surprises of postwar Eastern Europe. Just as, before the war, Czechoslovakia was the one country in the region which retained democracy until the end, so in the immediate postwar years it was the only one in which the Communists gained a measure of support at the polls. In the only free elections in postwar Czechoslovakia, at least until 1990, the Communists took 38% of the vote (40% in the Czech lands).

Why was this? It is true that there had been a strong Communist movement in the country between the wars, particularly in the Czech lands, where there was a sizeable industrial working class. The Communists had also gained prestige by their hostility to the Munich capitulation, by their acts of resistance to wartime German rule, and by the fact that it was the Red Army which had liberated most of the country. But perhaps most important was that in 1945–6 their programme seemed attractive. The Communists were not calling for revolution, for violent overthrow, but masked their real aims behind calls for reasonable reforms and national unity. Many of the proposals which had been discussed in Moscow during the talks with Beneš seemed very sensible to voters. Although the Czechoslovak Communist Party (CPC) had only some 50,000 members at the war's end – less than half its prewar membership – it worked hard to attract support, and by March 1946 could boast over 1 million members in the Czech lands alone.

Although the elections left them without an overall majority, the Communists were the largest single party. Their political opponents were divided among themselves, and in any case were bound by the coalition agreement which brought the National Front government into power. Few opposition politicians realized that their days were numbered, that they had come up against determined opponents who had clear objectives and were prepared to abandon principles in pursuit of them. The lack of a unified and coherent opposition enabled the Communists to strengthen their hold on power. Klement Gottwald, leader of the 'Moscow' group of Communists, became prime minister and out of the 26-member Cabinet, nine ministers were Communists.

Despite this evidence of their growing political muscle, the Communists were hesitant about carrying out a coup. They were worried that a violent seizure of power, going against the country's strong democratic traditions, might bring an outraged and hostile reaction from the community. Although they had increasing control of the mass media, the police and the security apparatus, made use of violence, blackmail and intimidation against political opponents, and encouraged marches and street demonstrations to exaggerate the strength of their support, the Communists were aware that, as things stood, they would not be able to capture power at the next election. Yet during 1947, as the political and ideological battlelines were drawn ever more clearly across Europe, the pressure from Moscow from a consolidation of Communist power became irresistible.

In the end the crisis which brought the Communists total control was

engineered by ministers of the 'opposition' non-Communist parties themselves. A threat of group resignation, which they hoped would curb the
excesses of the Communists and force them from office, backfired. Gottwald, by a mixture of cajoling and threats, managed to persuade the
ageing, sickly president, Beneš, to accept the resignations. The Communists were able to take power 'legally' through what was, in effect, a
bloodless revolution, and Gottwald was able to announce the victory to an
excited crowd in Prague's Old Town Square.

Consolidation of Communist rule

In the aftermath of the February coup, the Communists – as if to make up
for lost time – began to tighten their hold on the country by all the means at
their disposal. There was, as Hans Renner has written in a recently
published history of modern Czechoslovakia, a 'rapid metamorphosis of
Czechoslovakia into a totalitarian society of the Stalinist type'. In economic
life the first five-year plan (1949–53) covered the nationalization and
reconstruction of industry. Czechoslovakia was to become the foundry-
workshop of Comecon, concentrating on producing heavy machinery for
its socialist partners. The imposition of Stalinist orthodoxy also brought
with it a cultural purge. Hundreds of thousands of ideologically harmful
books were removed from shops and libraries, to be replaced with trans-
lations of Soviet literature and textbooks – not always of the highest
quality, but always in enormous quantities.

As in the rest of east-central Europe at this time, 'counter-revolutionary
elements' were arrested, evicted or thrown out of work. Some 130,000
people were despatched to prisons, labour camps and mines. The remaining vestiges of political tolerance vanished and many opposition politicians were forced into exile. Jan Masaryk, son of the country's first
president and the only surviving non-Communist in the government, died
in suspicious circumstances – widely presumed murdered by agents of the
Soviet or Czechoslovak security forces. The Church was also persecuted,
with members of religious orders and Catholic intellectuals among those
who were sent to labour camps.

But the terror did not only engulf the Party's opponents. In the early
1950s a bloody purge of the Party's own ranks was carried out, ordered by
Moscow and supervised by its advisers. Indeed, the purging of the 'inner
enemy' took a form which closely resembled the Stalinist show trials of the
1930s and 1940s. The purge claimed, among others, Rudolf Slánský (the
Party secretary-general) and Vlado Clementis (Minister for Foreign Affairs). Both were hanged in 1952. It seems that anti-semitism lay at the root
of the affair. Not only were most of the victims Jewish; when their names
were listed in *Rudé Právo* they were followed by the words 'of Jewish
origin'.

Gottwald, the architect of Stalinist rule in postwar Czechoslovakia,
died in March 1953, a matter of days after his political mentor, Josef Stalin.

In his place, Antonín Novotný became first secretary of the Party and, in 1957, took the post of president as well. But the death of Stalin and Khrushchev's leadership had little effect upon Czechoslovakia. In 1956 there was no 'thaw' as in Poland, no challenge to Communist rule, as in Hungary. Indeed, measures to consolidate the Communist system, such as liquidation of private trade, carried on apace, and in 1960 the country's new Constitution renamed the country the Czechoslovak Socialist Republic. Article 4 of the Constitution confirmed the Communist Party's 'leading role' in society and Marxism–Leninism was declared a cornerstone of cultural life.

The 1960s proved to be a decade of impatience with the chafing restrictions of Communist rule. Criticism emerged from within the party itself, particularly from the younger generation of intellectuals – those who had been in their teens and twenties at the end of the war. Economic failures led to calls for changes in policy, and, in turn, to pressure for liberalization in other areas. An internal power struggle developed in late 1967, with criticism directed at Novotný's leadership. When Leonid Brezhnev, visiting Prague in December of that year, pointedly refused to intervene, Novotný found himself isolated. His resignation as Party leader in January 1968 was followed by the election of the Slovak Party leader, Alexander Dubček, as first secretary of the CPC. The Party split into two camps – reformers and conservatives – and a bitter internecine struggle began for its soul.

'Socialism with a human face'

In April 1968 the reformers' manifesto – their Action Programme – was published. This blueprint for change envisaged greater democracy within the Party, a new constitution, rehabilitation of the victims of the 1950s purges, freedom of speech and of assembly, and devolution of powers to federal (Czech and Slovak) governments. Democratization of economic life was also foreseen, devolving power to workers' councils and restoring to trades unions the power to defend their members' interests. What came to be known as the 'Prague Spring' was accompanied by an unprecedented loosening of controls on the mass media, which began to report and debate political issues quite openly. Significantly, though, there were no moves to threaten the Party's position by ending its 'leading role'. Demands for the re-establishment of an opposition party, the Social Democrats, were stalled and subsequently overtaken by events.

There is no doubt that a majority of citizens supported the reforms – and supported Dubček, who attained a stature and popularity that no other Communist leader in postwar Czechoslovakia has even approached. But Dubček's moves to introduce 'socialism with a human face' were viewed with increasing concern, both in Moscow and by Czechoslovakia's Warsaw Pact neighbours. Moscow applied strong pressure on the Czechoslovak leadership during the summer of 1968, using such tried and tested methods as 'troop manoeuvres', but the reformists refused to alter course. On the night of 20–21 August, Czechoslovakia was invaded by troops from five of its Warsaw Pact allies – the USSR, Poland, Hungary, Bulgaria and the GDR; in all, 27 divisions.

The end of the Prague Spring

The world watched in astonishment and horror as Soviet tanks rolled into Prague. Older citizens could draw the parallels with the German takeover in 1938/9. The operation was not without casualties, and dozens died on both sides, but there was no mass resistance. The lasting impression is of a concerted, but peaceful, effort by the populace to convince the soldiers of the injustice they were doing. Attempts were made to confuse the operation by removing or altering road signs. Many of the troops were very shaken when they realized how they had been lied to, and units were rapidly recalled and replaced. The operation was accompanied by a campaign of misinformation in the Soviet bloc media. Meanwhile, Soviet theoreticians had worked hard to devise a rationale for the move. They came up with an answer. The brave experiment in seeking a Czechoslovak road to socialism had been suppressed in the greater interests of the 'socialist commonwealth' (the Brezhnev Doctrine).

Dubček and his supporters on the Politburo were treated disgracefully. They were arrested and taken to the Ukraine. Only when the ageing president, General Svoboda, who had decided to go to Moscow of his own accord, refused to begin negotiations without them, did the Soviets produce the Dubček group. During October the Soviet leadership bullied the reformers into reversing the reforms and signing a 15-point protocol, ensuring that Moscow's demands were met. The treaty also provided for Soviet troops to be stationed 'temporarily' on Czechoslovak soil (although as a small and rather hollow concession, there was agreement that they would not intervene directly in the country's internal affairs!).

To the ageing Kremlin leadership, the 'Prague Spring' represented a threat to the stability of the entire socialist bloc. But the return to orthodoxy, the process of 'normalization' which Moscow had indicated that it wanted set in motion, did not begin immediately. Slow to recover from the shock of the violent intervention, the reformists still believed that there was room for compromise and some of the gains could be retained. The desperation of reformist-minded Czechs and Slovaks not to return to the 'ice age' of Stalinist-style repression was tragically highlighted by the public self-immolation of student, Jan Palach, in January 1969. The one lasting gain was the confirmation of a federal structure, ensuring complete equality between the Czech and Slovak nations. Both were to have parallel institutional structures – a Czech National Council (200 members) and a Slovak National Council (150 members) – and were to receive a just allocation of seats in the Federal Assembly.

'Normalization' under Husák

Dubček was quickly relegated to obscurity. An initial posting to Turkey as Czechoslovak ambassador was followed by his expulsion from the Party's Central Committee. In June 1970 he was expelled from the Party and removed from the public spotlight to a lowly job with the state forestry administration in Bratislava. Dubček's fall was spectacular, but it was not isolated. In the months that followed, thousands of Party members were expelled and lost their jobs in a mass clear-out of the reformist elements. Some one and a half million members were interrogated by screening commissions. There were heavy casualties in the media and in cultural life, and large numbers of the persecuted (over 100,000 by the end of 1970) chose to leave the country.

Ironically, the man who took over as Party leader from Dubček and began to 'normalize' Communist rule was not only, like Dubček himself, a Slovak. Gustáv Husák had been arrested in 1951 – one of the victims of the Party's earlier purges of its own ranks. (He had been amnestied in 1960.) Husák had even at one time been a Slovak nationalist. He took over in April 1969, following prolonged 'armtwisting' of the Party hierarchy by the Soviet leadership.

The process of 'normalization' which took place under Husák meant inflexible, unresponsive leadership and public apathy. The stand-off which ensued can be compared to the situation after the 1981 suppression of Solidarity in Poland. People felt cheated of the freedoms they had tasted all too briefly. They resented the 'depoliticization' which followed. Many had begun for the first time to engage in true democratic debate and to interest themselves in the political process, as something they could influence, and which could bring change for the better into their lives. The Husák regime anxiously attempted to deflect unrest by engineering a rise in living standards. Private consumption rose considerably in the course of the 1970s and car-ownership alone increased threefold between 1969 and 1981. But this induced boom did not signify underlying economic health.

By 1980–81 there was a growing crisis in the economy and growth of national income had slowed to zero. The structure of the Czechoslovak economy had not been altered appreciably from its earlier Stalinist model. It was still functioning as the workshop of Comecon, producing steel and heavy machinery. Furthermore, much of the Czechoslovak industry was outdated and many of its products of low technical standard. The central planning restrictions and curbing of private enterprise stifled innovation and the growth of new industries – particularly the new technologies developing in the West and Japan. In the course of the 1970s Czechoslovakia lost one third of its share of Western markets. This meant an important loss of Western currency with which to finance imports.

Meanwhile the country was still having to import large quantities of raw materials and energy, and these were becoming increasingly expensive on world markets. Czechoslovakia's huge and inefficient consumption of energy led it to exploit large quantities of brown coal (lignite) to fire thermal power plants – but at enormous environmental cost.

Charter 77

The Husák period was marked by the growth of an intellectual and cultural opposition – dissident writers, academics, artists – who began to bypass the offical media by publishing their works in the unofficial (*samizdat*) press. The dissidents included both disaffected former Communists and those who had remained outside the Party, yet they had a common purpose, and their chief spokesman became playwright Václav Havel. In the spring of 1975 Havel wrote an 'open letter' to Husák in which he pointed out that far from returning to normality or order, Czechoslovakia was passing through a crisis – and the crisis was getting deeper. A continuation of present policies would only lead to disaster, and history would judge Husák and his colleagues most severely for driving Czechoslovakia into this impasse. This letter, like other products of the dissident press, was broadcast back to the country by Western radio stations. It remains an important testament to the courage of the man who was himself later to become the country's president.

In December 1976 Havel was one of the founders of a dissident group which became known as Charter 77 (the movement's declaration, written in large part by Havel, was dated 1 January 1977). Other founder members included Jiří Němec, Pavel Kohout and Zdeněk Mlynář. The movement was formed, like similar groups in neighbouring countries, to protest against abuses of human rights by reference to the Helsinki agreements and to draw infringements to the attention of the world media. A catalyst leading to the fusion of many dissident groups in just one movement was the regime's arrest, in March 1976, of a group of young rock musicians and fans. The youngsters, borrowing ideas from their Western counterparts of the 1960s, had decided to turn their backs on the sterile, official culture and develop an alternative one. They were, though, not a political opposition group, and the fact that the authorities should seek to extinguish all independent organizations, even an inoffensive group of musicians, struck many people as being both an appalling and a ridiculous misuse of power. The mobilization of opposition resources brought an awareness of how many groups there were and the realization that greater co-ordination was needed.

The founding of Charter 77 was the most significant political event in the period between the Prague Spring and the 'velvet revolution' of 1989. Charter 77 was not a political party, nor a trade union like Solidarity. It was not even an organization, but merely a loose association of like-minded citizens concerned that political and social life should be ordered along ethical lines, and that infringements of human rights should not be passed over in silence. It hoped, its manifesto stated, to engage in a constructive dialogue with the authorities over such abuses. This was too optimistic. In ensuing years the Charter signatories were threatened, harassed and hounded by the authorities. Some, like Jiří Lederer, were imprisoned early on (for 'undermining the republic'). Václav Havel received a prison sentence of four and a half years, Jiří Dienstbier (now foreign minister) one of three years. But those at liberty faced dismissal from their jobs, telephone threats against themselves or their families, or physical assault on the streets. A large number of Charter signatories were hounded out of the country. Despite such pressures, in the twelve years of its existence the 'Chartists' produced scores of letters, reports, pamphlets, analyses and declarations about a wide range of subjects – from history to nuclear power. Charter 77 did not become a mass movement – it had few working-class members – but gave hope to many and inspired others to form opposition groups.

The 'velvet revolution' of 1989

The 1980s in Czechoslovakia marked a change in the relationship between the Party and the people. There was a new spirit abroad of optimism and defiance which strengthened as the decade progressed. Three factors influenced the public mood. The first was the success – despite its suppression – of the Solidarity trade union in Poland in confronting the Communist authorities and attracting mass support. The second was Gorbachev's assumption of power in the Kremlin in 1985, and the introduction of a more liberal Soviet regime. The third was a resurgence of religious belief and activity – particularly among the Roman Catholic population.

The Soviet liberalization was perhaps the most important for the Prague authorities. The Czechoslovak censorship could hardly stem the flood of new articles appearing in Soviet party journals. Yet the unprecedented questioning and self-criticism ran directly counter to the stern, uncompromising approach of the Husák regime. The position of the Prague regime became increasingly awkward as Czechs and Slovaks realized that the changes taking place in the Soviet Union were more radical even than the modest reforms they had called for during the Prague Spring. In April 1967 when Gorbachev visited Prague he was generally complimentary towards the leadership but pointedly refused to endorse the Soviet intervention of 1968. His silence had a similar sequel to that of Brezhnev's visit in 1968. In December 1987 Husák resigned as Party secretary general (though he remained president). His successor was another hardliner, Miloš Jakeš. Jakeš had been right-hand man to Vasil Bilak, when the latter was charged with purging Party reformers in 1970.

In the course of 1988 and early 1989 Czechoslovakia seemed on the surface to remain almost unaffected by the historic moves towards dismantling of Communist rule that were taking place in her neighbours Poland and Hungary. True, the country saw the largest protest demonstration for twenty years in August 1988, on the anniversary of the Soviet-led invasion. Perhaps because of this, the government displayed nervousness the following January when a series of peaceful demonstrations in Prague to commemorate the death of Jan Palach were broken up by police. Václav Havel and thirteen other dissidents were arrested when they tried to lay flowers at the spot where Palach had set fire to himself. The 52-year-old playwright was originally charged with 'hooliganism', although he was later sentenced for breach of the peace and obstructing the authorities.

Yet Havel's arrest proved an embarrassment, particularly as the news broke that he had been nominated for the Nobel Peace Prize. Amid the international chorus of protest, over a thousand prominent figures from the Czechoslovak world of art and culture signed an appeal for Havel's release. Since they were all state employees, and faced loss of employment for their heresy, this was a move which demanded courage. On 20 February 1989 the premier Adamec returned from Moscow, evidently affected by the new mood of liberalization there. He told a Czech reporter, 'We want to hold a dialogue with all those who honestly desire to help socialism in a creative way . . .'

By the summer the Prague leadership was looking forward with apprehension to the twenty-first anniversary of the Soviet invasion. Three of the five Warsaw Pact countries which had taken part in the invasion had already condemned the act. The Czech leadership's response had been that such statements 'helped the cause of anti-socialist forces'. They could scarcely say otherwise. A repudiation of the 1968 invasion and attempts to rehabilitate Dubček called the legitimacy of the post-1968 regimes directly into question. (In fact, later in the year demonstrators were to taunt Jakeš with the chant that he was 'installed by tanks . . .'.) In the event the Prague demonstrations of 21 August 1989 were small. Only a few thousand people took part, probably due to the fact that opposition leaders, fearing a repetition of police violence (and no doubt mindful of the savage violence of China's Tiananmen Square), had advised people to stay away.

The Prague authorities began to take steps to soften discontent and to show that, along with the moves towards liberalization in its neighbouring states, Czechoslovakia too could show a human face to its citizens. On 1 August the Czech branch of International PEN Club held its first meeting since being disbanded in 1971. There followed in September a liberalization of the travel laws for those who wanted to visit the West. A greater openness was also evident on economic matters, belated recognition by the Party that economic failure lay at the root of much of the popular discontent. A government spokesman with responsibility for nationalized industry admitted that 30% of Czechoslovak industry was hopelessly uneconomic. The Party daily *Rudé Právo* reported on 30 August that there were 38 state enterprises for which bankruptcy proceedings had been started and 147 agricultural enterprises which had to balance their books within five years or be dissolved.

A turning point in the Czechoslovak situation came in October 1989 with the toppling of two hardline Soviet bloc regimes – in East Germany and Bulgaria. These developments brought to the opposition – and the hitherto uncommitted – the realization of how shaky were the foundations of Communist rule. At the same time, and in due proportion, the Party leadership began to lose confidence, finding itself to be an anachronism – an island of orthodoxy in a sea of reform and change.

Ironically, the event which led to the collapse of the Communist regime in Czechoslovakia had been approved by the authorities themselves. It was a student march in the centre of Prague on 17 November to commemorate the death at the hands of the Gestapo of a student, Jan Opletal. When the rally turned into an anti-government demonstration, the tens of thousands of people who had gathered in Prague's Wenceslas Square were attacked by riot police. Over 140 people were reported injured. Indignation at the news of the violence was increased when the rumour (later denied) spread that a student had been killed at the hands of the police. Instead of deterring opposition, the government's action provoked further marches, which grew in size on successive days. The Prague regime found itself confronting a new generation of dissidents – young people who had grown up since the 1968 events and had not the same fear of repression as their elders. In the early stages, though, the students had little support from working people.

On 19 November more than a dozen opposition groups met in Prague to form an opposition coalition, Civic Forum. (In Slovakia a parallel movement called Public Against Violence came into being.) They were joined by representatives of the Socialist Party and the People's Party, for 40 years the docile partners of the ruling Communists. Their joint resolution called for dialogue with the government and for the resignation of several Party leaders. Support came in the form of strikes and occupations of schools and universities throughout the country. Students prepared posters and made dozens of video copies of the film of the police violence, which were circulated to small towns and villages as a counter to the official, censored version. Actors, musicians and theatre staff also went on strike and theatres quickly became the scenes of public debates.

By Monday 20 November extraordinary scenes were taking place in Wenceslas Square as flowers were placed and candles lit at the foot of St Wenceslas's statue, the national flag waved and the national anthem sung. Keys were jangled, reminiscent of the closing-time ritual in Czech inns, to remind the leadership that their time, too, had come. Premier Adamec, clearly prompted by the paralysis that affected his older Party colleagues and wishing to dissociate himself from the earlier violence, met with opposition leaders and offered 'a different concept of the leading role of the Party', including the idea of non-Communists joining the government.

On 24 November both Havel and Alexander Dubček had addressed crowds in Prague. Dubček, speaking publicly for the first time in the current crisis, called for the resignation of the leadership. As he appeared on the balcony he was greeted by a huge roar of welcome. A two-hour national strike was called for Monday, 27 November. It met with the support of 60% of the workforce, and persuaded the Party leaders that the mood of defiance now extended to their traditional supporters.

Jakeš handed in his resignation and that of the entire Party secretariat. He was replaced as Party leader by a 48-year-old former railwayman, Karel Urbánek, who was relatively unknown and, because of his age, was untainted by association with the events of 1968. The opposition forces had developed a confidence and a momentum, however, and were not to be fobbed off by yet one more attempt to 'shuffle the pack'. Crowds continued to gather in the centre of Prague, to chants of 'Free elections'. Havel made clear to the crowds that dialogue with the Party must include abolition of the Party's leading role.

Although this was conceded by the Party – as was the demand for free elections – a government reshuffle on 3 December which still left 16 of the twenty Cabinet posts in Communist hands created an administration which lasted a mere seven days. Marián Čalfa was called upon to supervise the Party's retreat by forming a coalition with opposition leaders. Miloš Jakeš and Miroslav Štěpán, the former Party boss for Prague, were both expelled from the Party, after the public had been treated to the unedifying spectacle of the two men denying responsibility for the police violence on 17 November, while apologizing for it.

The new government dominated by non-Communists was sworn in on 10 December. Immediately afterwards the president, Gustav Husák, resigned. Premier Čalfa, a 43-year-old Slovak, soon left the Communist Party – as did two deputy premiers and a number of ministers of this Government of National Unity. It had become evident to many that in the rapidly changing political climate Party membership had become a liability and a hindrance to career prospects. Thousands of Party members at the lower levels returned their Party cards. (Between 600,000 and 800,000 – or 40% of the membership – are thought to have left the Party by the end of February 1990.) For the more active members, though – the editors, directors, heads of departments, ambassadors – there was nowhere to hide. Positions occupied by the *nomenklatura* during the Husák–Jakeš era were vacated – from government down to district and workplace level. They were quickly replaced by members of Civic Forum. Jan Czarnogursky, released from prison on one day, found himself deputy premier the next. Jiří Dienstbier, spokesman for the opposition movement, became Minister for Foreign Affairs. Havel's translator, Rita Klímová (before 1968 a professor of economics), became ambassador in the USA, while the son of Rudolf Slánský, victim of the Stalinist purges, became ambassador in Moscow.

President Havel

The election race for presidential office, following Husák's resignation, was initially between Havel and Dubček. Dubček, though, aware of the massive support for Havel, especially among the young, and having been promised the chairmanship of the Federal Assembly, made way to give Havel a clear run. On 29 December Havel, a man who had been imprisoned four times (the most recent sentence being at the beginning of 1989) and frequently detained by the regime, was elected president. He was the most popular and respected holder of that office since the country's founder Tomáš Masaryk, with whom he has since frequently been compared. The election result was important, since a legacy of the Communist years is that the presidency confers considerable powers. The president is not only Supreme Commander of the Armed Forces, he has the power to dissolve the National Assembly and name a new government. Havel undertook to use his new powers as a stabilizing force during the period of transformation to come and as a guarantee that full democracy would be restored to Czechoslovakia.

What made Havel such a popular figure? He is perceived by his countrymen as an unassuming and likeable person, in some ways otherworldly. He was an artist and philosopher rather than a politician and was not tainted by contact with the Party or political life. Indeed, he has made little secret of his dislike for politics. His word was believed, and he had a moral authority in a community which had need of a figure it could look up to. He had proved his integrity over many years through fighting for the principles he believes in. Also, he spoke out in a language that was free of the jargon and obfuscation that Czechs and Slovaks had become used to from the Party bosses.

In his New Year presidential address Havel told Czechs and Slovaks that their government had been restored to them. He undertook to raise the country from the mire of hypocrisy and restore the concept of morality to politics. Stressing that Czechoslovakia should be independent and never again 'an appendage or a poor relative of anyone else', he said that 'although small, we were once the spiritual crossroads of Europe. Can we not become so once again?' He invited both the Pope and the Dalai Lama, as spiritual leaders, to visit Czechoslovakia.

The first concrete steps towards the new morality had unfortunate results. The new president declared an amnesty for prisoners in the country's jails. The amnesty was to be broadly based – only those who had abused the power of an official post were excluded. It was planned to release some 200,000 prisoners – two-thirds of the prison population. (Until the 1989 revolution Czechoslovakia was one of the few European countries to have a proportionately higher prison population – at 195 per 100,000 – than Britain.) This caused an immediate problem on the labour front, since prison labour was used at many industrial works, including the Skoda car factory at Mlada Boleslav. But many of the freed immediately came into conflict with the law again. Cases of theft and violence were reported, and a group of 80 former prisoners vandalized a railway station at Olomouc. In the end Havel had to ask Interior Minister, Richard Sacher, to safeguard public safety 'by all possible means' from marauding gangs of released prisoners.

The Czechoslovak government had begun tearing down the country's 'iron curtain' – its border defences with the West – at the beginning of December. Immediately after his election, Havel visited East Germany, where he stressed his support for German unification and offered his country's help in tearing down the Berlin Wall. Controversy broke out in Czechoslovakia when Havel requested forgiveness for the brutality with which Germans had been expelled from the country at the end of the war. It was a wise move towards reconciliation, though, and was soon recognized as such by his countrymen. Havel has repeatedly said that he sees nothing to fear from a unified Germany, but his view is that the new, unified Germany should take its place within a unified Europe. Existing power blocs, he feels, should be be replaced by a European Security system.

Visits to Poland, Hungary, the USA, the Soviet Union, Britain and France were also to come within three months of Havel taking office. His Soviet visit at the end of February 1990 was of particular importance, since he went with the mission of persuading Gorbachev to remove one of the last vestiges of the 1968 invasion – the 'temporarily' stationed 75,000 Red Army troops – from Czechoslovak soil. Agreement was reached that all would be removed within eighteen months, i.e. by the beginning of July 1991.

Economic reform

Despite economic problems, Czechoslovakia has had a rather more successful economy than many of its Comecon neighbours, especially Poland and the Soviet Union. Food shops, for example, have usually been full and prices low (due to subsidies), although the choice of goods is poor by Western standards. The prospects for economic recovery are good. Czechoslovakia has an educated, skilled labour force. Its $8 billion of foreign debt is not as heavy as that of Poland or Hungary and is regarded as manageable by Western bankers, who regard the country as a good investment. It has a relatively low level of inflation, between 2.5% and 3.5%. But there is a need to rein in government spending drastically. The state budget accounts for a massive 70% of national income. Some 8% of this (50 billion crowns) is spent on defence and security, while further large sums are spent on government bureaucracy and state subsidies.

Deputy Premier, Valtr Komárek, pinpointed four major problems of reconstruction in a recent interview. First, Czechoslovakia needs to develop its industry away from the mining, steel and heavy engineering sectors into lighter areas such as electronics. Second, it must develop new markets for its products. The Soviet Union, Czechoslovakia's main export customer in the postwar years, is expected to buy 30% fewer of its heavy engineering products over the next few years. Third, in the interests of efficiency and innovation there will have to be some moves to break up the huge industrial conglomerates such as Tatra and Skoda, which produces everything from cars to nuclear power plants. Finally, some very important decisions will have to be made about environmental costs of Czechoslovak industry, which uses three times as much energy to produce one unit of net production as in Western Europe. The 100 million tons of lignite and the 26 million tons of coal burned in generating electricity are creating one of the biggest ecological disasters in Europe.

At the beginning of 1990 opinion was divided about how far-reaching a reform programme should be and when it should be implemented. While some (including Finance Minister, Václav Klaus) called enthusiastically for a tough budget and an early privatization programme, others were more cautious, fearing the effects such policies might have on their electoral chances. In the end the painful decisions were put off until a government with a proper mandate was returned.

The 1990 election

The 8 June election determined the composition of the bicameral Federal Parliament, and the two (Czech and Slovak) national councils. The run-up to the election proved eventful for the Civic Forum camp and their Slovak allies, Public Against Violence. First came a ridiculous and unseemly quarrel over the new name the Republic should bear in the post-Communist era; some of the more nationalist-minded Slovaks were so determined that their nation should receive equal prominence, that at one point a hyphenated form was suggested as a compromise (it is still officially used in Slovakia). Then the caretaker government came under fire for being 'soft' on the Communists. On the one hand there were calls for the Communists to be banned from taking part in the election; on the other hand, Interior Minister Richard Sacher (himself a member of the People's Party) was accused of failure to root out all vestigial influence of the state security police, the Statni Bezpecnost (St.B.). Rumours circulated that former security agents aimed to destabilize the new democracy. These were given substance by a bomb incident in central Prague during the election campaign.

As if to contribute to the uncertainty and further undermine the government's standing, it was revealed that the origins of the 'velvet revolution' of the previous November had not been as straightforward as popularly imagined. The police violence which triggered off popular protest had apparently been orchestrated by the KGB in an operation to unseat Husák and the hardliners in the Party. The attempt to bring in more moderate voices attuned to the new thinking in the Kremlin had gone out of control, paving the way for Civic Forum to step in.

All this might have damaged Civic Forum's chances. Indeed, at one point in mid-April opinion polls showed that support for the Forum/PAV allies had dropped to a mere 19% and that they were being pressed hard by the Christian Democrats. Observers began to wonder whether the more intellectual leadership which the Forum represented was beginning to lose its appeal to the masses. Yet if the Pope's visit to Czechoslovakia in April – the first papal visit since 1052 – gave the Christian Democrats a boost, Civic Forum candidates could derive satisfaction from the fact that their figure-head, Václav Havel (although, as president, neutral in principle), was constantly in the public eye.

The election result was a vote of confidence in the Civic Forum/PAV camp. It attracted just under 50% of the votes, yet owing to the nature of the voting system adopted, secured more than half of the seats in the Federal Parliament. The greatest surprise, apart from an impressive 96% turn-out of voters, was the fact that Civil Forum's improved showing was achieved not at the cost of the Communists, but at the cost of the Christian Democrats who were relegated to third place overall behind the Communists. Yet it is still the Christian Democrats with whom the Forum/PAV alliance will have to deal in future. In order to push through the more important pieces of legislation a 60% majority is required and Civic Forum has indicated its refusal to work with the Communists or with nationalist groupings (Slovaks, Hungarians). One of the tasks of the new government during its two-year term of office will be to frame a new Constitution. Another more immediate task is the selection of the President. At the time of writing, it seems almost certain that Havel will remain as president despite his earlier protestations that he is not a politician and finds the job worse than being in prison.

4 THE GERMAN DEMOCRATIC REPUBLIC

The people's revolution

Introduction

Towards midnight on 9 November 1989, Günter Schabowski, First Secretary of the ruling Socialist Unity Party (SED) in East Berlin, appeared on GDR television and announced to an incredulous population that the Berlin Wall was no longer a barrier to West Berlin. Most viewers were stunned by the news, but after some time decided to go to the Wall to discover whether Schabowski's words were true. As a human tide of East Berliners moved towards the hated symbol of division, border guards gave up any attempt to regulate the flow. East and West Berlin had reunited after 18 years. This reunion was the death knell of the GDR.

The death of the GDR was not solemnly observed. It was celebrated with a euphoria, joy and delight which knew no bounds. The scenes of emotion will long remain in the memories of those who experienced them. Everyone there was aware that they were participating in the making of history.

The German Democratic Republic (GDR) is a latter-day Holy Roman Empire, which was disparagingly referred to as neither holy, nor Roman, nor an empire. It foundered because it was neither German nor democratic. The ruling Socialist Unity Party (SED) tried to sustain the myth that Germans in East and West Germany belonged to different nations. The GDR occupies a unique place in contemporary European history. It is the only state which has voluntarily voted itself out of existence. The GDR declared proudly that it was the first socialist state on German soil. It may turn out to have been the first and last socialist state on German soil.

Historical background

The Republic was a war baby, and its father was Josef Stalin. It was born officially on 7 October 1949 but it had existed ever since the unconditional surrender of Nazi Germany on 8 May 1945 under the name of the Soviet Occupied Zone of Germany. The Allies had agreed that after defeat, Germany was to be occupied, and therefore three occupation zones (American, British and Soviet) were agreed. Berlin was to be divided into three sectors. Later, a French occupation zone and a French sector in Berlin were added, but Stalin insisted that they be taken from the American and British occupied territories.

Since the Red Army had conquered Berlin, the Soviets had a free hand in the city until the Western Allies arrived on 1 July. A Soviet Military

EAST GERMANY

Official name	German Democratic Republic
Area	108,333 sq. km (41,828 sq. miles)
Population	16,666,000 (1988) (annual growth rate 0%)
Capital	Berlin (East)
Language	German, Sorb
Religion	30% Evangelical Protestant, 6% Roman Catholic
Currency	mark of the GDR (Ostmark, DDR-M)

Administration (SMAD) was established to run the city and the Soviet zone. Its aim was to have a functioning city government in place by the time Berlin was again declared the capital of Germany. However, the Potsdam Conference could not agree on the future of Germany and the Allied Control Commission (ACC) fared no better. The Soviet Zone was stripped of many of its assets, which were declared by Moscow to be reparations. All important enterprises were nationalized in 1946 and a land reform eliminated large landowners. The onset of the Cold War in 1947 speeded up the Stalinist revolution and in March 1948 the Soviets left the ACC.

This ended the masquerade of a common German policy by the four occupying powers. All they had ever agreed on was their right as victors to determine the future of Germany, and that Germany should never again be a threat to European peace. Lying at the heart of Europe, the country was too important to be allowed to slip into the other camp. The Soviets wanted a socialist Germany, the Americans a capitalist one and the British and French were so concerned about resurgent German political and economic power that they preferred the country to remain divided.

The introduction of the deutschmark in the Western zones and Berlin in June 1948 divided Germany. The Soviet response was the Berlin blockade and the Western answer, the Berlin air lift. The longer the blockade dragged on, the more certain it was that a separate West German state, anchored in the Western alliance, would come into being. There was a real fear of the Soviets using their military power to expand westwards, and this gave birth to NATO, which obliged the USA to maintain troops in Western Europe.

Politically, the Soviets attempted to seize the initiative in Germany in 1945, and legalized parties in their zone in June without consulting the other occupying powers. The parties which came into being were conceived of as all-German ones; the Communists (KPD); the Social Democrats (SPD); the Christian Democrats (CDU) and the Liberal Democrats (LDP). Later, a National Democratic Party and a Peasants' Party were founded. Only in 1989 were more parties added to the list. The parties formed the National Front with the Communists playing the leading role.

Under the skilful leadership of Walter Ulbricht the Communists made headway but the SPD became more popular. It had always been the avowed intent of the KPD and SPD to merge, but when the fusion did come, in April 1946, it was a forced marriage. The relatively free elections later in 1946 did not provide the Communists with the mandate they desired, and thereafter only lists of candidates could be voted for.

When the GDR came into being on 7 October 1949 it was effectively a one-party state. The Communist Party then began the process of transforming the country into a socialist one. However, a Stalinist political and economic model was not to the liking of the great majority of the population. This led to a massive exodus of skilled personnel, but on 17 June

THE PARTITION OF BERLIN

REGIONAL ORGANIZATION IN EAST GERMANY

THE LÄNDER OF THE GDR (May 1945 – July 1952)   THE BEZIRKS OF THE GDR (July 1952)

1953 those who remained revolted against increased work norms. Without Soviet help, Ulbricht and the SED would have been swept from power.

By the late 1950s Ulbricht had ousted all his rivals and defeated efforts to retain aspects of the market economy. The border with West Germany had been closed but Berlin was still an open city. In order to complete the building of socialism by imposing collectivization of agriculture Ulbricht needed to close off the Berlin outlet. Khrushchev finally agreed, and on 13 August 1961 the building of the Berlin Wall began. The SED believed that only if the GDR were isolated from capitalist West Germany could social- ism be built at home.

Thereby began an isolation which was to last to 1989. In a world of increasing economic interdependence the SED attempted to do the impos- sible – build a modern, industrial state in isolation. In the 1950s and 1960s certain sectors of the GDR economy were on a European, even world, level but, over time, these achievements were lost. Autarchy became an ob- session with Erich Honecker after he succeeded Ulbricht as party leader in June 1971.

The drive for autarchy led to endless efforts to raise the legitimacy of the SED regime. The GDR proclaimed itself a separate nation, and attempts were made to engender a specific GDR state consciousness. The GDR evolved a specific economic model which was claimed as the most de- veloped anywhere. The leadership began a cult of past German heroes, including Frederick the Great, Luther and Goethe, but all in vain. Had the GDR become a vibrant, economically successful society it might have survived. However, economic malaise afflicted it from the early 1980s and the SED's inability to halt this condemned the GDR to accelerated decline. As the economic and social situation deteriorated, the regime descended to half truths and then lies. The educated segment of the population found the lack of dialogue with the regime extremely frustrating, and eventually assembled to debate the deteriorating position. With hindsight, the key variable in the collapse of the GDR was the Gorbachev phenomenon. His bold initiatives in the Soviet Union, at a time of leadership paralysis in the GDR, inspired many, and revealed that there could be an alternative to existing socialism.

Seven key factors led to the demise of the GDR:

1 The political, economic and social decline of the country during the 1980s and the startling revelations about the abuse of power and unbridled corruption of the GDR elite;
2 The advent of Gorbachev in the Soviet Union. His policies of *perestroika*, *glasnost* and democratization undermined the legitimacy of a GDR socialist model;
3 The swelling stream of GDR refugees during 1989. This led to the crucial decision by the Hungarian government on 11 September 1989 to permit GDR citizens to cross unhindered into Austria;

4 The events surrounding the 40th anniversary celebrations of the GDR state in October 1989. Gorbachev, as the main foreign guest, came not to honour Honecker and the SED regime but to contribute to their overthrow;

5 The power of the crowd;

6 The opening of the Berlin Wall;

7 The resurrection of politics and the march to German unity.

Political, economic and social decline

GDR published statistics were systematically falsified during the 1980s and presumably long before that. The SED's legitimacy rested on its ability to fashion an economically successful state as a viable alternative to West Germany. The GDR had significant achievements to its credit, especially in the realm of social policy, but these were all achieved before 1980. Competitiveness *vis-à-vis* West Germany declined. The technological gulf between East and West increased as East German industry failed to invest in new equipment and keep pace with world technology. Labour productivity was a critical factor. In an economy in which there were no labour reserves, economic output could only grow through productivity gains. Annually the gap widened between labour productivity in East and West Germany. There were islands of excellence, such as Carl Zeiss Jena, but the overall picture was one of gloom. This led to a rising curve of mendacious statistics. While these fooled many foreign observers, they increased the frustration felt by most GDR citizens. They knew their living standards were declining but the state insisted that things were rather rosy. The lack of investment led to critical shortages of housing, medical and other social services. Many citizens were shocked to hear, on 13 November 1989, that the state had run up debts of 130 billion ostmarks. Most industrial enterprises were also in debt, as were most local authorities. Hard currency debts, on 3 January 1990, were put at US$20.6 billion.

The person rightly blamed for this monumental mismanagement of the national economy was Günter Mittag, SED secretary for the economy since 1976. Deeply unpopular, arrogant and dictatorial, Mittag ran the GDR like a family firm – *his* family firm. Like several other members of the GDR elite, he became addicted to hunting and delighted at shooting at anything that moved. (Finding a factory on his game reserve he ordered its removal! This makes clear his economic priorities in the 1980s.) Other members of the elite enjoyed unheard-of privileges, and could be likened to feudal robber barons. They had special residences built for themselves at Wandlitz, just outside Berlin, the whole area being out of bounds to ordinary GDR citizens, and every luxury imaginable was available to them. The state's hard currency reserves were plundered to pander to the whims of the elite. One device for adding to the stock of imported goods was the annual Christmas barter deal. Freedom for political prisoners in GDR jails could be bought by West Germany at princely sums. Some of the negotiators began to confuse state and personal profit during the 1980s. Alexander Schalck-Golodkowski was said to have been involved in illegal arms and currency deals. Other leading politicians were less expensive. Harry Tisch, head of the trade union movement, was so obsessed about cleanliness that he had a shower installed in his garage! Needless to say, Honecker had most. He even had his own island in the Baltic.

During the 1980s Honecker and his elite gradually lost contact with reality. They all lived under Communism, where money was no longer necessary. Wealth and luxury sapped the moral fibre of even the most resilient Communist. Only those who deliberately avoided becoming members of the elite, such as Hans Modrow, evaded its deadly embrace. Top officials could not complain of being kept in the dark. Honecker dismissed the criticisms of one First Party Secretary by advising him to concern himself with matters in his own district.

The SED claimed that it was building real socialism in the GDR, but the party permitted no debate about priorities or policies within its ranks. Frustration built up, and churches became an alternative venue for discussions. As disillusionment grew with the Honecker regime so, too, did police brutality. Honecker appears to have believed that he was facing a counter-revolution which, by definition, had to be controlled from abroad. He was quite incapable of appreciating that it was not an exogenous force which was threatening socialism in the GDR but the SED's own incompetence and corruption, undermining it from within.

Enter Gorbachev

The advent of Gorbachev in the Soviet Union was an embarrassment to the SED leadership. It had become accustomed to setting its own priorities under the ailing Brezhnev and his successors. Gorbachev began to undermine the legitimacy of the SED by offering a fresh vision of socialism. Honecker found the principles of *perestroika*, *glasnost* and democratization deeply distasteful and alarming in their implications for the SED regime. *Neues Deutschland*, the party organ, censored Gorbachev's utterances, especially those which attacked party and governmental corruption. This did not prevent East Germans from discovering what the Soviet leader had said, since West German radio and television carried full coverage. Honecker's message to his members was that party discussion was to be restricted to the excerpts printed in *Neues Deutschland*. When *perestroika* was on the agenda many party and trade union officials insisted that it only applied to the USSR.

Honecker argued that the SED did not need the changes being introduced by Gorbachev since its economy had not declined. However, the increasing shortages and poverty of political life transformed Gorbachev into a symbol of hope for many GDR citizens. He was greeted with genuine warmth during his visits to the republic.

Events in Poland and Hungary began to isolate the SED. The GDR congratulated the Chinese leadership on slaughtering students in Tiananmen Square in June 1989. Gorbachev made no secret of the fact that he believed that the present kind of socialism had no future. Although all socialist regimes were sovereign, he expected them to follow in his footsteps and introduce a more democratic system.

Given the opportunity, Honecker lectured the Soviet leader and party on the virtues of East German socialism, and was quite incapable of grasping that his analysis of GDR reality was ludicrously wrong. Other members of the SED elite found original ways of justifying the do-nothing policy. Kurt Hager, Central Committee Secretary for Ideology, asked rhetorically if one's neighbour papered his house, was one supposed to do the same? He was forever dogged by this unfortunate remark.

Emigration

A tangible measure of the dissatisfaction felt by East Germans was the increasing numbers trying to emigrate to West Germany. A rising flood began to seek refuge in West German embassies in Eastern Europe and in the West German mission in East Berlin. On 3 August 1989 the Hungarian Foreign Ministry stated that it was considering granting GDR citizens political asylum. Hungary began to turn a blind eye to East Germans crossing the Austrian frontier, and by 10 August about 1,600 had reached Austria. Bonn was forced to close its mission in East Berlin and its embassy in Budapest to stem the flow of those seeking to move to the West.

Animated diplomatic discussions between Bonn, East Berlin and other capitals failed to staunch the flow of refugees. Remarkably, the GDR authorities did not cancel visa-free travel to Czechoslovakia. Most refugees then moved on to Hungary. The Hungarian government regarded the refugees as a German problem and eventually presented the GDR with an ultimatum. Either solve the problem or Hungary would open its frontiers to Austria.

At about midnight on 11 September Hungary did this, and over 25,000 East Germans crossed into Austria *en route* to West Germany. This unilateral decision infringed a 1969 agreement, but the Hungarians had come to the conclusion that the SED regime could not survive very long. The decision to open the frontier was of enormous political and psychological significance, since it was the breaking of the first link in the chain which had isolated the GDR since 1961. This decision had a catastrophic impact on SED morale, and led to a flood of refugees making for Hungary. The GDR responded by dragging passengers off trains and raiding flats to seize identity papers. East Germans, in turn, made for West German embassies in Warsaw and Prague. East Berlin capitulated, and on 30 September special trains, accompanied by West German officials, carried 800 refugees from Warsaw to Helmsted and 5,500 from Prague to Hof in Bavaria. The following day, over 6,000 more travelled by special trains from Warsaw and Prague to West Germany. There was no respite for the embassies, since new refugees immediately replaced those who had left. On 4 October over 7,600 refugees travelled to West Germany in special locked trains. Their departure had been delayed while all the stations they were to pass through in the GDR were cleared of would-be emigrés. On 4 November the Czechoslovak authorities secured an agreement from the GDR government that permitted GDR refugees to cross into West Germany. Over 40,000 people made use of this between 4 and 9 November. By 31 December 343,854 GDR citizens had moved to the West.

Alarmingly for the GDR, the refugees were predominantly between 25 and 45 years old. They and their families had chosen to turn their backs on their homeland and abandon their flats, cars and most worldly possessions. The refugees included many doctors, teachers, engineers, railway workers and others desperately needed in the GDR. This produced a knock-on effect throughout the economy. Medical services, for instance, were badly hit as doctors and nurses left.

Gorbachev's visit

The chief guest at the celebrations marking the 40th anniversary of the GDR in 1989 was Mikhail Gorbachev, but he came not to praise but to criticize. At a gala meeting on 6 October, the eve of the anniversary, he said he expected the 'SED to find political answers to the questions on the agenda being posed by all social forces and which concerned the population'. On 7 October Honecker and Gorbachev met for discussions, but there was no meeting of minds. According to Soviet sources, considerable attention was paid to the 'changes which were taking place in many socialist countries'. After his return to Moscow Gorbachev stated, in an interview on Soviet television, that he had pressed for reforms in the GDR.

Official parades and demonstrations marked the anniversary but counter-demonstrations, involving tens of thousands of people in favour of reform and freedom of opinion, took place in East Berlin, Leipzig, Dresden, Plauen, Jena, Potsdam and many other cities, and were broken up by police, often with great brutality. Many of the demonstrators were injured and over a thousand arrested. Foreign journalists were also caught up in the violence; they were beaten and their equipment smashed. Renewed demonstrations took place on 8 October and again the security forces dispersed them by force. Many were arrested.

The power of the crowd

Those who wished to practise free speech in the GDR had to go to church. In a party-run state, churches were the only buildings not directly licensed by the SED. Over the years, a dialogue had developed between the churches and the regime and a certain amount of free speech was tolerated. Many clerics were embarrassed by their role but gradually, over time, the churches evolved a social theology which was based on dialogue, opposition to violence and reconciliation between conflicting groups.

Various pastors emerged who enjoyed great authority and represented an alternative way of life to the increasingly moribund Marxist–Leninist dogma of the SED. During the 1970s there was considerable contact between the churches and Honecker, but this stopped in the 1980s. The Roman Catholic Church was more conservative than Evangelical churches in the 1970s but gradually became more radical. However, it never produced clerics who were as prominent as Rainer Eppelmann, for instance. The fact that Catholics made up about one in six believers in the GDR also played a role.

It is a custom for believers to pray for peace, but this began to assume greater significance as political tension rose. Leipzig became a focal point and St Nicholas's Church the source of a new movement. Regularly on Mondays after prayers, believers and others assembled outside and demonstrated peacefully. This was copied in many other cities and the security services became alarmed and dispersed the crowds. On 29 September 1989 church authorities in Leipzig stated that eleven demonstrators had been sentenced to up to six months' imprisonment and that about two dozen had been fined up to 5,000 ostmarks. Instead of this intimidating protesters, a remarkable phenomenon developed. Each successive Monday evening saw an increase in the number of demonstrators in Leipzig. On 2 October over 20,000 demonstrated and were attacked by the security services, with many injuries and arrests. Large demonstrations took place throughout the GDR on 6, 7 and 8 October with security forces dispersing the crowds. Again, many were injured and arrested. On 4 October over 3,000 demonstrators and police clashed violently in front of Dresden's main railway station, and the following day the same happened. Demonstrators in Magdeburg were also attacked by the security forces.

The violent conduct of the security forces became a focus of protest. On 9 October the crowd in Leipzig had swollen to 70,000, but this time the police did not intervene. This was due to the fact that three Leipzig SED secretaries, Kurt Masur, conductor of the Leipzig Gewandhausorchester, Pastor Peter Zimmermann and the artist Bernd Lutz Lange, had signed an appeal which had been read out in churches and broadcast. The appeal stated that a 'free exchange of views about the further development of socialism in our country was needed. Therefore the signatories promise all citizens that this dialogue will not be restricted to Bezirk Leipzig but will also be conducted with our government'. The same day, Wolfgang Berghofer, Mayor of Dresden, received a delegation of 20 who were acting as spokespersons for the thousands of demonstrators who had been on the streets the day before. A nine-point programme was presented which demanded an explanation for the violent behaviour of the police on the previous day; the right to freedom of opinion, demonstration, travel and free elections; and the legalization of the political grouping 'Neues Forum'. Berghofer offered to examine the demands and to pass them on to higher authorities. On 10 October 500 of those arrested in Dresden were released.

In the Gethsemane Church in East Berlin, Gottfried Forck, Bishop of Berlin, read an appeal signed by leading members of the Evangelical Church in Berlin-Brandenburg. It requested the GDR leadership to come up with credible suggestions which could serve as a basis for 'broad general agreement about a democratic, socialist future'. On the same day, Honecker received Yao Yilin, Chinese deputy Prime Minister, and drew parallels between the 'counter-revolutionary uprising in Beijing' and the 'present hate campaign against the GDR'.

On 15 October thousands demonstrated in Halle and Plauen for democratic reforms and Walter Leich, Bishop of Thuringia and chairman of the GDR Evangelical Church Union, in a circular, warned the GDR leadership against classifying demonstrators as 'enemies of the state' and to refrain from the use of force.

By 16 October the Leipzig crowd, demonstrating for reforms and democratic renewal, had grown to 120,000. Again, the police did not intervene. In Dresden about 10,000 people assembled in front of the Rathaus (town hall) to hear about the second round of talks between the mayor and city representatives and Church leaders. The results were to be read out the following evening in five Dresden churches. *Neues Deutschland* carried an interview with Berghofer on 18 October. The party newspaper also reported worker dissatisfaction with the information policy of the regime. However, it did not report the meeting of the leadership of the Writers' Union on 11 October. It called for 'revolutionary reform' in the GDR and demanded that an 'open democratic dialogue' at all levels of society should begin.

On 17 October over 20,000 packed five Dresden churches to hear reports on discussions with Wolfgang Berghofer which had taken place the day before. In Leipzig Mayor Bernd Seidel and other councillors met Church representatives for discussions. *Neues Deutschland* reported that talks between the SED, the government and trade unions had been taking place. It underlined that everything should be openly spoken about but socialism was not to be undermined. One of the National Front parties, the Liberal Democrats, proposed more freedom of travel and the ability to renounce GDR citizenship as well as greater legal protection for citizens.

The resignation of Erich Honecker on 18 October and his replacement by Egon Krenz accelerated demands for reform. On 20 October about 50,000 demonstrated in Dresden and over 5,000 in Karl-Marx-Stadt. In East Berlin the deputy police chief met the press and answered allegations about police brutality on 7–8 October. He stated he had many complaints against police officers and every complaint would be investigated. In Dresden, Bishop Johannes Hempel, addressing the Evangelical Synod, cast doubt on the right of the SED to rule.

On 21 October tens of thousands demonstrated in East Berlin, Plauen and other cities. In the capital Erhard Krack, Mayor of East Berlin, and Günter Schabowski, SED First Secretary, engaged in debate for over an hour with demonstrators. Schabowski promised that a new travel law had 'top priority'. He also lamented the fact that everything the SED did in the short term would be perceived by the population as a 'trap'.

Bishop Johannes Hempel called on the GDR leadership to apologize for brutal police behaviour against demonstrators. The Dresden Church authorities had prepared a document which included statements by eye witnesses. The report called for an independent enquiry, and this was supported by other groups, such as Demokratischer Aufbruch (Democratic Awakening). The report had been held back until after Honecker's resignation because of the appalling story it had to tell. The feeling was that had it been published beforehand it would have inflamed passions and led to possibly more bloodshed.

On 22 October 1989, in the Gewandhaus in Leipzig, over 500 people debated the situation in the GDR with Kurt Masur, Klaus Höpcke, deputy GDR Minister of Culture, and SED officials. It was agreed that similar meetings would take place on future Sundays.

On 23 October, on the eve of Egon Krenz's election as the GDR's head of state, about 300,000 demonstrated in Leipzig for free elections and against a 'new concentration of power'. Thousands also protested in Dresden, Magdeburg, Zwickau and East Berlin. Demonstrations against Krenz's election were called for the following day.

On 25 October in a live television interview on West German television Günter Schabowski stated that discussions with opposition groups had been under way for some time. He had also asked Church authorities to use their influence to ensure that demonstrations remained peaceful. In Neubrandenburg, after prayers for peace, 20,000 took part in a 'march of hope'. Mayor Heinz Hahn proposed discussions during the weekend and on following Saturdays.

On 26 October about 100,000 people attended a meeting in Dresden at which the mayor reported on a special session of the city council. Specialist groups, including citizens among their members, had been set up. On 28 October tens of thousands demonstrated in Plauen, Greiz, Rostock, Senftenberg and elsewhere for 'meaningful reforms in all areas of social life'. On 30 October over 200,000 in Leipzig cross-examined Mayor Seidel and other officials about the 'desolate housing situation' and the slow 'processing of complaints'.

On 4 November in East Berlin over 500,000 attended a demonstration for reform in the GDR, the largest ever demonstration in the GDR not organized by the SED. At the five-hour event, called by the artists' associations, 26 speakers, including the writers Stefan Heym and Christa Wolf, accused Erich Honecker of 'mistakes, omissions and crimes'. Similar demonstrations, stressing the urgency for political, economic and cultural change, took place throughout the country. On 7 November in Wismar 50,000 and in Meiningen 20,000 demonstrated for 'free elections and against the power monopoly of the SED'.

On 18 November over 150,000 demonstrated in East Berlin, Leipzig and Dresden against the power monopoly of the SED and for free elections. Over 50,000 attended the first legal meeting of 'Neues Forum'. Forum speaker Jochen Lässig called Egon Krenz an 'election falsifier and a friend of Chinese terror'.

On 11 December over 100,000 Leipzigers participated in the tenth Monday demonstration since 7 October; 90,000 came together in Dresden, 40,000 in Karl-Marx-Stadt, and there were large crowds in many other cities. At all demonstrations there were calls for and against German reunification. On 18 December 150,000 took part in Leipzig in the traditional Monday evening demonstration. On the initiative of Kurt Masur, it was dedicated to the 'victims of violence and spiritual oppression under Stalinist rule'. In East Berlin several hundred people commemorated the 'victims of Stalinism' in a silent march.

The traditional Monday demonstrations continued to take place in Leipzig and other cities, but the focus of attention changed. They orientated themselves more towards policy and the future. Issues such as German reunification became very important and, with elections brought forward to 18 March, West German politicians began to take part. This became very widespread in February and presented Federal politicians with a ready-made opportunity to address electors.

The power of the crowd played a major role in destroying the power of the SED. The party's refusal to enter debate about priorities was circumvented by large crowds, week after week, demanding reform and dialogue. The cradle of this revolution was Leipzig, and contributed to the weakness of the SED there. SED tactics were to disperse the crowds, but this could only be done if they remained relatively small. Once a crowd exceeded 100,000 in a city centre it became extremely difficult to control it. This was one of the reasons the security forces became so brutal and violent. A crowd of 200,000 or 300,000 could not be dispersed by them, and then the question of the use of the military had to be faced. Krenz has maintained that he was given an order by Honecker to use the military to break up the demonstrations in Leipzig but he refused to carry it out. Worker militias placed a statement in the *Leipziger Volkszeitung* to the effect that they would use force if ordered to do so. The fact that so little blood was spilt in Leipzig is due to the role of the Church and others, especially Masur, who became one of the heroes of the revolution. After Honecker had warned the population to remember what had happened in China Masur turned the Gewandhaus into a place for debate, and he and many other musicians tore up their SED party cards. The crowds throughout the GDR forced SED politicians to debate with them, and under these circumstances it is not surprising that they enjoyed little credibility and authority.

The inability of the SED to formulate cogent responses to popular demands handed the initiative over to other groups whose aims differed radically from those of SED socialism. The continued flow of refugees testified to the lack of hope about the future and the revelations about the corruption of the SED elite led to a precipitate decline in SED fortunes. Seldom has a political party lost power so rapidly.

Breaching the Wall

The opening of the Hungarian–Austrian border to GDR refugees on 11 September was the first link to break in the chain which isolated the country from the West. Breaching the Berlin Wall on 9 November tore the rest of that chain asunder. It also broke the spell of SED power. Before the opening of the Wall almost all East Germans had regarded the collapse of SED power as inconceivable. Now the impossible might happen, and with it the end of the fearfully efficient security police, the Stasi. Moreover, the holes in the Wall revealed that there was only one German nation. Honecker had previously defended the existence of the GDR by pointing to the achievements of existing socialism. He conceded that without such socialism the state had no reason to exist. He never expected socialism to fail, but his words proved very prophetic in November. Its collapse meant that it would have to give way to an economically more dynamic system – capitalism. The SED paid a high price for failure – extinction.

The resurrection of politics

The longer Honecker stayed in power, the more likely it was that all he stood for would go with him. His destructive role can be likened to that played by János Kádár in Hungary. Both men hung on too long, and in so doing failed to address all the key questions on the political agenda. They belonged to the Brezhnev generation, and their parties could only have survived if they had ruthlessly removed both men from power in the mid-1980s.

Honecker was in hospital several times during 1989 and when he left the Berlin Charité hospital after an operation for a malignant kidney tumour on 29 January 1990 he was judged too ill to be arrested. The lack of decisive action by the leadership to staunch the flow of refugees during the summer (such as ending visa-free travel to Czechoslovakia) was remarkable. This may have been due to Honecker's state of health, which paralysed decision-making, or to an inability to decide whether making concessions or using force was more likely to resolve the crisis. Using force was only an option while the size of the crowds did not exceed 100,000. But only a certain number of medium-sized crowds could be controlled by the security forces. The opposition realized that the authorities could not cope with demonstrations in many GDR cities simultaneously. Hence Monday evenings became a focal point for protest.

Since there could be no dialogue with the SED, initiative groups, such as New Forum, began forming. They were composed of artists, intellectuals, clergy and others who expressly avoided using the word 'party' to describe their group. The first opposition group to apply for recognition as an association was the New Forum. Their application was rejected by the Ministry of the Interior on 21 September 1989 on the grounds that they were 'hostile to the state'. New Forum actively recruited new members, and those involved were often fined. By 14 October, when 100 New Forum representatives met in East Berlin to co-ordinate their efforts, there were about 25,000 members.

After Gorbachev's visit it was only a matter of time before Honecker was forced to resign. However, he was determined to cling on to power as long as possible, and this split the SED Politburo. Some of his supporters remained loyal to the bitter end, and thereby ended their own political careers. Honecker commented publicly on the flight of refugees for the first time on 13 October. His lame comment was that no one could be 'indifferent' to the loss of citizens. All he could offer the beleaguered party and state was the promotion of the 'strategic concept of continuity and renewal'. No tangible reforms were in sight.

The in-fighting ended on 18 October at the 9th Plenum of the SED Central Committee, when Honecker asked to be relieved of all his functions: as SED First Secretary, Member of the Politburo, Chairman of the GDR Council of State and Chairman of the National Defence Council. Joachim Herrmann and Günter Mittag, who had stood shoulder to shoulder with Honecker, were also dismissed from their functions as Politburo members and Central Committee Secretaries. The new party leader was Egon Krenz, long regarded as the *Kronprinz* (crown prince). Krenz's career pattern was almost identical to that of Honecker's. He was a previous leader of the FDJ, the Communist youth movement and afterwards Central Committee Secretary for Security. He had been cultivated by the Soviets, and although Gorbachev would have preferred a clone, he had to make do with Krenz, who remained a prisoner of his own background and proved quite incapable of imaginative leadership.

Krenz had several crosses to bear from the beginning. Due to a previous illness, he had dark shadows under his eyes, and this gave him the appearance of being always the worse for drink. He was linked to the blatant falsification of the results of the May 1989 elections, which purported to show that the SED was as popular as ever. Then there was his ill-advised trip to China. But worst of all, he was the overlord of the Stasi. On the following day, Krenz met Bishop Werner Leich, chairman of the GDR Evangelical Church Union, and resolved to 'engender trust and to dare to build up trust'. The official communiqué was silent about demands for an open and very frank dialogue with the population and the involvement of reform groups such as New Forum.

On 22 October the first Soviet criticism of the Honecker leadership appeared in the trade union newspaper *Trud*. This was scathing in its condemnation of the old regime, and in a nice turn of phrase claimed it had 'erected a wall without windows and doors' to keep out GDR reality. The result of this short-sighted policy was that tens of thousands had quit the country.

On 24 October the Volkskammer (Parliament) elected Krenz as Chairman of the Council of State (President) with 26 voting against and 26 abstaining. The votes all came from the non-socialist parties. Only eight voted against and 17 abstained when he was elected Chairman of the National Defence Council. Krenz spoke of a possible change in the electoral law, but the same evening 12,000 demonstrated in East Berlin against his election to the two high state offices.

On 1 November, on his first visit to Moscow as Party leader, Krenz referred to *perestroika* and the new political thinking as a 'constant stimulus to social progress'. Gorbachev was confident that the SED was capable of 'boldly pursuing the course of renewal'.

The Central Committee plenum on 8 November 1989 opened with a sensation. The whole Politburo resigned and a new, slimmer, Politburo replaced it. There were up to 66 votes against some of the candidates. The new Politburo had eleven (formerly 21) full members and six (five) candidate members. The new full members were Hans Modrow, First Secretary in Bezirk Dresden and soon to succeed Willi Stoph as Prime Minister; Wolfgang Herger, chairman of the Volkskammer youth committee; Wolfgang Rauchfuss, deputy Prime Minister; and Gerhard Schürer, chairman of the State Planning Commission. All the others were from the old Politburo. Among those dropped were Kurt Hager (responsible for ideology); Erich Mielke (Stasi chief); Willi Stoph (Prime Minister) and Harry Tisch (trade unions). This did not satisfy Party members, and thousands demonstrated in front of the Central Committee building in East Berlin for a 'party leadership that listens to the people'.

This was the plenum which took the decision to open the Berlin Wall. Hundreds of thousands crossed into West Berlin, most of them without any checking of documents. By 30 November another 50 crossing points had been opened.

The Central Committee plenum ended on 10 November with an 'action programme' which included free elections, a new criminal code and freedom of association. It was also announced that four Politburo members, elected two days before, had been forced by pressure from below to resign. They included three district first secretaries who were obliged to resign these positions as well. Also, as a result of pressure from below, the Party Conference called for mid-December was transformed into an extraordinary Party Congress.

On 17 November Hans Modrow presented his new government to the Volkskammer. There were 28 (previously 44) ministers, of whom 16 were from the SED. Four were Liberal Democrats, three Christian Democrats, two National Democrats and two from the Peasants' Party. Nine ministers, including Oskar Fischer, Foreign Affairs, survived from the old government. The Ministry of State Security (Stasi) was dissolved and replaced by the Office of National Security under Wolfgang Schwanitz (SED). The Volkskammer also set up a commission to examine 'abuses of power, corruption and personal enrichment' of members of the Honecker regime.

Modrow built up a solid reputation as prime minister mainly because he emphasized that he spoke for all GDR citizens. Nevertheless, the government had limited authority, since it still excluded the new political groupings. Pressure told, however, and the first meeting of a Round Table was called by the SED for 7 December 1989.

Turmoil within the ranks of the SED resulted in the whole Politburo and Central Committee resigning on 3 December. This astonishing move was necessary in order to protect the party from 'extinction'. A working committee was set up to guide the party until the extraordinary Party Congress. It was also decided to expel Honecker and eleven other members of the old party and state leadership from the SED. Gregor Gysi, later to become Party leader, headed a commission to examine illegal activities by previous and present officials. Gysi reported on 5 December that his commission already had 'thousands of examples' of malfeasance.

On 6 December Krenz resigned as Chairman of the Council of State and Chairman of the National Defence Council. On the same day, the SED Congress was brought forward a week and was due to open on 8 December. It began its deliberations during the evening and stayed in session for 17 hours. Gysi was elected Party Chairman with over 95% of delegates in favour. The Party Congress concluded its deliberations on 16–17 December. It still claimed 1.7 million members, and in an attempt to change its fortunes it changed its name. The new party was called the SED-Party of Democratic Socialism (SED-PDS). This mouthful would last until party members agreed on a new name.

A new leadership (Parteivorstand) was elected with a ten-member Presidium. The SED-PDS was only nominally one party. Several groups established themselves with their own platforms. Krenz's party career ended on 21 January 1990, when he and 13 former full and candidate members of the Politburo were expelled from the party. Forty-seven members, expelled under Ulbricht, were rehabilitated. On the same day, Wolfgang Berghofer, Mayor of Dresden and deputy chairman of the SED-PDS Parteivorstand, and 39 other Dresden party members, resigned from the party and called for its dissolution. It did not dissolve, but on 4 February 1990 changed its name to the Party of Democratic Socialism (PDS). Gysi reported on 15 February that the PDS had about 700,000 members – a long way short of the 2.3 million the SED had had in mid-1989.

Gysi, a bespectacled Berlin Jewish lawyer, totally lacked charisma but was accepted as a comrade with clean hands. He failed to revive the fortunes of a party racked by deep antagonisms between the base and the leadership. One of the reasons for this was the daily revelations of corruption of the SED elite. The announcement of criminal charges against Honecker and others did not help matters. Probably the only SED official who could have salvaged something from the wreck of a once-omnipotent party was Hans Modrow, but he was politically too astute to try.

If Gysi's task was well-nigh impossible that of Modrow, the Prime Minister, was almost as difficult. Head of a government which was composed of the old political forces, he had to contend with the rising authority of the new political parties and groups. The front-runner had been the New Forum. It made a breakthrough on 26 October when Schabowski, Berlin First Party Secretary, met two of its leaders, Jens Reich and Sebastian Pflugbeil. Its first officially sanctioned meeting, which attracted 50,000 people, was in Leipzig on 18 November 1989. New Forum was a coalition of opponents of SED rule but did not develop into a political party. There were in reality two CDU parties until the elections of 18 March 1990. One consisted of those members elected to the Volkskammer under Honecker, many of whom continued to support the SED-PDS. The other CDU was modelled on its Western sister party and developed, against all expectations, into the strongest party in the GDR. On 10 November 1989 Lothar de Maizière, later to become GDR Prime Minister, was elected chairman. On 20 January 1990 twenty conservative Christian, liberal groups came together in Leipzig to form the German Social Union (DSU), and Pastor Hans-Wilhelm Ebeling was elected its first chairman. Democratic Awakening (DA), another conservative group, led by Wolfgang Schnur and Pastor Rainer Eppelmann, also had its base in Leipzig. These three formed a coalition on 1 February to fight the elections of 18 March. On 5 February in West Berlin it was given the name of Alliance for Germany, and thereby declared its main aim to be the rapid unification of Germany.

The Social Democrats chose 7 October 1989, the 40th anniversary of the founding of the GDR, to re-emerge from their long-enforced cohabitation with the SED. A Social Democratic Party in the GDR (SPD) was founded in Schwante, near Potsdam. The historian, Ibrahim Böhme, was elected leader. It developed close relations with the West German SPD and on 27 October, in Bonn, Steffen Reiche, one of its leaders, stated that the West German party would support its application for membership of the Socialist International and 'preferred' it as future discussion partners in the East.

A major problem for the Social Democrats was their attitude to the reunification of Germany. They proposed at their programme congress on 18 December in Berlin that a community treaty be negotiated between the two German states. This would then lead to a confederation. At the founding congress of the GDR SPD in Leipzig on 25 February Böhme was elected chairman and Willy Brandt, honorary chairman. An SPD aim was to ensure that the tender plant of democracy in the GDR would be allowed to flourish before the two Germanies embraced one another tightly. Despite the eloquence of Brandt and other leading Social Democrats, this message fell on deaf ears. The economic plight of the country swayed many workers to vote for the Conservatives, who promised economic union and the introduction of the deutschmark.

GDR liberals could count on the support of Hans-Dietrich Genscher's party in the Federal Republic, the FDP. An Alliance of Free Democrats, consisting of the German Forum Party (DFP), the Liberal Democratic Party (LDP) and the Free Democratic Party (FDP), came together to fight the election. The original front-runner, New Forum, moved to the left and linked up with Democracy Now and Peace and Human Rights Initiative to form Alliance 90 for the election.

On 7 December 1989 an 'alternative' government came into being, one which represented the new constellation of political forces. Called a Round Table, it met on the initiative of the Evangelical Churches in the GDR and twelve parties and groups were represented. The CDU, Peasants, LDP, National Democrats and New Forum had three representatives. The SED, Democracy Now, Democratic Awakening, the Greens, Peace and Civil Rights Initiative, SDP and United Left each had two. After protests by trade unionists, two FDGB members joined as did two from the Independent Women's League. Three other organizations were granted observer status. The Round Table proposed Volkskammer elections for 6 May 1990 and the preparation of a new constitution to be confirmed by referendum. It also demanded that the Office for National Security be dissolved under civilian control, that the true ecological, economic and financial plight of the country be revealed, that the government informed the Round Table of key pending decisions and that members participated in the decision-making process. The election date was subsequently brought forward.

The Round Table met 16 times under the able chairmanship of the theologian Wolfgang Ullmann. A founder-member of Democracy Now and a minister in Modrow's government, Ullmann deftly brought the often acrimonious debates back to basic essentials. When an embarrassed Krenz apologized awkwardly for falsifying the May 1989 election results Ullmann, in the silence which greeted these words, replied: 'I accept, as a citizen and as a Christian, your apology.'

The worsening economic situation made Modrow's position almost untenable, and on 29 January 1990 he announced the formation of a 'government of national responsibility', which would run the country until the 18 March elections.

The change of mood towards German reunification emerged from opinion polls. A *Neues Deutschland* poll of East Berliners, published on 24 November 1989, found that 83% were in favour of the continued existence of a sovereign, socialist GDR but only 19% would be willing to vote SED. A poll of young people in Leipzig between 20 and 27 November found 16% strongly in favour of a united Germany and 29% strongly against; 31% would vote SED, 17% for the New Forum and 10% for CDU. Also in late November a poll in Neubrandenburg revealed 39% in favour of a united Germany. On 29 December a poll in East Berlin resulted in 34% saying they would vote for the SED-PDS and 7.9% for the CDU. A Leipzig poll, published on 6 February 1990 about the forthcoming elections, found 59%

preferring the SPD, 12% the PDS, 11% the CDU but only 4% the New Forum. By then, the SPD and PDS were in favour of a united Germany, but the crucial question was how quickly this would come about.

The election results of 18 March stunned the SPD and delighted the Alliance for Germany and the PDS. It overturned all the opinion polls, since it had been expected that the Social Democrats would gain most from the discomfiture of the Communists. The Alliance lost a few votes due to the revelation that Wolfgang Schnur, chairman of Democratic Awakening, had been a Stasi informer for over a quarter of a century. The campaign was a personal triumph for the West German Chancellor Helmut Kohl. During the week before the elections he addressed over a million people in six cities, ending with a huge rally in Leipzig attended by up to 300,000 on 15 March.

The first and probably the last democratically elected GDR government was agreed on 9 April. A grand coalition of the Conservatives, Social Democrats and Liberals, it was headed by Lothar de Maizière. Social Democrats obtained the key posts of Foreign Affairs, Health and Employment.

The contentious issue of the exchange rate between the ostmark and the deutschmark was decided on 23 April 1990, when Bonn stated that salaries, wages and savings up to 4,000 ostmarks would be exchanged at parity. This paved the way for monetary union on 2 July.

End of an era

Many people will be sorry to bid farewell to the GDR. It represented a Germany which had developed distinct characteristics. Life for the opposition was never easy, but it engendered a camaraderie which may now be lost. Politics in the new GDR is softer than in the West, but the hard reality of raising living standards will change all that. The GDR has a distinct smell about it. Most of the odours are life-endangering – such as in Halle and Bitterfeld – but there is often an old-world charm which reminds one of pre-war Germany. In many towns the cobbled streets and shops have hardly changed over the last half century, and the country must have the largest collection of antique railway stations in the world.

Not all party members will mourn the passing of the SED. Under the leadership of Erich Honecker it managed to lead the country to ruin. Possessed of immense power and a population which knew the limits of dissent, it nevertheless ended in oblivion. In postwar Eastern Europe the Polish Communists were held to be the least gifted, to put it politely, but there must now be some doubt about this. The SED must be in the running for the prize for incompetence, corruption and stupidity. During his many appearances before the commission of enquiry into party behaviour, Honecker never conceded that he had been wrong. He appears to have led a life apart, and to have become detached from reality. After he left hospital in January he was judged too frail to be imprisoned. A pastor and his family offered to welcome Honecker and his wife Margot (the long-serving Minister of Education) into their family circle. Eventually the Honeckers had to leave since there were too many people who wanted to send them to the next world.

The Honeckers and the GDR elite lived under Communism – they had everything they wanted and did not need money – but they forgot that the population had to live under socialism. Only one or two of the elite were capable of showing remorse about the past. The others blithely defended themselves before the commission, arguing that they performed their functions and the leader led. Krenz claimed that the Soviet ambassador in East Berlin made them believe that Moscow would rescue them. This is one reason why the SED failed. At some point of time during the 1980s it passed the point of redemption. The GDR was the SED's child. It was most healthy in its thirties (in the 1970s) but at forty it was senile, and expired soon afterwards.

5 HUNGARY

From Kádárism to democracy

The roots of modern Hungary

The reason Communism fell apart in Hungary, according to the Budapest version, is that it rotted away. This contains an element of truth and begs a number of questions as well. Above all, it demands, almost insistently, why? What made conditions in Hungary so different from the other Communist countries that the Soviet-type system disintegrated quietly? Why did the ruling Communists not put up much of a fight? What determined the composition of the forces that replaced them?

The answers are partly to be found in the remote past, in the origins of the Kádár régime and in the way in which the system was put together after the revolution of 1956, and partly in the particular circumstances of the mid-1980s, when the system needed a new infusion of energies, which was impossible because of the way in which it had been put together. Crucially Kádár's own role as a conservative innovator who could not move with the times requires particular scrutiny.

The modern Hungarian state emerged from the ruins of the Austro-Hungarian Empire in 1918. It was much reduced in size, however, losing some two-thirds of its territory (to Romania, Serbia and Czechoslovakia) at the Treaty of Trianon in 1920. A four-month Communist regime, headed by Bela Kun, ended in August 1919 when the Romanian army marched into Budapest. Hungary subsequently came under the virtual dictatorship of Miklós Horthy, a former admiral in the Austro-Hungarian Navy.

In the course of the 1930s Hungary came under German influence. When war came it profited from German goodwill by regaining some of the territories lost in 1919. It also sent a contingent to fight alongside the Germans on the eastern front. Its loyalty was ill-rewarded when, after Horthy had signed a treaty with the Soviets in October 1944, he was arrested and replaced by a fascist stooge, Ferenc Szalasi. By April 1945 Hungary had been liberated by the Red Army.

Hungary emerged then from the war under Soviet occupation and was reduced to its pre-war territory. Its people were exhausted and eager for reform of the social and political order. The Communist Party had been declared illegal for most of the interwar period. At the end of the war some of its members (Mátyás Rákosi, Ernö Gerö, Imre Nagy) returned from abroad, while others (Laszló Rajk, János Kádár, Gyula Kállai) came out of hiding. Although its base of support was weak – it had only 3,000 members in November 1944 – within twelve months this figure had grown to almost half a million. It was not sufficient to gain them political hegemony. In the

HUNGARY

Official name	The Republic of Hungary
Area	93,030 sq. km (35,910 sq. miles)
Population	10,569,000 (annual growth rate 0.2%)
Capital	Budapest
Language	Hungarian
Religion	54% Roman Catholic, 22% Hungarian Reformed Church, Lutheran and Orthodox minorities
Currency	forint

first, largely free, postwar elections in November 1945, the Communists received support from only 17% of the electorate. The outcome was a victory for the Smallholders Party (KGP) but Soviet pressure led to the inclusion of Communists in the government.

By the next elections, in August 1947, although Communist support had increased only to 22%, the Communists formed the largest single party. At the beginning of the following year they exercised effective control of the Hungarian state and government having used their notorious 'salami tactics' to eliminate the rival parties one by one as serious opponents. In the May 1949 election, the Hungarian 'People's Front for Independence' was able to put forward a single list of candidates before the electorate. Following their predictable successes the Communists found the way clear to introduce a new constitution modelled on Soviet lines. Hungary became a republic of 'workers and peasants'.

Under Stalinist rule, Hungary followed a predictable pattern; it became a police state, with all opposition crushed and dissent stifled. In the economic sphere there was emphasis upon the development of heavy industry, agriculture was collectivized, and there was a rapid shift from private to state ownership. Following Stalin's death in 1953 a struggle developed between Imre Nagy and Mátyás Rákosi, Party first secretary, for political supremacy. In 1955 Rákosi regained political dominance, and Nagy was expelled from the Party. By the time the Soviets realized their mistake and removed him in mid-1956, Rákosi's hardline regime had stirred up so much hostility and opposition that the Party and its security apparatus were unable to control it. What began as a student demonstration in Budapest at the end of October turned into a full-scale uprising and a battle for the capital.

Although Imre Nagy was restored as premier and victory seemed assured (the secret police was disbanded and Soviet tanks withdrew), it was only the first stage of the campaign. While the country prepared to take a new political course, which included a multi-party system and neutrality (Nagy issued a declaration on 1 November that Hungary was leaving the Warsaw Pact), the Soviet leadership was planning how to crush the revolution. The second and decisive stage of the campaign began on 4 November when the Red Army returned in force, inflicting heavy damage on the capital and thousands of casualties. Dozens of the insurgent leaders were arrested and tried. Imre Nagy and a handful of close collaborators were executed for their 'treason' – martyred in the eyes of the overwhelming majority of the nation.

In the wake of the revolution the Soviets chose János Kádár to be the new premier and Party leader. After 1956, Kádár had a complex task and little time in which to do it. He had to re-establish his power, reorganize the Communist Party that had fallen apart in the revolution, break down the resistance of the population, end the general strike and liquidate the institutions that the revolution had created. He could not be too discriminating about the means and he did not have much of a choice either. He had to use harsh methods and to rely on discredited Stalinist elements, who wanted revenge for the shock they had suffered in the revolution. Kádár's tactics were to use every possible lie in negotiating with the Workers' Councils, the strongest representatives of the people, and to arrest and imprison opponents.

He had to convince the population that resisting the might of the Soviet Union was useless and that the Communist system was there to stay. For five years, he operated or presided over a reign of terror, in which thousands were executed, imprisoned and interned. Kádár targeted different social groups – the workers, the intellectuals and the peasants – until the completion of collectivization in 1961 signified a kind of pacification. He had already organized a major show trial, after which the principal leaders of the revolution – Imre Nagy and four others chosen almost at random – were executed. By the early 1960s, Hungarian society was thoroughly cowed.

Kádár, however, was not Stalinist himself and he did not want to rule over a country run solely on the basis of terror, always assuming that this was possible. He had, after all, been a victim of Stalinism personally and his vision, presumably, was of an orderly, economically prosperous, disciplined system, in which everyone accepted his version of 'socialism' and worked towards it. Pivotally, he drew the lesson from the 1956 revolution that the people were not to be trusted with power. If they were given a choice, they would not exercise it in the way that he wanted. On the contrary all sorts of undesirable political aims would be pursued, such as a multi-party system, workers' self-management and spontaneity. In Kádár's view – and this can be deduced from the kind of political system that he subsequently established – political choice was to be the preserve of the few, of individuals like himself, honest socialists.

Depoliticizing society

From that time, Kádár's tactics could be described as having evolved towards a strategy – depoliticize society and keep the population happy through economic concessions. To this end, the system needed both economic and administrative adjustments, many of which had political implications. The Communist Party would continue to insist on its monopoly of power, but this would no longer be defined in Stalinist terms as an absolute monopoly. The Party no longer claimed to be omniscient and omnipotent, in charge of all social, political, economic and moral agendas.

The individual could now have some choice, as long as this did not impinge on the power of the Party, and when such trespasses took place was something defined solely by the Party. In other words, political monopoly was retained under a new and considerably more sophisticated redefinition. This dispensation was arrived at in its final form more by good luck than by good management, but it proved to be a most successful one from the Party's standpoint.

It offered a considerable flexibility in dealing with society, in the management of power and in the routinization of administration. Essentially, it gave the power elite wide-ranging discretion in the exercise of power – there were no fixed criteria for anything. This meant that every concession remained a concession and could not be transformed into a right. It provided opportunity for pragmatism – much admired by those in the West who entirely failed to understand the true nature of the system – and created just enough social space for different groups to find satisfaction. The satisfaction of social aspirations was, of course, made much easier by their previous forcible suppression after 1956 – people expected much less.

The trouble with this degree of discretion was that it gradually undermined the system of power itself. A power elite is not a small club of people who know each other personally, but a complex organism and, as such, it requires basic ground rules, some relatively clear and understandable criteria for the exercise of power. In Hungary, as in other Communist countries in the 1970s, the official ideology lost this cementing quality and it was not replaced by anything other than the ideology of power itself, coupled with the external threat of Soviet intervention. In the mid-1980s, the latter vanished and the former proved too weak to sustain the edifice of power for long. But in the 1960s, it still held.

In effect, the foundations of Kádárism were laid by the early 1960s. The peasantry, once it had reluctantly accepted that collectivization was there to stay, was left alone and given an incentive to produce. The output of the private plot could be sold on urban markets and the urban population's consumption of foodstuffs was secured thereby, unlike Poland where the rulers failed completely to achieve this. Collective units are notoriously inefficient in producing fruit, vegetables, poultry and eggs, but private enterprise, by relying on cash incentives for work done, could do so. At the same time, sections of the peasantry also prospered.

The industrial working class was offered the prospect of high levels of collective consumption through a variety of welfare provisions, coupled with lenient labour discipline, low productivity and a steady improvement in the standard of living. Egalitarianism, the crude levelling down of the 1950s, on the other hand, was off the agenda.

Intellectuals and intelligentsia

The deal extended to intellectuals and the intelligentsia (the former create values, the latter administer them as teachers, lawyers, managers, engineers, etc.) was the most complex, and went to the heart of the Kádár system. One of the roles of intellectuals in one-party systems is to act as the mirror in which the ruling elite sees itself reflected. The elite's self-confidence and morale depend crucially on this, in the absence of genuine legitimation through elections. Under Stalinism, the creative independence of intellectuals and the administrative autonomy of the intelligentsia were brusquely ended because the system had no need of them – it regarded the supposed perfection of Marxism–Leninism as its sole source of legitimacy. They were expected to sing the praises of socialism and that was all, for the Party, through its control of the past and the future, had the answers to everything.

Kádárism recognized the utter futility of this and sought to incorporate these social-professional groups in order to use their talents instead. So the word went out that anyone honestly ready to use his or her talents would be deemed to be engaged in 'the construction of socialism'. This dealt adequately with the intelligentsia, which did not have serious aspirations to gain autonomy as well.

The creative intellectuals were more problematical, but here the system found a brilliant device. Instead of being forced to proclaim, as in the 1950s, that 'socialism was the most marvellous system in the world', they could say, in effect, 'the system that we have here in Hungary is full of defects, it does not work very well, it is open to criticism on a whole variety of grounds; but it is the best that we can hope to have'. This formula completely immobilized critical intellectuals and built self-censorship into their public utterances.

To secure its position, the Party let it be understood that there were two rules that had to be strictly observed – neither the basics of the system nor the relationship with the Soviet Union could be questioned. Not, the Party would hasten to add, because this was something that the Hungarians liked, but because the Soviet comrades preferred it that way. This subtly mendacious system of blackmail and self-deception was augmented by giving intellectuals and the intelligentsia access to material privileges, to information, to the outer fringes of power and *de facto* control over entry to higher education, which meant that those who had succeeded could live secure in the knowledge that their children would inherit their privileges and status.

The character of the system was, therefore, deeply opportunistic. There were no fixed standards. Everything was subject to the needs of the day, decided on by a political leadership that had largely lost its vision. It knew it wanted to hold on to power, but it could no longer justify it in any terms other than those of power. As the 1970s progressed, the official ideology was increasingly emptied of content. The ideals of equality, modernity and rationality – central to the Marxian idea of the future – were gradually lost as power-holders and intellectuals recognized that the system could not be adapted any further to meet these goals.

The forcible suppression of the 1968 Czechoslovak experiment in using Marxist socialism to meet the challenge of change sent out an unmistakable signal, to the effect that no East European country – Hungary included – had the freedom to go farther and faster than Moscow. Ideology was dead except as rhetoric. The Party then tried to legitimate its rule by insisting that it was the repository of rationality and efficiency, a claim that was increasingly difficult to make good in practice and, as far as the population was concerned, disproved by everyday life.

To make the mixture more palatable, the Party added a judicious amount of nationalism to it: that the Communist Party's rule was the most successful expression of Hungary's national destiny. This, too, was disproved by practice. Apart from the inherent implausibility of a self-proclaimed Marxist party pretending to be the best representative of the nation and of nationhood, the fate of the Hungarian minorities in the neighbouring states increasingly exercised Hungarian opinion, and the country's rulers were seen as incapable of doing anything to help the ethnic Hungarians in Czechoslovakia and Romania.

This left the Party with the threadbare proposition that it was the agent of a 'revolution', which no-one took very seriously, though it did make it impossible for Kádárism to come to terms with the (genuine) revolution of 1956. For Kádár, the events of that year were forever a 'counter-revolution', because it had defined its own myth in having seized power as a Marxist–Leninist party against the anti-Communists. That was the limit to the Kádárist integration strategy.

Declining legitimacy

As far as justification by power was concerned ('we rule because we rule'), this was vulnerable to any direct challenge to that power or threat of a challenge. Essentially, legitimation by power alone was a dangerously thin support, because any loss of power would weaken the core of the Party's rule, as eventually happened. Buying peace through economic expansion proved to be exposed to economic failure. Hence the successful management of the economic system was crucial for keeping it together.

The Kádár system earned many plaudits from Western observers for its apparent ability to run a reformed economy and to have discarded Marxist dogmas about central planning. The 1968 New Economic Mechanism (NEM) appeared to many to be a well-intended and intelligent attempt to combine central planning with market instruments, to mix the best of capitalism with socialism. It gave up physical allocation, instructing enterprises what and how much they should produce, and no longer treated the country's economy as a vast, single firm, the functioning of which could be known precisely by the country's central planning office. It appeared to accept that complexity and unforeseen transactions, conflicts of interests and individual choice were normal parts of a modern economy.

The authorities sought to reach their stated goals by indirect means. That was the theory. In practice, neither enterprise managers nor the central bureaucracy was ready to give up power and live with the risk of market failure, constant adaptation, technological change and high information flows required by the market model. But unlike Czechoslovakia, where the post-1968 restoration actually reversed similar reforms overtly, in Hungary the backward move took place behind a façade of reform-oriented language. This was a deception, but it had the advantage that the language of reform was never excluded from public discourse, so that the limits of debate were significantly wider than in Czechoslovakia. Nor did the Party attach issues of ideology and prestige to non-reversal of Marxist–Leninist orthdoxy, as happened in Prague, where the very word 'reform' was excluded from public utterance for the best part of two decades.

The reality was also different in Hungary, though not that different. The central plan was replaced by the 'plan bargain', by which every enterprise did a deal with the relevant branch ministry to regulate conditions for its operations – supplies, subventions and market shares. In this system, no-one ever had an incentive to make improvements. On the contrary, it favoured conservatism and bureaucratic politics rather than economic efficiency, though it maintained the external appearance of market operation.

It also left the economy firmly fenced in by political constraints. What enterprises could do were, beyond a certain point, determined by political power. When an enterprise was plainly uneconomic, its fate was decided not by financial criteria but by the economic power of the manager and his patrons in the Party and the branch ministry. If they had enough power, the enterprise would not be closed down but would be rescued and 'reorganized', and then helped to stay afloat through ever-higher central subventions. Clearly, there was no economic incentive to operate more efficiently, by, say, cutting costs or improving productivity.

The consequence was that the level of central support for much of industry was dangerously high – dangerously, because it could only be sustained by continuous and increasing foreign borrowing. It was evident by the late 1970s that the country's heavy industry was a severe burden, that it cost the country more than it produced and that restructuring, including closure, was the best way of saving the economy the large subsidies that it was paying to keep these firms alive. Politics, as ever, intervened. The heavy industry lobby was well entrenched politically. It was the source of power and patronage for Party secretaries and managers, so that the last thing they wanted was bankruptcy. Political power predictably won the day over economic rationality. Despite the sophisticated public relations job performed by Hungarian spokesmen in the 1970s and 1980s, the economy was declining, and only a steady infusion of Western credits kept it afloat. The legacy of this was a foreign debt of $21 billion by 1990 and the highest per capita indebtedness in Eastern Europe.

The New Economic Mechanism

The principal milestones of the rise and fall of the NEM are simply chronicled. The reform project came on stream on 1 January 1968 and looked dangerously bold on 21 August that year, the day when Czechoslovakia was invaded by the Warsaw Pact, including Hungarian troops. In November 1972, the Central Committee of the Hungarian party introduced a variety of restrictions on the reform, largely depriving it of its marketizing qualities while pretending that these were little more than course-corrections.

Two years later, the main architects of the reform were dropped from the Politburo and the new strategy was to give subventions to enterprises whose weaknesses had been exposed by the NEM and by the growing openness of the Hungarian economy to the world market. The size of central support increased quickly, until by 1979 even Kádár was convinced that a move back towards economic rationality – supply and demand – was advisable. The outcome was a cautious, conservative course that eliminated the worst excesses but left the main problem – the political obstacles to market rationality – untouched. Kádár's conservatism, as ever, got the better of him.

At this point it is worth noting again how significant it was that reform language (and hence the potential for re-opening the debate on reform) remained within the ambit of politics. Criticism of the situation began to grow and sections of the elite were influenced by this, so much so that the pressure to introduce more radical measures resulted in Kádár declaring in 1983 that there would be 'no reform of the reform'. Unlike Czechoslovakia, the intellectuals were not tied down by a narrowly circumscribed political system but had some leeway for thought and debate. The habits of criticism had not been marginalized by political power.

This had two consequences. The political leadership needed the intellectuals up to a point, more than they had thought, in order to legitimate their own ideas and strategies and were, as a result, vulnerable in this respect. Second, the intellectuals themselves were aware that they could make an impact on the political system. This was the sense in which the decay of the Kádár system took place from within, with only minimal popular participation.

From that point on, it was evident (though few accepted this in public) that as long as Kádár remained at the helm the system could only disintegrate from within. The external proprieties were maintained, but by the mid-1980s the stagnation was unmistakable. When, instead of adopting a market-oriented course, Kádár launched yet another 'acceleration' in 1986 (an investment drive with funds that he did not have but had to borrow from abroad), he was really saying that, despite his reputation for flexibility, he was no longer capable of changing with the times. From having been a conservative reformer he had become an opponent of all change, a true reactionary. That was the moment when Kádárism lost the backing – political, intellectual, psychological – of those supporting intellectuals who had played such a vital role in sustaining him from the early 1960s onwards.

Because the process in Hungary was a gradual one, there was no clear, visible, dramatic moment from when it is possible to date the beginning of the end. Nevertheless, the last months of 1986 saw increasing signs of the growing alienation from the regime of the previously supportive intellectuals. At the end of November, the country's writers, who traditionally enjoyed the role of being a surrogate opposition, met at the Writers' Union Congress and rebelled against the wishes of the Party, which essentially told them not to meddle with politics, as this was not their concern. On the contrary, the writers insisted, the alarming state of deterioration in Hungary was something that concerned all responsible intellectuals.

The economists, who formed an influential group and on whose ideas the Party and the economic bureaucracy leaned heavily (even if much of their advice was ignored), likewise withdrew its support from the Kádár system. In a wide-ranging document entitled *Turning-point and Reform* the economists strongly argued that, without radical changes in the direction of marketization, Hungary would head towards inevitable decline and collapse. 'Collapse' was, of course, a metaphor, but the physical reality of collapse was represented by next-door Romania, which had been dragged into an appalling state of poverty by Nicolae Ceauşescu's misconceived development strategy. What was particularly striking and influential in the document was the argument that the Communist model of development, when viewed in a perspective of four decades, had been much less effective than the market-based strategies employed in the Pacific Rim countries – Taiwan, South Korea, Singapore – which had already overtaken the Communist world economically.

Finally, the Kádár system also lost the support of the country's journalists at this time. Their role was an important one in reporting the general state of affairs, and their growing consternation at the state of the economy and society, coupled with the apparent complacency of the political leadership, represented a major loss to the regime. The journalists could not, of course, simply write what they saw, but whereas until then they had been prepared to live with the Kádárist constraints and respected the rules, they now insisted on writing more freely. This resulted in a constant battle with editors, who acted on Party instructions as censors, and over the months the editors' resistance was worn down. The result of this was that, by 1987, the Hungarian media were reporting more of the real situation. This major gap in the Party's control of the information available to the public made it possible for alternative, competing ideas to circulate and gradually, but irreversibly, undermined the Party's hold on public opinion. By the beginning of 1988 it was widely accepted that a change was essential, but the way in which this was to happen remained contested.

The central issue was, of course, that economic reform on its own was not enough. In order for the economy to respond effectively to supply and demand, the political impediments to this would have to be removed, and that obviously meant that the Party's control over the political system and power would have to be loosened. The recognition of this was the key element in the changing consciousness of the intellectuals. There were two broad strands – the work of the Party reformers and of the democratic opposition.

The Party reformers

The group known as the Party reformers were historians, jurists, sociologists and political scientists, with official posts, who had for some time been calling for a transformation of the Party's political monopoly into something more responsive to public opinion. The democratic opposition, on the other hand, had consciously taken a stand outside officialdom and chose marginalization. It had launched itself tentatively in 1977 and, in its earliest phases, relied on Polish and Czechoslovak models. After 1982 it embarked on a more directly political form of activity, mostly through *samizdat*, in calling for a transformation in Hungary on the basis of human rights and democracy. Their influence was hard to assess or quantify, but in the 1985 elections to parliament they were pleasantly surprised to discover that many of their ideas had been espoused by independent candidates who otherwise had no links with the democratic opposition at all. The implication was that the *samizdat* writings of the democratic opposition had much wider currency than they had imagined.

At more or less the same time, both the democratic opposition and the Party reformers launched a concept that has come to be known as 'constitutional Communism'. The idea behind this was that of one-party pluralism. The Communist Party would retain power, but this would no longer be absolute or a monopoly. Rather, it would be circumscribed by legal and political constraints, thereby enabling the market to function in the economy and the political leadership to gain greater legitimacy. The key document from the democratic opposition was entitled 'Social Contract', and it came from the group around the *samizdat* journal *Beszélö*. Its most striking feature was a call for Kádár to go. Without Kádár's removal from the leadership, the document recognized, no change was possible. The Party reformers were more circumspect in this respect, but they too demanded a political system with constraints on the power of the Party. Both groups proved to be influential, especially on sections of the Party itself, which was not, of course, immune to the growing ferment in the country.

By the early months of 1988 the atmosphere in Hungary had changed beyond recognition. The tight control of the Party over intellectual opinion was a thing of the past. There were dozens, if not hundreds, of discussion groups, many of them formally constituted, with explicitly political objectives. The most significant of these at the time was the Hungarian Democratic Forum.

The Forum, which subsequently went on to become the largest single political party in the 1990 general elections, was initially a loose discussion circle set up by the populists. The populists (in many respects a uniquely Hungarian phenomenon) were drawn from writers rather than social scientists, and they addressed their message to the country as a whole rather than to the intellectuals. They were a part of opposition, but were in many ways more ready to deal with the Party than the democratic opposition proper, something which resulted in constant tension between the two. Both were committed to democracy, but the language of the populists was more nationalistic and more concerned with returning to true Hungarian traditions than the democratic opposition liked.

The social background of the two groups also set them apart. The democratic opposition was drawn primarily (though not exclusively) from the urban, Budapest, Jewish middle class and intelligentsia. Many of them were the children of established Communist figures and had had a Communist background themselves. They had abandoned this by the time they moved into opposition, of course, and were committed to human rights and democracy. The populists, on the other hand, were generally from the country, of a more humble background, mostly non-Jewish and had had no part in Marxism at all. This social difference also contributed to the tension between them.

Opposition rivalries

Over the years, some co-operation between the opposition currents did take place, though it was never easy. In 1987, in part as a direct response to the 'Social Contract' document (in the drafting of which they had played no role), the populists held a meeting at Lakitelek, a small town outside Budapest, from which the democratic opposition was largely excluded. This had long-term and highly negative consequences, and explained much of the rivalry between the two groups. The reason for the exclusion was that the Forum had succeeded in persuading the Party reformers to go to Lakitelek and, crucially, the leader of the Party reformers, Imre Pozsgay, had agreed to take part. Pozsgay had asked that the most radical members of the democratic opposition not be invited, calculating that thereby he could legitimate at least a section of the opposition without excessively offending the Party hardliners.

In this Pozsgay was successful, and the Forum thereafter had a recognized existence, neither legal nor illegal, but the price of this was a final and fatal breach with the democratic opposition. From September 1987, when the Lakitelek meeting took place, until November 1988, when the democratic opposition constituted itself as the Alliance of Free Democrats, the Forum held the initiative. It organized more or less monthly meetings (open forums) at which the democratic opposition was free to speak, but which were dominated by the populists. Various topics were debated – the state of the country, the national minorities in the successor states and the media. In this way, the Forum made a major contribution to the political radicalization of the intelligentsia.

By the spring of 1988, the situation in Hungary was widely described as 'fluid' and 'decaying'. The Party leadership (above all, Kádár himself) had no response to the increasing ferment except to make threatening noises. When four well-known intellectuals, who were also Party members, attended meetings of the Forum, all the Party could do was to expel them from its membership. This, if anything, made things worse. In effect, the leadership was not leading, and the ferment in intellectual life was beginning to affect the Party membership, which was far from immune to the country's problems and the changing mood.

The personality of Kádár became an important factor in this complex situation. Born in 1912, he was 75 years old at this time and was manifestly losing control. His speeches had become hesitant, repetitive and unconvincing. There were rumours circulating about his mental and physical health. Whether these were true or not was irrelevant. The fact that they were circulating was a symptom of his declining authority. When two senior Party figures came to him to suggest that perhaps he might like to retire, he is said to have retorted, 'You know what will happen then. They'll rehabilitate Imre Nagy'. It was like Banquo's ghost at the feast. This obstinate refusal either to change or to go evidently persuaded his opponents in the party to prepare a coup for his removal.

In one respect, Kádár made it easier by a speech that he made in March 1988, which destroyed all lingering respect for him. He insisted, in the face of all the evidence, that there was no crisis in Hungary. As far as the Soviet Union was concerned, the Kremlin had already signalled that there were no objections to getting rid of Kádár. At the 1987 celebrations of the anniversary of the October Revolution, Kádár was given a very low protocol position, a significant pointer to the declining esteem in which he was held.

The fall of Kádár

The Kádárist leadership was forced to make the concession of permitting the convening of a Party Conference (an event where all the Party bodies are represented, but without the weight of a Party congress) and this was scheduled for May 1988. Kádár's opponents used this to remove him, and relied on classic tactics. They established unity among themselves, agreed on a candidate of their own to succeed Kádár (Károly Grósz, the prime minister) and indicated that the post-Kádár leadership would be open to major changes. It went as expected, with only one surprise – the Conference was more radical than anyone had thought and sacked not only Kádár but all the senior Kádárists as well, so that eight out of 11 Politburo members were voted out.

The new leadership, however, turned out to be much weaker and more divided than expected. It seemed afterwards as if removing Kádár was the only point on which they were agreed. Grósz essentially looked towards some kind of an authoritarian model of economic efficiency and high levels of coercion. Pozsgay and the party reformers, on the other hand, were increasingly attracted by an open, democratic system. For all practical purposes, the outcome was a stalemate.

Grósz did nothing during the summer months, while Pozsgay accepted that the media could widen their already extensive freedom to comment. The situation deteriorated very rapidly and by August the questioning of Grósz's leadership had begun. Then Grósz made a mistake, which destroyed virtually all his authority. Hungarian opinion was increasingly worried over the fate of the ethnic Hungarian minority in Romania in connection with the 'systematization' policy of forced resettlement pursued by Ceauşescu. Grósz agreed to a one-day meeting in Arad with the Romanian leader and returned empty-handed, and was also rather offhand about it. This was enough to make him unacceptable to public opinion, and the signs of a widening political vacuum were unmistakable. Within a few days of the Arad meeting, the Hungarian Democratic Forum announced its existence as a political movement.

The months between the beginning of September and the end of November represented the watershed. In September, with a more determined leadership, the Communists might just have been able to seize the agenda and push through a reform programme of their own. By the end of November, it was too late. During those weeks, Hungarian society became aware of the weakness of Communist rule and of its own mounting political weight. Thus at a Central Committee meeting in early November the hardliners in the Party launched a major attack on the media, in the expectation of halting the trend towards greater openness. This was simply ignored. In addition, the Soviet Union, the conservatives' last redoubt, had also kept silent. In the past, the hardliners had always been able to eliminate criticism by referring to Soviet disapproval. This pretext for doing nothing had gone, as Gorbachev's reform programme progressed. To underline this, as it were, Hungary was visited at this time by the Soviet Politburo reformer, Alexander Yakovlev. From fragmentary evidence, it seems likely that Yakovlev told his hosts that the Kremlin had no objections to the Communist Party abandoning its monopoly, if that was the only way of revitalizing the country.

From the end of November, overtly political organizations began to emerge. Hungary had begun to assume the appearance of a multi-party system. The democratic opposition established itself as the Alliance of Free Democrats at this time and the so-called 'nostalgic parties', the Smallholders and the Social Democrats, which had taken part in the post-1945 coalition and briefly revived in 1956, once more returned to the political stage.

It was still far from clear, though, that the Party reformers had won the battle. Pozsgay had some supporters, but the Party as a whole was hesitant about accepting pluralism. In January 1989 Pozsgay made a major move, when he announced that a Party commission, working on the history of the previous 40 years, had concluded that Imre Nagy had been correct in 1953–5, when he sought to introduce liberalizing reforms, and that the events of 1956 were not a 'counter-revolution', as the Kádárists had insisted, but a popular uprising. There was a major row in consequence, the outcome of which was a fudged compromise coupled with the simultaneous announcement that the Party accepted a multi-party system. The Party recognized that its strength was draining, and its strategy at this time was to try to guarantee itself a reserved position in the political structure, while allowing other parties to exist.

The Party loses control

The contest turned on a number of interlocking factors. The reformers argued that change was urgent and would only work if pluralism was accepted. Otherwise Hungarian society would not accept the authority of the political leadership and hence its energies could not be mobilized. The conservatives disliked this, but were stripped of all counter-arguments by their fear of popular upheaval as in 1956 and the fact that they did not have an intellectually viable alternative strategy. The break-up of political monopoly was merely a question of time.

Nevertheless, it was not all over by the spring of 1989. The conservatives' retreat was a step-by-step affair. While the celebration of 15 March as Hungary's national day (in commemoration of the 1848 revolution and, as such, a potent symbol of freedom) was fairly easily accepted, the ceremonial re-interment of Imre Nagy was much more contested. By acceding to this, the conservatives tacitly acknowledged that everything that had happened after 1956 was, in some senses, illegitimate. In fact, on 16 June, the thirty-first anniversary of the execution, Imre Nagy and the others who died with him were formally reburied, thereby symbolizing reconciliation, the relegitimization of the values of 1956 and the acceptance of democracy.

In the summer, the Party finally sat down with the opposition parties at a round table (in reality, the two sides sat opposite each other) to try to work out the method of handing over power and to construct a new political system. Work on drafting a new constitution had been going on for some time in the Ministry of Justice, but the political sanction came from the round-table agreement in September. This approved a political structure with an over-strong parliament and a weak presidency. The thinking underlying this was the expectation that the Communists would retain much of the strength even after the forthcoming elections, so that the position of the government *vis-à-vis* parliament would be a weak one.

No-one actually expected what happened in October – the complete collapse of the party-state, the Communist system in its entirety. The Communist Party held a congress at the beginning of October and was deeply split between reformers and conservatives. A dubious compromise was patched up, by the terms of which the Party reconstituted itself as the

Hungarian Socialist Party. This appeared to break the spell, and the control exercised through the *nomenklatura* system vanished. Party discipline over parliament and government went too, so much so, that in the middle of October, parliament passed a series of laws depriving the Communists of their power, abolishing the Factory Guard (the Party's private army), banning the Communists from organizing cells in places of work and insisting that the Communists disclose all their assets. Finally, on 23 October, the anniversary of the outbreak of the 1956 revolution, Hungary was formally declared to be a 'Republic' and no longer a People's Republic. Communist rule was over.

Between October and March 1990, the time was spent on a long election campaign. The chief antagonists did not include the successor to the Communists, the Hungarian Socialist Party, but were the Forum and the Free Democrats. The conflicts outlined above now bore fruit in the bitter and often vindictive hostility between the two. The Free Democrats discovered that they could widen their appeal by offering the voters a radical anti-Communist programme, based on the rapid introduction of a market system. At the same time, the Free Democrats also included a strong Social Democratic element, offering social protectionism. How these two were to be reconciled was never made clear. The Forum, representing provincial, small-town middle classes and entrepreneurs, as well as a strand of Christian Democracy, also had to contend with the national radical populists in their ranks. In this sense, both parties were conglomerates, incorporating contradictory political elements.

In the elections, which were held under an unbelievably complex voting system, the Forum emerged decisively as the largest single party and the Free Democrats failed to match the promise of their vote in the first round of polling. This left the Forum with the task of forming the government.

On 2 May the newly elected parliament assembled for the first time and learned that the Forum and the Free Democrats had reached a deal over a wide range of issues on the running of parliament and political life. They agreed that the president of Hungary would be elected by parliament and that it would be a noted Free Democrat, Árpád Göncz. There was agreement, too, on the personnel of the ten permanent and five special parliamentary committees; on establishing an independent body to supervise radio and television; on limiting the range of issues for which a two-thirds majority vote was required to basic laws affecting the system itself; and one or two other, lesser issues. This deal essentially excluded the smaller parties and, indeed, there was some hostility to it within the Forum itself, but the pre-eminence of the leader of Forum, József Antall, was sufficient to overcome this.

Antall emerged as prime minister designate, as the leader of the largest party, and he successfully persuaded the Smallholders and the Christian Democrats to join him in a coalition. This gave the government a comfortable majority. While the composition of the Forum's parliamentary faction was partly populist-radical and partly Christian Democrat, the wing of the Forum to which Antall belonged, the government was dominated by the Christian Democrats.

The new government was announced on 16 May. Eight portfolios went to the Forum, including Interior, Foreign Affairs and Defence; three to the Smallholders; one to the Christian Democrats; and three independents were invited to take on Finance and Foreign Trade. Antall stressed that the government would pursue a policy of introducing an all-encompassing marketizing reform, whereby the share of the state in the economy would decrease from 80% to an eventual 20%, though this would take time. In this process, the Hungarian government looked to participation by foreign capital. The emphasis was in gradual rather than sudden change. Both the new government and its programme were approved by parliament by 218 votes in favour, 126 against and 8 abstentions. Overall, Hungary made a reasonable start to the democratization programme on which it had embarked, though there was some scepticism at what appeared to be the rather comfortable pace of economic reform that was adopted.

6 POLAND

A step-by-step revolution

The political transformation which occurred in Poland during 1989 has been called a 'step-by-step revolution'. Although Poland produced the first non-Communist prime minister in the Soviet bloc, and the first government not controlled by Communists, the changes which occurred were not so much an overthrow of Communist power as a negotiated withdrawal by the Party. In order to understand the historic compromise which occurred in Poland, we must know what went before.

Prewar Poland

Modern Poland is the descendant of a powerful and prosperous kingdom which once stretched from the Baltic to the Black Sea. Its decline in the seventeenth and eighteenth centuries ended in partition at the hands of three powerful, imperial neighbours – Russia, Austria and Prussia. Released after over a century of captivity, when the three empires collapsed during World War I, Poland was reborn in 1918.

Poland's short-lived period of independence between the wars was plagued by political, economic and social problems. Rapid attempts were made to unite the three partition zones – their economies, administration and transport systems. The early years, however, were marked by political instability, and in 1926 a *coup d'état* was carried out by Marshal Józef Piłsudski. Subsequently government, although more stable, became increasingly less democratic and tolerant. Poland's economic plight grew worse in the wake of the Depression, and the position of her large minority populations also deteriorated.

In 1939 Poland became the first nation to resist Hitler's territorial demands. The Nazi–Soviet Pact paved the way for the invasion of Poland and the outbreak of World War II followed. Partitioned again by two powerful neighbours, Poland succumbed to a long and bloody occupation. Some six million of Poland's inhabitants died, including virtually the whole of its Jewish population. Material damage and cultural losses were also severe. Polish resistance was stout and heroic – but was treated with savagery. The Warsaw Rising in August 1944 resulted in a quarter of a million people killed and the capital being razed to the ground by the Germans. The Polish government took up residence first in Paris and later in London. Throughout the war its soldiers, sailors and airmen fought alongside the Allies, under British operational command.

At the end of the war Poland faced once again the consequences of its

POLAND

Official name	The Republic of Poland
Area	312,685 sq. km (120,695 sq. miles)
Population	38,210,000 (annual growth rate 0.9%)
Capital	Warsaw (Warszawa)
Language	Polish
Religion	95% Roman Catholic
Currency	złoty

geographical position. Strategically located on the Soviets' route to Berlin, the country found itself under Red Army occupation. At the 'Big Three' wartime conferences of Teheran and Yalta it had been agreed that Poland would come under Soviet influence. The Polish government, although a wartime ally, was not consulted. In a sense one could say that Poland was the price the West paid Stalin for the Red Army's successes, and sacrifices, on the eastern front.

Postwar

The postwar Polish state was a very different structure from that of 1939. First, it was moved bodily to the west, losing half of its territory to the Soviet Union and being compensated at the expense of Germany with territory in the north and west. The transfer of territory was accompanied by massive exchanges of population – 3½ million Germans were expelled from the 'recovered' territories in the west, while almost 4½ million Poles 'returning' from Soviet-acquired territory took their place. Second, Poland was now a remarkably homogeneous state, with relatively small numbers of non-Poles and overwhelmingly Roman Catholic.

The Western leaders hoped that Stalin would be content with this settlement (he gained virtually the same area of Poland that he had been allotted under the 1939 Nazi–Soviet Pact), would consider that Soviet security interests had been satisfied and would not feel it necessary to communize Poland. Their hopes were misplaced. Stalin was unsure of whether Communist rule could be imposed on Poland or whether it would be wise to try (he once likened it to 'putting a saddle on a cow'). There was a long legacy of hostility in Polish–Russian and Polish–Soviet relations, which had not been assuaged by Stalin's cynical and brutal policies from 1939 onwards. Indeed, if it is true that Poland suffered more than any other nation during World War II, then much of that suffering was due to Soviet actions; the mass deportations to the USSR, the murder of Polish officers at Katyn and failure to help the Warsaw insurgents during the 1944 Rising.

In addition, there were few native Communists Stalin could count on, since he had liquidated the leadership of the Polish Communist Party in 1938. The few Party members who had survived the purge were those who had been in Polish jails or else who had refused the summons to Moscow and gone to ground. The pro-Soviet Poles who had gathered in Poland towards the end of the war and formed the Lublin Committee (a pro-visional government under Soviet auspices) were a poor bunch of non-entities, who had little following. Indeed, they were regarded as traitors by many of their own people. Their great virtue from Moscow's viewpoint, though, was that they would do Stalin's bidding. The word 'Communist' was intentionally dropped.

The Communist Party was recreated in 1942 as the Polish Workers Party – later (in 1948) to become transformed into the Polish United Workers Party (PUWP). It did not start from any significant base of support, although from an estimated 8000 members at the beginning of 1943 the Party had built up its membership to some 20,000 in mid-1944 and 30,000 by January of the following year. As people saw which way the wind was blowing, more and more decided to join the Party as the road to political or vocational advancement. In the summer of 1947, some six months after the elections, there were one million members (out of a population of some 24 million).

In July 1945 the USA and Britain recognized a 'Provisional Government of National Unity', in which both 'Moscow' Poles and members of the Polish exile government in London took part. Stanisław Mikołajczyk, leader of the Peasant Party, was the most prominent of the 'London' group, and his return to Poland was something of a test of Soviet intentions and good faith. The distribution of Cabinet posts was significant; some two-thirds of the portfolios, including the key posts of Internal Security and Defence, went to Moscow nominees.

The Yalta formula provided for 'free and unfettered elections' in Poland, but not for any mechanism for international monitoring of these elections (as in Greece). It was to be a year and a half before elections took place (in January 1947). They were preceded by a campaign of terror and intimidation against opposition parties, including the murder of many supporters of Mikołajczyk and the splitting of his party. Even so, the election results when they appeared were grossly falsified, the Communists and their allies receiving 80% in official figures. Western protests that the conditions set out in the Yalta agreement had not been met were rejected by Moscow. A few months after the elections, Mikołajczyk fled to the West, fearing for his life.

Poland's period of Stalinism lasted until 1956 and was relatively bloodless, by comparison with neighbouring Czechoslovakia. In 1948 a campaign was mounted on Moscow's orders against Władysław Gomułka for advocating a 'Polish road to socialism'. Gomułka had objected in particular to the demand that agriculture be collectivized. In the flurry which followed Tito's heresy in rejecting the Stalinist line, Gomułka became a victim of Moscow's clampdown on all forms of national deviationism. He was denounced publicly and in the following year removed from his position as deputy premier and from his seat on the Party's Central Committee.

In 1956 the first Polish protests against deteriorating economic conditions took place. Following Khrushchev's intervention, Gomułka was rehabilitated and assumed the mantle of Party leader, but despite his popularity the reforms he introduced were ineffective. The economy became increasingly inefficient and declining living standards resulted in further outbreaks of popular unrest, notably in 1970, when Gomułka himself was removed from office and replaced by Edward Gierek.

Gierek's period of office was notable for three factors, all of which were setbacks to Communist rule and were to stimulate the Polish drive for freedom and democracy. First, Gierek's policy of a massive, investment-led drive for growth – funded by Western banks and governments – failed miserably due to the structural inadequacies of the Polish economy. Debts accumulated and the huge interest repayments required to service this debt handicapped later attempts to improve investment and trade performance. Gierek stated at the XVI Party Plenum in October 1979 that the 1980s would be 'the decade of the greatest progress (economic and social) in the history of People's Poland. We have created a fine basis on which to build the future of our country.' The future was anything but sure or rosy, and within a year Gierek himself was forced out of office, the victim, once again, of popular protest.

The second major event was the formation in September 1976 of KOR, the Workers' Defence Committee, following the arrest of striking workers at Radom. It was the first organized body to oppose the Communist authorities and to defy them in the name of the workers. Although its members were harassed by the authorities (one of them, a young student named Stanisław Pyjas, was killed in Kraków in May 1977), the movement, nevertheless, gathering confidence from the Helsinki accords, extended its activities to include defence against all infringements of human rights. It provided a training ground for many of the dissidents (such as Adam Michnik and Jacek Kuroń) who were later to advise the Solidarity trade union.

The third event was an act of God – the election in October 1978 of Kraków's Cardinal Wojtyła as Pope. Not only was Wojtyła (or John Paul II as he chose to become) the first Pole to ascend the Throne of St Peter, he was a living contradiction – the head of a universal church numbering hundreds of millions of adherents who came from a formally atheist, Communist-bloc state. It is difficult to overstate the emotional effect that Wojtyła's election had on the people of Poland. It was a matter of national pride that a son of Poland had been elected to such an illustrious position, but it was also a reaffirmation of Poland's place in Christian and Western civilization – to which Poles had always felt they belonged. What is more, henceforth ordinary Poles were to feel the confidence that they had a stout and powerful defender on their side. The Pope's first return visit to his homeland in June 1979 inspired scenes of mass enthusiasm, and seasoned observers of the Polish scene were not slow to contrast them with the dour demeanour of marchers on the Party-orchestrated May Day parades.

The rise of Solidarity

In the summer of 1980, instigated by sudden food price rises, a wave of strikes swept across Poland, from Lublin in the south-east, to Silesia and the Baltic Coast. The mood of protest reached the Lenin Shipyard in Gdańsk, where a Strike Committee was set up on 16 August under the leadership of a shipyard electrician named Lech Wałęsa. The Committee drew up a list of 21 demands which included the 'acceptance of free trade unions independent of the Party and the employers'. Following much-publicized negotiations with the government, agreement was reached, although at a political cost. Prime Minister Babiuch was removed and at the beginning of September, Gierek himself stood down as Party First Secretary. The official reason given for his departure was 'health grounds'. A caretaker leader, Stanisław Kania, was brought in.

Moves towards the creation of independent unions did not go smoothly. The authorities dragged their feet over registration and were clearly unhappy about licensing unions to act on a national, as opposed to a local, basis. Nevertheless, the success of the union in forcing the government to talk and then to recognize it officially was considerable, and a landmark in the history of postwar east-central Europe. At last the Party, self-professed champion of proletarian interests, was forced to admit that it did not command the loyalty or support of the working masses. The momentum which had been created by the historical agreement in Gdańsk did not slacken. The 'Solidarity' union increased its following across the country until it had an estimated 10 million members.

As Solidarity attracted the hopes and the loyalty of millions of Polish citizens, so the morale of the Party membership, ashamed and disenchanted by the incompetence of their own leaders, plummeted. Many Party members flocked to join the ranks of Solidarity. A movement within the Party for reform and renewal scarcely got off the ground. In the course of 1981 it became clear that events in Poland had moved too fast for the Soviet leadership. A power vacuum had formed in Poland, as those holding the reins of power proved impotent to control events and those who enjoyed popular confidence and support were blocked from the positions of true authority.

A state of martial law was declared on 13 December 1981 and was accompanied by the arrest and internment of several hundred Solidarity activists. The move came as a complete surprise, although it had clearly been planned well in advance. The operation was put into effect by General Wojcich Jaruzelski, Kania's replacement as Party leader. It was essentially a move by the military wing of the Party to bolster the sagging morale of the civilian Party's leadership and to restore order and discipline, on both the political and the economic fronts.

It now seems clear that Jaruzelski and his colleagues acted to forestall possible Soviet intervention, along the lines of Budapest in 1956. At the time, however, the repressive measures which came into force were greeted with a chorus of protest both inside and outside the country. The protest demonstrations and strikes which broke out were put down harshly and a number of deaths resulted. In the international arena, the Jaruzelski leadership became a diplomatic leper – shunned by all except its extremely relieved socialist bloc allies. Most damagingly, the USA imposed economic sanctions on Poland, thereby considerably hindering the task of economic recovery.

Indeed, although martial law ended a period of extreme uncertainty, it is arguable whether its introduction facilitated the task of governing Poland. The formation of a Military Council of National Salvation (Polish acronym, WRON) was designed to override the established structures and political – and Party – rule. Jaruzelski added the chairmanship of WRON to his Party first secretaryship and several other posts, concentrating power in his own hands. He faced though a sullen and unco-operative people whose history had taught them that, if it was unwise to engage in any dramatic and fruitless gestures of resistance against such overwhelming military force, they could not be compelled to do any more than the bare minimum by way of co-operation. The spirit of wartime occupation was revived among a younger generation as a flourishing underground press sought to evade the censor's blockade.

Indeed, the Communist regime, having proceeded to outlaw the Solidarity opposition, found that it had no-one to talk to. Wałęsa, as the Polish media and Party spokesmen insisted, was merely a private citizen. (For a while, he had been detained by the authorities, but never subjected to long-term imprisonment or internment, like other Solidarity figures.) The desire of the Communists to relegate him to obscurity proved unsuccessful. He had already achieved too great a status, having become famous far beyond Polish borders. When eventually foreign leaders began to make their way to Warsaw they made a point of visiting Wałęsa during their stay. This meeting with the unofficial opposition leader was always made during the private section of their visit. (In 1983 he was awarded the Nobel Peace Prize.)

Although Solidarity was outlawed in October 1982, martial law itself was lifted some nine months later. The Communist leadership made strenuous efforts to achieve 'respectability' and to convince world opinion that the situation in Poland had returned to normal. Unfortunately, the leadership's hopes that a mood of reconciliation and unity would result from the Pope's second visit to Poland during June 1983 were disappointed. In October 1984 news of the brutal seizure and killing of the pro-Solidarity priest, Father Jerzy Popiełuszko, shocked the world. The fact that the murder was carried out by agents of the Interior Ministry drew attention to the murky role of the Polish security forces in establishing 'order' in the country. In the course of the decade scores of deaths were to occur in mysterious circumstances.

Economic reform

Gradually, following successive amnesties of interned Solidarity activists, there was a slight thawing of the diplomatic atmosphere which resulted in the lifting of US trade sanctions in 1983. The sanctions certainly damaged the Polish economy, and helped exacerbate the most serious underlying economic problem – foreign debt repayment, the legacy of Gierek's profligacy. Although the economy had picked up from its low point of

1981–2, shortages and queues remained. Attempts undertaken during 1983–5 to decentralize economic decision making had no noticeable effect and the poor foreign trade performance indicated that more radical measures were called for. At the beginning of 1988 the Polish authorities launched a new initiative – the 'second stage' of economic reform – having first appealed to the population in a referendum. This was received by a weary community with scepticism. Party organs also began to voice the opinion that there was no way out of the morasse if the traditional forms of one-party rule were not relaxed.

Throughout the 1980s thousands of Poles left the country, seeing no future for themselves. They went abroad as tourists and remained as refugees. Special camps were created in Austria, a favourite destination, to house them. From there they sought to move on to Canada, South Africa and Australia. They included large numbers of trained and qualified personnel – engineers, for example – which Poland could ill afford to lose.

In mid-January 1988 the Party weekly *Polityka* published an open letter to both Jaruzelski and Wałęsa from the Warsaw historian, Professor Jerzy Holzer. Holzer's message was apocalyptic. He pointed out that the crisis which had engulfed Poland was rapidly reducing it from membership of the mid-developed group of countries to that of a backward state in terms of civilization. A feeling of helplessness and apathy hung over the country. The authorities had not managed to enlist the support of the majority of the population since the introduction of martial law. Their struggle with Solidarity had undermined the authority of both sides and left a gulf. It was important, continued Holzer, that those who were able to influence the future of Poland should meet and – if only temporarily – overcome their animosities. Otherwise, he warned, Poland stood before a threat equal to that which faced the country in the eighteenth century (i.e. extinction). History would not forgive those who had a chance to save Poland and failed to act.

Other analysts pointed to the cyclical nature of Polish upheavals, and the pattern that these confrontations demonstrated. While there was no doubt that each crisis had left some permanent change to the system of government, Poles could perhaps hope for a more evolutionary, less painful and damaging means of bringing about change. Even political commentators from the Party ranks admitted that the era of ideological confrontation was in the past. The vocabulary of socialism was bankrupt; no-one now wanted to talk about 'improving socialism' or 'introducing real socialism'. The need for greater co-operation with the opposition had dampened polemics.

The 'second stage' of economic reform, the attempt to rally support for one more 'push' on the economic front, was undermined by ill-conceived price rises in the early part of 1988. A further wave of strikes in the spring and summer of 1988 forced Jaruzelski and his advisors to the conclusion that Poland could no longer be governed by force. Some kind of compromise had to be found with the opposition.

The consultations begin

The breakthrough came in August 1988 on the eve of the Party's VIII Plenum, when Interior Minister General Czesław Kiszczak offered to convene a series of meetings with 'representatives of various social and workers' organizations' to take the form of round-table talks. This face-saving formula – stressing 'various' groups, including 'workers' groups, but omitting the name of Solidarity – was intended as an olive branch to the opposition, which, nevertheless would not unduly alarm hardline Party elements (or Moscow). The Plenum agreed to base the system of government in Poland on a wider national understanding.

Kiszczak's offer of talks was quickly taken up. The Interior Minister had a series of meetings with Wałęsa and opposition leaders (including Church representatives) during the late summer. At the same time, Wałęsa invited groups of expert advisers to consult with him in Gdańsk about the way in which negotiations with the authorities should be conducted. Meetings had begun in 1987, and the fifth such conference took place on 18 December (of 135 people invited, 119 attended). These advisers represented more than purely political and economic expertise; they included Church representatives, and figures from the world of culture. In Western terms, the consultations amounted to the drawing up of a political manifesto by a party's policy-making committee. This loose assembly of experts was eventually transformed into a 'Citizens' Committee' linked to the Solidarity leadership. It developed fifteen sub-commissions dealing with specific topics such as political reform, trade union pluralism and the national minorities.

When, on 19 September 1988 the Sejm passed a vote of no confidence in the government of Zbigniew Messner, Poland's eighth prime minister in the postwar period, he was replaced by Mieczysław Rakowski. Rakowski, formerly editor of the Party weekly *Polityka*, took the unusual step of consulting with Cardinal Glemp before appointing his Cabinet. In another departure from orthodoxy, he appointed a millionaire private business-man, Mieczysław Wilczek, his Minister for Industry.

The year 1988 proved a crucial one for the ending of one-party rule in Poland. (The decision to enter into round-table talks was, as one political commentator wrote, like 'giving the opposition the ball and inviting them to play . . .') Communists themselves voiced their perplexity at times that there should be a crisis of confidence in the government at precisely the moment when it had attempted to introduce new policies of openness and consultation, when radical economic reforms were being attempted, and when people could say and write almost what they wanted. This was naive, though, and if genuine, indicated how little they understood the strength of the distrust and resentment that lay beneath the surface. The desire to get the Communists out after years of mismanagement, of official lies and of subservience to Moscow was overpowering.

Although formal round-table talks had been planned for November 1988 they did not take place until February of the following year. The talks lasted for nine weeks and the legislative proposals which resulted were far-reaching. They involved significant changes to the Constitution and to political structures. First, they recommended the creation of a second, upper chamber (Senate), which meant a return to the bicameral system of government abandoned by the Communists in 1946. Second, they foresaw the restoration of the presidency, the candidate to be elected by a National Assembly (i.e. a joint session of the Sejm and Senate). Most importantly, they recommended multi-party, competitive elections – the first in Poland since 1947, and a departure from the 'plebiscites' by which the Communists had formerly called on the populace to support a closed list of Party nominees. There were also far-reaching economic proposals. The Sejm approved the measures in April 1989.

The elections

The elections were held in two stages in June 1989. All seats to the Senate were fought competitively, but in the Sejm only 35% of seats were 'open'; the other 65% remained reserved for the Communists (PUWP) and their allies (ZLP and SD). While this meant that the Communists were guaranteed a continued presence in government, it was conceived as an interim measure – a period of coalition or 'guided democracy', leading to completely free and competitive elections planned for 1993. All parties were to be free to conduct their own election campaigns. In May 1989 a new independent daily newspaper, *Gazeta Wyborcza* (*Election Gazette*), came into being with official approval. Its chief editor was Adam Michnik, historian and long-term dissident who had been imprisoned under martial law. The *Gazeta Wyborcza* was founded to report the election campaign and especially the point of view of the opposition candidates.

The course of the two-stage June elections and the subsequent manoeuvring to form a government was unprecedented for a state in the Soviet bloc. As expected, Solidarity candidates virtually whitewashed the Communists, securing 99 out of 100 seats in the Senate and all the 35 seats which they were able to run for in the Sejm. However, this still left them in a minority in the lower chamber, and most onlookers expected that Solidarity would be content to continue its opposition role, except this time in a more formal setting. Statements from Wałęsa and other Solidarity leaders confirmed that they would bide their time, and not participate in any Communist-led administrations.

In the aftermath of the elections the office of presidency had to be filled. General Jaruzelski, the architect of martial law, made an early announcement of his decision not to stand, fearing that his record would count against him and would result in a humiliating defeat. When it became clear, though, that Wałęsa was not standing for office, the general reversed his decision. On 19 July he was elected president after an eight-hour televised debate, having received 270 votes against 233 votes opposed to his candidature (34 deputies abstained). The majority of Solidarity deputies voted against him.

Jaruzelski's subsequent decision to ask former Interior Minister, Kiszczak, to form a government was greeted with hostility. It was a blow to Solidarity, since Kiszczak was the person responsible for interning so many people during martial law. With the prospect that they would capture both the presidency and the premiership, many felt that the Communists were merely taking over where they had left off. Wałęsa issued a statement opposing the choice, which deepened the crisis. Faced with such firm opposition, Kiszczak found it impossible to form a government. Solidarity persuaded the Communists' formerly loyal allies, the Democrats (SD) and the Peasant Party (ZSL), to turn against them. Kiszczak was forced to admit defeat.

The way now became clear for adoption of the formula proposed by Adam Michnik in the columns of *Gazeta Wyborcza* – 'Your President, Our Premier'. On 24 August 1989 Tadeusz Mazowiecki, a Catholic journalist and one of Wałęsa's advisors since the early days of confrontation in the Gdańsk shipyard, was appointed prime minister. He immediately set about constructing a Cabinet. By 12 September he was able to submit 23 names to the Sejm. While eleven of the Cabinet posts were allocated to Solidarity deputies, and only four to the PUWP (Communists), the latter were granted key ministries of the Interior and Defence. (Since control of the military and security forces had been the springboard from which the Communists had taken power in the period 1945–7, this raised some eyebrows, but it was a necessary part of the compromise.) Other Cabinet posts were allocated to the Democrats (3) and to the Peasants' Party (4), with one portfolio going to an independent.

The assumption by Mazowiecki of the premiership, the first non-Communist prime minister in the Soviet bloc, was received with justified acclamation and even incredulity in the West. Within the Communist world reactions varied, from the guardedly welcoming to the openly hostile. It was the Romanian leader Ceauşescu whose hostility went furthest. While Ceauşescu had not supported the Warsaw Pact invasion of Czechoslovakia in 1968 and had broken with Moscow over it, he now tried to persuade Soviet leader Gorbachev that intervention in Poland by friendly socialist states was necessary. Such entreaties were futile, of course. The Soviet leader had been hinting for some time that he was not in sympathy with the Brezhnev Doctrine and had made his rejection public in a number of speeches during the summer. The Poles immediately made soothing noises, by stressing their intention to honour existing agreement, and specifically to remain members of Comecon and the Warsaw Pact.

'The first comprehensive market-oriented reforms in Eastern Europe'

The new government rapidly set about rolling back the frontiers of Communism. This process began with changes to the Constitution, including the deletion of Article 3, concerning the leading role of the Communist Party. A team was charged with drafting a new Constitution, which, it is hoped, will be ready by May 1991 – the 200th anniversary of Poland's, and Europe's first. Poland's official name reverted to the prewar 'Rzeczpospolita Polska' (that is, Polish Republic, rather than People's Republic). The country's symbol, the white eagle, had its royal crown – a legacy of the Polish monarchy – restored. Across the country, the symbols of Communist rule were stripped or torn down. Busts and statues of Lenin were toppled, and there was great satisfaction when the statue of Feliks Dzierzyński, the Pole who created Lenin's secret police, was taken down in the Warsaw square that had borne his name.

The most difficult task facing the incoming administration was that of tackling the economy. In addition to the crippling burden of overseas debt which aproached $40 billion by the end of 1989, inflation had accelerated dramatically and was estimated at 1000%. Part of the boost to prices had been caused by the Rakowski government's attempts during August to 'marketize the food economy'. While the measures had given producers free rein to raise their prices, they had not been able to ensure an adequate supply of goods to satisfy market demand.

The young Finance Minister and Deputy Premier, Leszek Balcerowicz, had to consider with his colleagues how to control the rampant inflation, and at the same time put the Polish economy on the road to recovery. Negotiations began with the International Monetary Fund (many loans from Western governments are dependent upon IMF approval of the restructuring arrangements). The package eventually agreed was the most radical break with socialist policies ever attempted, and in the words of *The Economist*, 'the first comprehensive market-oriented reforms in Eastern Europe'. There was to be an end to price controls and remaining subsidies. Prices would be determined by the market, but wages would be held down to avoid a wage–price spiral that would accelerate inflation. The private sector would be freed from government restrictions, while the state sector would be slimmed down by privatizations, and subjected to the discipline of the marketplace. The government undertook to adopt responsible monetary and fiscal policies (e.g. balanced budgets), and stressed its eventual aim to bring about convertibility of the złoty.

The measures were introduced on 1 January 1990, in a mood of both excitement and apprehension. As the Polish economy moved into uncharted waters, what would the effect be on employment levels, production, the trade situation, household budgets? Forecasters estimated that by holding wages down while prices rose, real incomes could decline as much as 20% by the spring before the situation began to improve. Price rises had in the past so often tolled the death knell for Communist administrations. Could support for Mazowiecki's government survive such draconian measures? The government has already planned welfare provision (such as benefit payments) for those most in need, and soup kitchens have been established.

Early evidence (May 1990) indicates that the reforms are having the desired effect in bringing down inflation. However, as expected, unemployment is rising too; by the end of May the figure had reached 443,000, which was 3.3% of the total national workforce; more pessimistic forecasts are that it will rise to 1 million. Production has dropped more heavily than expected, and the first bankruptcies of state and private concerns occurred in February 1990.

The medicine is certainly beginning to hurt, and as the pain increases, so will pressure on the government. A strike of Silesian miners, complaining about the eroding value of their wages, was only called off when ministers explained their case to the workers. In Łódź, a textile town, large numbers of factory workers have been laid off. Many of these are women, and in some cases they are the sole family breadwinner. Suicides are reported to have occurred. Disaffection in the countryside, where farmers are unhappy at the government's agricultural policy, has gone so far that there have been calls from within the Peasant Party for its single Cabinet representative, Agriculture Minister, Czesław Janicki, to resign.

Understandably, former Communists are both smug and astonished. Smug, because the capitalist system so many Poles ardently desired has brought a worse shock to the system than ever administered under Communist control; and astonished, because despite it all, there is still widespread support for Mazowiecki and belief in what he is trying to do.

International relations

On the foreign relations front, Poland made an early undertaking to respect its membership of Comecon and the Warsaw Pact—looking to calm fears in Moscow. But Poland has also been in the forefront of Eastern bloc moves to establish links with Western economic organizations, such as the European Community. (It has already rejoined the International Monetary Fund.) Suggestions of central European federation with Czechoslovakia revive an idea that was last mooted during World War II – when the political authorities of both states were in exile. Now, as then, the Czechs seem less keen on the idea. (Then they were worried about the disapproval of the Soviets, now they seem more interested in joining the EC.) Poland has been less vocal than some neighbours about the removal of Soviet troops on Polish soil – perhaps due to the uncertainties which have grown up about the future of its western borders following the inevitable German reunification.

Indeed, it is relations with West Germany which are likely to prove the most sensitive aspect of Poland's foreign relations over the next few years.

The continental balance of power is shifting around Poland, and the centre of equilibrium is moving from Poland's eastern neighbour, the Soviet Union, to its western neighbour, a reunifying German Republic. While Poland is eager to establish good relations with the new Germany, Polish fears about a renewal of German territorial designs on its western frontier were revived by the insensitivity of Chancellor Kohl's remarks on the subject. The Poles are also wary about economic domination – they want to attract foreign investment, but fear the buying up of large sectors of the Polish economy by German capital.

Elsewhere Poland's foreign policy under the Mazowiecki administration has seen diplomatic relations re-established with the Vatican after a 45-year break, and moves towards establishing relations with Israel. Contacts have also been made with the white regime in South Africa – something unthinkable in the past.

The future

What is the future likely to bring for Poland? Much depends on the progress of the economic reforms over the next twelve to eighteen months. In February 1990 the 17-member 'Paris Club' of international creditors agreed to defer interest payments on the massive Polish debt for 12 months, in order not to hinder the Balcerowicz reforms. The interest, though, is not being written off; it is being added to the $40 billion sum outstanding. A later Polish attempt to reduce its debt-servicing commitments by 80% had a surprisingly rapid and positive response from the USA, with ideas for a relief plan being floated by the American administration in May. If it comes to fruition this will be a considerable boost to Poland's long-term economic prospects. However, more tangible evidence is required if the Polish electorate is to be persuaded that there is light at the end of the tunnel and that their present sacrifices are going to result in lasting benefits.

The political map is still changing. The Polish United Workers' Party (Communists) disbanded itself in January and became the Social Democratic Party of the Polish Republic. A breakaway faction named itself the Social Democratic Union. (More suspicious but historically minded observers have commented that the Communist Party has changed its spots before, but remained the same animal. They recall that the Party led and inspired before World War I by Polish Communist Rosa Luxembourg was also called Social Democratic.) The efforts of these successor parties to inherit the massive estate of the defunct PUWP have been largely foiled. A government commission discovered that the Communists and their allies had occupied some 5000 buildings, only 86 of which, however, were legally in their possession; the remainder had been appropriated from the state. In early April, the great majority of these were reclaimed by the state.

As in the other post-Communist states of the region, a multitude of political parties has come into being, including Greens and even Monarchists. The process of crystallization is far from complete, though, and in the June 1990 elections to some 2383 local councils, many of the smaller parties were still campaigning under the Solidarity banner. The election itself, an important further step in the gradual removal of the Party *nomenklatura*, resulted in a disappointing turnout (42% may compare well with the turnout in British local government elections, but this was the first completely free election in Poland for more than half a century). Solidarity-backed candidates, as expected, did well, winning 59 out of 60 seats in Gdańsk and 72 out of 75 seats in Kraków. Elsewhere, their support was considerably reduced from the level of June 1989. There was a high level of support for independent candidates (many of whom were claimed to be former Communists), while in the rural areas the Peasant Party (PSL) made a respectable showing. Indeed, the unification of various peasant factions under one umbrella organization (at a Warsaw Congress on 5 May) is likely to be one of the more significant political developments of the year. They claim to be the natural successors of the Peasant Party of wartime Polish premier, Stanisław Mikołajczyk. Under their 44-year old leader, Roman Bartoszcze, they are sure to increase pressure on the Mazowiecki government for more favourable rural policies, and are indeed committed to presenting an alternative economic plan by autumn 1990. They may prove to be one of the major players on the Polish political scene in future years.

The single most puzzling question in Polish politics is over the future of Solidarity. During the period of its infancy (1980–81), Solidarity was a broadly-based movement. It attracted people of widely differing views and beliefs, who were united only by their opposition to the Communists. As Communist power recedes in the memory, so this glue which bound the movement together is disappearing. A division has already become apparent between the trade union and the political front (the Citizens' Parliamentary Group); Lech Wałęsa's attitude towards his former advisors in government has been ambiguous, but he is increasingly voicing criticism of their performance. The June 1990 local elections showed cracks beginning to appear between more right-wing, Catholic, nationalist elements and centre-left factions. The links which bind the groups together are being sorely tested as the austerity measures of the Mazowiecki government take effect. It now seems that the free general elections provided for in the 1989 round-table talks may be brought forward from the planned date of 1993. Many commentators feel that once the new Constitution is framed (in 1991), the desire to oust the former Communists and abandon all traces of the former regime will be irresistible. A general election will doubtless see the splintering of Solidarity into more coherent political groupings.

Uncertainty exists, too, over the figure of Lech Wałęsa. Officially, he is chairman of Solidarity's National Committee, having been re-elected to the post during the movement's national congress in Gdańsk in May 1990 (the first national congress held since 1981). He has vacillated about whether or not to enter government in some formal capacity, and those who are close to him say that he regrets not having seized the opportunity to become premier in August 1989. Some people see him as the next president. However, his rather clumsy demands early in the year that Jaruzelski should resign as president were not well received. Wałęsa claimed to be merely 'testing the water' of support for his candidacy, but he will have been disappointed with the result. Opinion polls reflecting the popularity of possible candidates for the presidency had Wałęsa in fourth place. Not only did he trail behind former advisors, Mazowiecki and Geremek – now, of course, both government ministers – but even his old adversary, General Jaruzelski, in third place, was preferred. Wałęsa is still a figure of immense charisma and influence in Poland. There is no-one who could have talked railway workers into ending their week-old strike as he did in May. But he is increasingly being seen as self-indulgent, exasperating and disruptive – as a mercurial figure who lacks both the education and discipline needed for the detailed day-to-day work of high office. Critics also claim that after years of leading the Solidarity union in an autocratic style he lacks the ability to compromise and the personal qualities necessary in a national leader. In his more resigned – perhaps more realistic – moments, Wałęsa has said that he sees himself as first and foremost a trade union leader. There must be many Poles who, while they admire the Solidarity leader for his achievements, fervently hope that this will remain the limit of his ambitions.

7 ROMANIA
A reign of terror – then ethnic unrest

Romania as we know it today is, territorially speaking, largely the product of the Paris Peace Settlement which followed World War I. Much of the country was under foreign imperial rule until 1918. Transylvania and Bukovina had been part of the Habsburg Empire, and Bessarabia, having been lost to Russia in 1812, was regained in the turmoil produced by the Bolshevik Revolution. Even the Black Sea coast province of Dobrogea had only been severed from the Ottoman Empire and awarded to the infant Romania by the European Powers in 1878.

The legacy of a different historical experience of the Romanians in these constituent lands, coupled with the diverse ethnic mix of the large Hungarian, German and Jewish minority populations which they contained, posed major problems of harmonization and consolidation in the enlarged Romanian state, problems which, in the brief interlude of the interwar period, Romania's leaders had little time, capacity and will to address. The failure to solve them (and the Western democracies provided little help to this end) was to blight the country's progress towards modernization and the exercise of genuine democratic rule.

Although a radical land reform was introduced after World War I, the economic and social reforms sought by the peasantry (80% of the population of 18 millions lived in villages) were not introduced by governments, which remained subservient to the sectional interests of the banks and prominent industrialists. The economic recession of the 1930s doomed such hopes and fostered a decade of instability in which the xenophobia of the impoverished peasantry was exploited by right-wing movements, principally by the Iron Guard, and directed against the Jews. The growth in support for the Guard, which stemmed in part from a widespread disillusion with the experience of parliamentary government, led King Carol II to institute a personal dictatorship in 1938. At the same time, Romania's geographical position, and its economic predicament, forced it into Hitler's arms.

Involvement with Germany
After the Munich agreement of 1938 Romania found itself increasingly drawn into the web of German military and economic policies. With Britain unwilling to buy Romania's wheat in large quantities, and with Germany in control of the Czech Skoda works with which Carol had placed orders for arms, Romania was now dependent on Hitler for the means to save its

ROMANIA

Official name	Romania
Area	237,500 sq. km (96,699 sq. miles)
Population	23,050,000 (1988) (annual growth rate 0.4%)
Capital	Bucharest (Bucureşti)
Language	Romanian, Magyar
Religion	70% Romanian Orthodox Church, 10% Romanian Uniate Church, 5% Roman Catholic, 5% Lutheran
Currency	leu

economy and territorial integrity in the face of threats from the Soviet Union and Hungary.

In June 1940, on German advice given in accordance with the Nazi–Soviet pact of August 1939, Carol agreed to the Soviet demand for Bessarabia and Northern Bukovina, and two months later he accepted Hitler's own imposition of the Vienna Award, by which Romania was forced to cede Northern Transylvania to Hungary. The loss of these provinces cost Romania almost one third of its territory and population of whom half, some 3 million, were ethnically Romanian. Unable to resist popular demands for his abdication following these supine concessions, Carol renounced the throne in favour of his teenage son Michael, after having appointed General Ion Antonescu as Prime Minister. In January 1941 the Iron Guard, which had shared power with Antonescu, rose against him and Hitler, anxious to have a stable Romania as a springboard for his attack upon the Soviet Union, allowed the general to crush the rebellion. Antonescu now assumed supreme powers and willingly joined the German invasion of the Soviet Union on 22 June 1941 in order to gain the lost eastern provinces.

As the military situation steadily deteriorated after the battle of Stalingrad, in which Romanian losses were put at 155,000 dead, wounded and missing, Antonescu tolerated the emission of peace feelers, both from within his own government and from the opposition leader, Maniu. These efforts foundered on the Anglo-American insistence upon 'unconditional surrender', which could not be reconciled with Antonescu's desire to guarantee Romania's postwar independence from the Soviet Union. Antonescu's reluctance as a soldier to abandon his German ally who was now on the defensive forced the opposition parties to plot his overthrow, and with Soviet troops rapidly advancing on Romanian territory the young King Michael boldly arrested the general on 23 August 1944. This *volte-face*, the most decisive of World War II, exposed the German Army's southern flank and opened the whole of south-eastern Europe to the Red Army.

The Russians arrive

When Soviet troops entered Bucharest on 31 August they found an interim Romanian government ready to negotiate an armistice and to hold free elections. To regain the initiative, Stalin fashioned from the Soviet–Romanian armistice a legal framework for securing a dominant political and economic interest in Romania, one conceded to him by Churchill at their meeting barely a month later in Moscow under the so-called 'Percentage Agreement'. The British and American co-signatories, and their representatives on the aptly titled Allied (Soviet) Control Commission in Romania, were reduced to the role of spectators in the application of the armistice according to Soviet dictates.

In order to impose Stalin's will on the Romanian people the Soviet authorities employed blatant political engineering. On the grounds that they needed stability in a country that was behind their lines in their continuing war effort against Germany, they installed a puppet government under Petru Groza on 6 March 1945. This government oversaw the first steps to communize the country, which involved abolishing the freedom of the press and of political assembly, and the arrest and imprisonment of virtually all political opponents. Most of the Romanian army was demobilized and the policing of the country placed in the hands of the Soviet Army of occupation. At the insistence of Britain and the USA, elections were finally held in November 1946. The results were not announced for three days, and the government was suspected of having falsified the returns in presenting a total defeat as a major victory. The subjugation of Romania to the Soviet Union was completed at the end of the following month, when King Michael, on being presented with an ultimatum by Groza to abdicate or face the prospect of civil war, renounced his throne. On the same day, 30 December 1947, the Romanian People's Republic was proclaimed.

The postwar period

The principal political figure of the early postwar period in Romania was Gheorghe Gheorghiu-Dej, General Secretary of the Romanian Communist Party (from 1947 the Romanian Workers' Party) between 1945 and 1954, and First Secretary from 1955 to his death in 1965. Under his leadership, Romania emerged from subservience to the Soviet Union to challenge the latter's supranational pretensions by resisting pressure to become the granary of Comecon and by rapidly developing its own industry. Underlying the emphasis given to rapid industrialization was also a political goal: that of enabling Romania to break its dependency upon the Soviet Union. The achievement of the greater economic self-reliance needed to underpin the political autonomy from the Soviet Union sought by Dej and his party in the late 1950s and early 1960s was based not only upon the further development of agriculture but also upon an extension of the industrialization drive to the countryside. The policy had important sociological, occupational and economic consequences, generating a movement of labour from the land to the factory and increasing the urbanization of the population. The proportion of the urban population rose from 22% in 1948 to 30% in 1965 and 49% in 1983, and was projected to rise to 75% in the year 2000.

The autonomous policies inaugurated by Dej were continued by his successor, Nicolae Ceauşescu, who was elected First (later General) Secretary of the Party in March 1965. Romania developed relations with China, who became its principal partner in the international Communist movement, was the first country in the Eastern bloc to establish diplomatic relations with West Germany in 1967, and did not break diplomatic ties with Israel after the Six-Day War. The most forceful affirmation of independence from Soviet dictates was Ceauşescu's refusal to participate in, and condemnation of, the Warsaw Pact intervention in Czechoslovakia in 1968. Growing recognition of Romania's political usefulness as a thorn in the flesh of the Soviet Union opened a period of increasing Western courtship of Ceauşescu, exemplified by President Richard Nixon's visit in August 1969. Ceauşescu returned the visit in December 1970. There followed a succession of economic favours. In 1971 Romania was admitted to GATT (General Agreement on Trade and Tariffs) and in 1972 it was accepted into the International Monetary Fund and the World Bank. Romania's trading position was further enhanced when the country acquired preferential trading status with the Common Market in 1973. In March 1975 President Gerald Ford granted Romania Most Favored Nation status and Ceauşescu visited the USA again in April 1978. Three months later he was given an honour unprecedented to the head of a Warsaw Pact country – a state visit to the United Kingdom.

Economic decline and 'systematization'

At the same time, disturbing trends began to emerge in the country's economic performance. Soviet opposition to Romania's rapid industrialization was translated into a refusal to provide financial aid for the programme and therefore Ceauşescu turned to the West for loans. Romania's creditworthiness was assessed on over-optimistic estimates of its ability to repay through exports which were generally of poor quality. Not only did exports fail to generate the income anticipated, but the energy-intensive heavy industry plants became increasingly voracious due to inefficient running. In the mid-1970s Ceauşescu expanded Romania's oil-refining capacity in excess of the country's own domestic output, and in 1976 was forced to begin importing crude oil. When the price of oil soared on the international market in 1978 Romania was caught unprepared, and soon faced a major trade deficit. The problem was exacerbated by the revolution in Iran, a chief supplier to Romania of oil, which interrupted deliveries. With the Soviet Union refusing to make good the oil deficit unless Ceauşescu showed greater conformity in foreign policy, a third of Romania's oil-refining capacity became idle in 1981.

Nature was also against the regime. A severe earthquake in 1977 and floods in 1980 and 1981 disrupted industrial production and reduced the exports of foodstuffs which Ceauşescu now looked to in order to reduce the foreign debt incurred through industrialization. In late 1981 Romania's foreign debt rose to $10.2 billion and Ceauşescu decided to request its rescheduling. On the recommendation of the IMF, imports were reduced and exports, especially of machinery, equipment and petroleum products, increased. The implications of this reduction of imports has not been fully appreciated, since in 1981 Romania was a net importer of food from the industrialized West (Romanian food imports from the West in 1981 totalled $644 million and exports $158 million; in the same year Soviet statistics show that Romania exported 106,000 tons of frozen meat to the USSR).

Therefore in order to reduce Romania's hard currency debt Ceauşescu reduced food imports from the West from a peak of almost $1 billion in 1981 to $300 million in 1982 and $27 million in 1984. Cutting back on food imports, while at the same time continuing to export meat to the Soviet Union, forced Ceauşescu to introduce meat rationing.

More importantly, the very act of having to accept conditions from the Western banks was a great blow to Ceauşescu's inflated pride. He declared defiantly in December 1982 that he would pay off the foreign debt by 1990, and to achieve this introduced a series of austerity measures unparalleled even in the bleak history of East European Communist regimes. Rationing of bread, flour, sugar and milk was introduced in some provincial towns in early 1982, and in 1983 it was extended to most of the country, with the exception of the capital. The monthly personal rations were progressively reduced to the point where on the eve of the revolution they were, in some regions of the country, two pounds of sugar, two pounds of flour, a half-pound pack of margarine, and five eggs. At the same time, heavy industry was also called upon to contribute to the export drive, but because its energy needs outstripped the country's generating capacity drastic energy-saving measures were introduced, which included a petrol ration of 30 litres per month for private car owners. Other strictures stipulated a maximum temperature of 14°C in offices (in winter outside temperatures usually drop to well below zero) and periods of provision of hot water (normally one day a week in state-owned flats). In the winter of 1983 these restrictions were extended, causing the interruption of the electricity supply in major cities and reduction of gas pressure during the day so that meals could only be cooked at night. During the severe winter of 1984–5 it was calculated from medical sources in the capital's hospitals that over 30 children had died as a result of unannounced power cuts affecting incubators.

Ceauşescu's relevance on the world stage was undermined by the accession to power of Mikhail Gorbachev in March 1985. A number of the very positions which Ceauşescu had been adopting in his foreign policy, and which had gilded his 'liberal' image in the West, now became features of Soviet policy; withdrawal from Afghanistan, removal of short-range nuclear weapons from Europe, and reductions in nuclear arsenals. Ceauşescu's usefulness as a bridge between East and West rapidly evaporated. Furthermore, the reforms to the Communist system advocated by Gorbachev were rejected by Ceauşescu, who continued to apply his Stalinist policies in an even more draconian manner by introducing in November 1987 a seven-day working week and reduced domestic heating quotas. On the very day when the Party newspaper reported the proceedings of a Central Committee plenum at which Ceauşescu dismissed the idea of Gorbachev-style reform, the first major challenge to Ceauşescu was launched by several thousand workers in Braşov, the country's second largest city, when they sacked the local Party headquarters on 15 November in protest at his new measures. The leaders of the protest were rounded up, beaten and jailed as Ceauşescu defiantly refused to make any concessions.

Ceauşescu's fanatical commitment to modernizing the country was exemplified by his announcement of the 'systematization' policy, and in this respect he scored a spectacular own goal. With it disappeared the popular image of him in the West as a benign figure, as 'one of Europe's good Communists' as Vice-President George Bush described him after a visit to Romania in September 1983. In March 1988 Ceauşescu announced plans to complete by the year 2000 the urbanization or 'systematization' of the country which would involve a reduction by half in the number of Romania's 13,000 villages. How the number of villages was to be reduced soon became clear from the demolition, in one case at only 48 hours' notice, of a handful of villages around Bucharest.

As the pace of reform grew within the rest of Eastern Europe the president became more and more defiant. The extremism of his thinking found expression in his attempt at the July 1989 Warsaw Pact meeting in Bucharest to obtain support for armed intervention against the Solidarity government in Poland when his most sympathetic listener was Erich Honecker. He found another partner in the resistance to reform in Deng Xiao-ping, to whom he offered free holidays in Romania for Chinese soldiers and policemen who had suppressed the demonstrating students in Tiananmen Square. Deng was one of the few Communist leaders to send a high-ranking representative to the Fourteenth Romanian Party Congress in November 1989, where Ceauşescu received 67 standing ovations during his opening address, which once again made no concession to *perestroika* and *glasnost*. The popular despair and frustration at Ceauşescu's re-election as General Secretary manifested itself a month later.

The pastor in Timişoara

The spark which ignited the revolution against Ceauşescu was a local protest in the western Transylvanian town of Timişoara against the harassment of a Hungarian pastor, Laszlo Tokes. Members of his flock maintained a vigil on the night of 15 December outside his house to prevent Tokes being taken away for questioning by the security police. On the following day the vigil turned into a major demonstration, when several thousand Romanians joined the Hungarian parishioners and began shouting 'We want bread'. These calls were then replaced by chants of 'Down with Ceauşescu' and the protesters marched into the town centre. They were dispersed by baton-wielding militiamen but no shots were fired, even though Ceauşescu had given orders that the security police and the army should fire on the demonstrators. The demonstrations continued on 17 December, but on that afternoon the army did open fire on the crowd. The number of casualties was initially put at several thousand, but subsequent investigations put the figure at less than 200. On Elena Ceauşescu's orders, 40 of the dead were transported by lorry to Bucharest and cremated to make identification impossible.

On 20 December Ceauşescu returned from a brief visit to Iran and made the first of three fatal errors. In a televised address to the nation he completely misjudged the mood of the people by displaying no hint of compassion for the victims of Timişoara and by dismissing the demonstrations as the work of 'fascists' and 'hooligan elements', inspired by Hungarian irredentism.

His second mistake was to convene a public meeting of support on the next morning in Bucharest, when the public was incensed by his lack of humanity. To his amazement, his speech was interrupted by cries of 'We are not hooligans' and the live television and radio coverage was cut for several minutes. When he resumed his speech, Ceauşescu attempted to placate the crowd by announcing salary and pension increases, but this stratagem only angered them further. At the end of his speech large groups of young people remained in the city centre and, encouraged by the warm, unseasonal weather, lingered into the evening. It was at this point that they were fired upon by the army and security police, and many of them were shot dead.

On the following morning of 22 December Ceauşescu committed his third error. He summoned yet another public meeting of support and attempted to address it. Stones were thrown at the balcony of the Central Committee building and Ceauşescu fled from the rooftop in a helicopter accompanied by his wife and two of his closest allies, Manea Manescu and Emil Bobu, and two bodyguards. Ceauşescu ordered the helicopter pilot to land at Snagov, some 30 kilometres to the north of Bucharest, where he had a country villa, and it was from here that he and his wife collected a suitcase of clothing. Manea and Bobu remained behind as the helicopter took off again with the Ceauşescus and their bodyguards in the direction of Piteşti, but shortage of fuel, and the danger of being spotted by radar, prompted the pilot to put down on a main road just outside Titu, some 35 kilometres to the south of Tîrgovişte. Here they parted company with their bodyguard and highjacked a car driven by a doctor, who took them to the outskirts of Tîrgovişte. They then commandeered a second car and tried to reach the local party headquarters, but were recognized. The driver took them to an agricultural centre, where they were locked in a room until the local police arrived. The couple were eventually taken to the Tîrgovişte military garrison, where they were tried and executed on Christmas Day 1989.

The Front for National Salvation

In the wake of Ceauşescu's flight from the roof of the Central Committee building on 22 December the Council of the Front for National Salvation was set up to run the country. Comprising 145 members, it represented an alliance of reform-minded Communists and prominent dissidents which initially enjoyed widespread support for its declared aim of steering the country towards free elections. On 26 December Ion Iliescu was declared president, and Dumitru Mazilu vice-president, of the National Salvation Front (NSF) and a government appointed with Petre Roman as prime minister. All were members of the Communist Party. An eleven-man Executive Bureau of the NSF was set up to act as a 'Cabinet', but in effect all major decisions, including the one to execute Nicolae and Elena Ceauşescu, were taken by a small group centred around Iliescu, Mazilu and Silviu Brucan, a leading Party critic of Ceauşescu and the *eminence grise* of the Front. It was this concentration of power in the hands of an inner circle of Communists and the secrecy of its decision-making processes that created a climate of suspicion about its intentions.

The turning point in the public's acquiescence in the NSF came with its decision on 23 January 1990 to stand as a political party, despite the pronouncement on 29 December of its ideologue, Silviu Brucan, that 'it is not necessary for us to become a political party'. On the following day the leading dissident, Doina Cornea, announced her resignation from the NSF Council, accusing it of being 'demagogic'. The Front's *volte-face* was also criticized by the three leading opposition groups, the National Peasant Party, the National Liberal Party and the Social Democratic Party, and prompted a large anti-Front demonstration in Bucharest on 28 January 1990. This was followed by a pro-Front demonstration by workers, many of whom were brought in by buses and brandished cudgels and chains. A number of them besieged the National Peasant Party leader, Corneliu Coposu, in his headquarters, and when he left he had to be taken away in an armoured car. The day after, on 31 January, Ana Blandiana, the dissident poet, announced her resignation from the Front's Council, opining that her membership was not compatible with her position as a writer who wanted to distance herself from the 'aggression, hatred and lack of tolerance produced by the struggle for power'.

This turbulence forced the NSF to open discussions with the opposition parties in order to enlarge the Council of the Front, which had been set up on 22 December 1989 on an *ad hoc* basis as an interim government. The new Council was set up on 1 February 1990 with the name of the Provisional Council for National Unity (PCNU), and its 241 members were to be drawn from representatives of the major parties and national minorities, together with figures 'active in the revolution', workers, intellectuals, and students. Nevertheless, the Front continued to dominate the new body, with 106 members, compared to the 105 representatives of the 35 registered parties (three from each) and the 27 members representing the nine national minority bodies. The membership of the PCNU was increased to 253 on 10 February to incorporate extra representatives from the Front and from two newly formed parties. The proliferation of new parties (on 19 April their number stood at 82) might be seen as a reaction to almost half a century of single-party rule, but many of them are regarded by the opposition as cover organizations for the Front and six of them indeed declared their support for it in late January. Such developments invite parallels with the tactics used by the Soviet Union to impose Communist rule in Romania at the end of World War II, when a National Democratic Bloc incorporating several Communist front bodies was used to bring a Communist regime to power.

On 19 March the PCNU passed a decree confirming 20 May as the date for parliamentary and presidential elections. In a statement the Council's chairman, Ion Iliescu, said that the electoral campaign, which would start the next day, would lead to the election of a bicameral parliament whose main task would be to draft a new constitution. According to the electoral law the parliament will operate as a constituent assembly with two chambers: an assembly of deputies with 387 seats and a senate with 119 seats.

Public distrust of the NSF's intentions and its anger at the Front's failure to grant equal air-time to the opposition parties led to the resignation of the president of Television and Radio, Aurel Dragoş Munteanu, on 9 February while a week later the Minister of Defence, General Nicolae Militaru, resigned following demonstrations outside the government's headquarters by young army and air force officers and civilians protesting at his association with the Ceauşescu regime. Reports of attacks in February on National Peasant Party officials and offices throughout the country heightened suspicion that the NSF was resorting to intimidation and violence in order to dampen opposition, and once again raised the spectre of the brutal authoritarian rule associated with the Communists.

Fears that the NSF's ultimate aim, if elected, is to engineer a return to single-party rule have been strengthened by its reliance on officials who served Ceauşescu and on senior *securitate* officers. Prime minister Petre Roman has countered that it is impossible to form an interim government without including figures who were members of the Communist Party and who have some administrative experience. Mistrust of the NSF is compounded, particularly in the eyes of the younger generation, by the prevalence of opportunism which so ravaged Romanian public and intellectual life during the Ceauşescu era, and which still threatens to turn the revolution sour. Dumitru Mazilu has been a victim of such a charge. A Communist turned dissident, Mazilu was appointed vice-president of the NSF Council on the morrow of the revolution, but when he appeared on the same platform with President Ion Iliescu to answer critics at an anti-Front demonstration on 12 January he was accused of attempting to manipulate the crowd to his own advantage. Three days later a number of letters appeared in one of the principal national dailies, claiming that Mazilu had some years earlier been Director of the State Security Training School. Despite his threat to sue the newspaper for libel, public suspicions were not allayed, and he resigned from the Front on 26 January, claiming that he was the victim of 'Stalinist' methods adopted by those who had access to *securitate* files.

In the degree of attention given to criticism of the NSF it is tempting to believe that it is completely lacking in public support, but this is not the case. The miners who came to Bucharest to show their support for the Front on 19 February 1990 did so, despite President Iliescu's plea to them to stay at home, and threatened to destroy the local railway station in the mining centre of Petroşani if trains were not provided for their transport to the capital. In the miners' view the Front's reformed Communist policies offer a better guarantee of their jobs than the market-orientated programmes of the other major parties. These parties have claimed that the miners are easy prey to manipulation by the Front for its own ends, but they have been far from docile in the past, and they staged the first major strike in protest at working conditions under the Ceauşescu regime in July 1977.

Ceauşescu's legacy

While the crisis of morality and the political problems of Romania might be alleviated by impartial and dignified conduct of the May elections, the solution of the economic problems left by the Ceauşescu regime will require drastic and painful measures. All the major political parties are agreed upon the need for decentralization, the transition to a market-based economy, and the dissolution of collective farms. Where there is a difference is over the speed at which these changes should take place, and the NSF, with its largely Communist composition, is in this respect the most cautious, for it derives most of its support from the industrial working class who stand to lose their jobs in any market-orientated rationalization of the economy, and who cannot fall back on a non-existent unemployment benefit.

The most comprehensive statement on the state of the Romanian economy was given by the prime minister, Petre Roman, on 4 January 1990. He told the National Salvation Front Council that the economy was in 'profound crisis'. Production targets had been imposed without any regard for the country's 'raw material and material resources'. Money was thrown away on 'lunatic investments . . . with no technical or economic justification'. Industry was using 'obsolete technologies', particularly the metallurgical and chemical industries, which had not been modernized since 1948. 'In the energy field we are working with pre-war technologies.' Due to the policy of rapid debt repayment, no new technology had been imported for 10 years, and for the same reason, health, education and transport services had all been starved of investment during the same period.

Roman announced at the same time that a number of Ceauşescu's prestige projects would be abandoned, including the construction of a canal linking Bucharest to the Danube, the Călăraşi iron and steel combine, and the second stage of the heavy-water plant at Turnu Severin. While the cancellation of these projects, and of the systematization programme announced on 26 January, will release funds for investment, they will not be sufficient for the modernization which Romanian industry so desperately requires. Industrial modernization can only be achieved with foreign collaboration, but the Front's declarations in this regard are less than encouraging for prospective partners, for they will not allow majority Western equity participation in Romanian companies. Roman seems to fear that aid from the industrialized West will not only bring a transfer of capital and technology but also concomitant divisions of wealth, privilege and labour.

The most immediate problems for the economy arise from energy production. Over the last decade the power supply network was not developed sufficiently to meet the needs of the energy-intensive and wasteful metallurgical and chemical industries, and as a consequence, draconian restrictions and quotas were imposed on domestic consumers. These restrictions were annulled on 1 January, but the subsequent diversion of power supplies to the household has badly affected industrial production. Domestic consumption of electricity rose in January 1990 by 50% compared with the same month last year, and now represented 12% of total electric power generation, according to the Minister for Electric Power. In February it was announced that street lighting, which had been cut by 80% between 1972 and 1989, would be restored. In Bucharest alone 40,000 lamps would be reinstated by 1992.

The impact of these measures upon industry has been considerable. In January the Minister for National Economy, Colonel-General Victor Stănculescu, reported that factories were suffering from shortages of natural gas, electricity, coal and other raw materials. It is clear from the minister's remarks that industrial output fell in the first two months of 1990, and these difficulties make the case for economic reform even more cogent. The interim government's commitment to improve household supplies will further reduce the amount of energy available to industry unless the deficit is made up by imports from the Soviet Union.

The miners' protests in support of President Iliescu suggest a favourable response from the industrialized working class to the Front government's measures to protect workers' interests. They have been told that they will not have their wages stopped for failure to meet unrealistic targets, as was the case during the Ceauşescu period. Where production was halted due to shortages of energy or raw materials, 75% of wages would still be paid.

It was upon the workers that the Front pinned its hopes for victory in the May elections. The Front was to emerge victorious only by maintaining its support from large numbers of workers, and we can expect only a very gradual transition from a centrally planned to a market economy, unlike the developments in Poland. There are advantages in this. A slow restructuring of industry will reduce the threat of massive and rapid unemployment which could create political instability. Furthermore, Romanians' economic expectations are less ambitious at the moment because of their experience of Communism. Having endured the insanity of the Ceauşescu regime, they are relieved to have survived, and even though we can hardly describe the situation at present as one of even relative normality, it is undeniably preferable to what preceded it. Romanians will be happy to make do with half a capitalist loaf after having been completely denied the Communist one. The disadvantages in apply- ing a slow pace to industrial change are that there will continue to be shortages of consumer goods, and that this will give little incentive for the new private peasant farmers to invest in agricultural machinery and increase production for the market if they have nothing to spend their income on.

Chronic shortages of consumer goods were a feature of the latter years of the Ceauşescu era, and the Front has frozen the export of foodstuffs. But despite the arrival of emergency food aid, many areas do not have food supplies sufficient to satisfy local needs. The abolition of rationing, intro- duced in 1982, has aggravated the problem, for there has been panic buying of meat, sugar, edible oil, butter and eggs, and stocks of these products are low. Food supply in the long term will be eased by the creation of private holdings of plots on state and collective farms. Two decrees issued by the Front on 31 January 1990 permitted collective farms in mountainous regions to allocate land to farmers for private use with production being delivered to what were termed 'the state's specialized units'. In lowland regions collective farms would be allowed to allocate up to 5000 square metres of land for private use to collective farm mem- bers, and up to 2500 square metres to those who were not collective members but who wished to return to the countryside, provided that they cultivated the land and paid rent to the collective. State farms would also be able to allocate up to 5000 square metres of land to agricultural labourers. The produce of these private plots could be sold in the market and the plots themselves, together with the farmers' houses, sold and inherited.

Private enterprise, albeit on a very limited scale, has also been permit- ted by the Front in industry. Under a decree issued on 6 February small enterprises with a maximum of 20 employees may be set up, and individ- uals who are already employed in state industry may move to private enterprises. The products of these businesses may be exported through the state foreign trade concerns and 50% of the hard currency income may be retained by the business. The rest will be credited in lei converted at the official exchange rate. What the decree does not address is the problem of obtaining investment capital for these small businesses, and the Front's cautious attitude towards Western economic co-operation, coupled with the unstable political situation, make the prospects for investment gloomy. The need for Western involvement in modernizing Romanian industry was recognized by prime minister Roman himself in an economic report which he gave on 5 February. Lack of investment had created conditions in factories which were 'impossible' while machinery had not been maintained and had broken down. Imports of what he called 'key technologies' would be needed in order to raise living standards: 'For these technologies we must and have already started to turn openly to the West, Western Europe in particular.' Exactly how this technology would be acquired was not made clear, although his reference in this context to the provision 'of proper laws for joint societies, for co-operation' seemed to indicate a preference. Under pressure from the opposition parties the proposed decree for attracting foreign capital in Romania was modified in the interim Parliament in March to allow Western companies to own outright Romanian enterprises, but profits from such companies must be reinvested in the country.

The threat of nationalism

The problems of underinvestment, of modernizing a backward economy, of creating a civic society undivided by generation divisions and ethnic tensions – difficulties which Romania's politicians faced at the end of World War I – must be confronted again today. If they remain unsolved, as they did in the interwar period, we shall witness a period of political turmoil. In such conditions nationalism, which has been a feature of Romanian politics for over a century, is likely to flourish.

The greatest threat to stability in Romania is posed by ethnic differences, and failure to solve them will endanger all efforts to set the country on the path to democracy and to economic reform. Sadly, the spirit of partnership shown by the Hungarian and Romanian communities in Tranvsylvania in the anti-Ceauşescu demonstrations in Timişoara which set off the revolution in December rapidly evaporated as the Hungarians used their newly gained freedom to present demands for more cultural autonomy. These included a restoration of secondary and university education in their native tongue and greater provision for the publication of Hungarian-language books and newspapers. Initially, the provisional government promised to meet these demands. A ministry for ethnic minorities was to be set up and a Hungarian, Attila Palffy, was appointed Deputy Minister of Education. However, measures to revive former Hungarian-language schools in Transylvania were resisted by local Romanians, especially those who had been settled by the Ceauşescu regime to provide manpower for the newly developed industries of the province. Palffy was dismissed, the provisional government abandoned plans for an ethnic minorities ministry, and the proposed educational reforms were postponed on the grounds of lack of money.

A hardening of the Romanian attitude was prompted by the creation in February 1990 of an ultra-nationalist Romanian cultural association in

Transylvania called Vatra Românească (Romanian hearth), which has attracted a considerable membership among professional people and workers by exploiting Romanian fears that the Hungarian agitation is a sinister stratagem to revive territorial claims to Transylvania, and by encouraging anti-Hungarian sentiment. Hungarian frustration at this change of direction by the provisional government found expression in a sit-in, organized by Hungarian students at the Institute of Medicine in the Transylvanian town of Tirgu Mureş in March, who demanded the restoration of teaching in Hungarian, as indeed had been the case in the pre-Ceauşescu era. The Ministry of Education countered that medical graduates must have a fluent knowledge of Romanian in order to practise throughout the country.

The problem is not just one of language. Behind it lies a mutual mistrust felt by the Hungarian and Romanian governments, which is the legacy of Transylvania's position as part of the ancestral homeland of both peoples, and, more basically, a differing conception of respect for minority rights. Until 1918 the province formed part of Hungary, and following World War I was awarded to Romania on the basis of its considerable Romanian majority. The Romanian government fears that granting separate education in Hungarian will encourage the 2 million Transylvanian Hungarians to then press for greater political autonomy and for a closer association with Hungary. The Hungarians feel that they can only reverse the process of forced assimilation and integration carried out by Ceauşescu by first protecting and then asserting their national identity, and in the event of opposition, calling upon Hungary to aid them in these endeavours.

The question of minority rights strikes at the heart of a democratic society. The principle of equal rights for all citizens is fundamental for any democratic society, and the guarantee of these rights has been given by all the political parties created since the revolution. However, Romanians of all social classes still show sympathy with the Romanian nationalist propaganda generated by the Ceauşescu regime, which was based on two premises. The first was the primacy of group rights over individual ones, and the second, that a people's group rights were to be accorded upon the basis of their historical antiquity in Romania. In support of the second premise, the theory of Romanian historical antecedence over Hungarians in Transylvania was consistently adduced to the exclusion of all other views on the subject. Linked to this idea was the slogan 'Romanians must be masters in their own home', which was interpreted by the regime to mean that since the Romanians were in their own home, they must therefore be masters in it. For the Romanians the idea of 'mastership', or supremacy, was confirmed by the measures taken under Ceauşescu to place minority institutions, such as schools, institutes of higher education, and theatres, under the aegis of Romanian ones, whose governing bodies were almost exclusively made up of Romanians. For most Romanians this system seemed perfectly normal, 'For after all', the argument went 'we live in Romania'.

This mentality is still exhibited by supporters of the nationalist association Vatra Românească, who see the relationship between the Romanians and Hungarians in terms of subordination of the minority to the majority. Hungarians want this relationship to become one of co-ordination, one of tolerance and not dominance. In their view, loyalty to the Romanian state, to have any meaning, must be one that is freely given and not extracted from them, and to give their loyalty they too must be allowed to feel at home in the ancestral homeland which they share with the Romanians. Hungarian demands for greater cultural autonomy have encountered powerful resistance from many Romanians in Transylvania, who see them as an attack on their own interests, which can be defined as both national and economic. It is precisely to defend these interests that Vatra Românească was established, drawing its support from members of the Romanian professional classes, who see the Hungarian demands as a threat to the position of supremacy which Romanian culture has been accorded in public life in Transylvania, and from the Romanian industrial working class, many of whom were brought from other parts of Romania during the last two decades as industry expanded in Transylvania and who fear the loss of their jobs. The latter have been encouraged by the leaders of Vatra Românească to believe that the restoration of Hungarian cultural autonomy will lead to greater Hungarian control of the local economy and that positive discrimination in favour of the Hungarians will leave many Romanians jobless. The association's manipulation of Romanian fears has contributed in a major way to the ethnic unrest in Transylvania.

In essence, Vatra Românească seeks to maintain the Romanian position of supremacy in Transylvania, and appeals to all those who still share Ceauşescu's aim of creating a uniform, homogeneous state. It is obvious that such an aim is alien to a democratic society, and the association's propaganda campaign of what can only be termed incitement to ethnic hatred threatens, in practical terms, to effectively undermine the process of democratization in Romania as a whole. It is in the interests of both Romanians and Hungarians to create a democratic society in which these ethnic tensions disappear, and yet the ethnic divide continues to be reinforced by the composition and character of the political parties which have emerged since the revolution. The largest of these, the Front for National Salvation, the National Peasant Party and the National Liberal Party, have drawn very little support from among the Hungarian community, which has identified itself almost exclusively with the Hungarian Democratic Union. Very little dialogue has taken place between this Hungarian party and the other political groupings, with the result that its pleas in the provisional parliament to discuss minority demands have fallen upon deaf ears. The failure of the Bucharest government to address the issue prompted a series of peaceful demonstrations by Hungarians in

Tirgu Mureş, but tension increased after celebrations on 15 March 1990 of Hungary's national day, when buildings in Transylvania were draped with Hungarian flags and thousands of Hungarians from Hungary joined their co-nationals in the ceremonies. On 19 March Romanians in Tirgu Mureş marched in peaceful protest at what they regarded as the connivance of local Hungarian officials in staging ceremonies which were considered provocative, but in the evening a crowd of several hundred Romanians stormed the local headquarters of the Hungarian Democratic Union party. After sacking the building, they beat party officials as they tried to leave, including the prominent Hungarian Transylvanian writer, Andras Suto, who was blinded in one eye. At the same time, the local headquarters of the predominantly Romanian National Liberal Party were attacked by a mob armed with staves and axes. On the following day, as some 5000 Hungarians staged a peaceful demonstration against the violence of the previous evening, they were charged by an estimated mob of 2000 Romanians armed with scythes and clubs. The attack left six people dead and more than 300 injured. It was only after the bloodshed that the army intervened with tanks to separate the rival groups.

Apart from the ethnic dimension to these clashes and the harm which they have done to community relations, there is the separate issue of the violence which was used on both sides. Violence has not been restricted to Transylvania, but has characterized political manifestations in other parts of the country, notably the attack on the National Peasant Party headquarters in Bucharest on 30 January 1990. The failure of the interim government to intervene on these occasions suggests, at best, weakness, and, at worst, collusion. How was it possible, for example, in Tirgu Mureş for several thousand Romanians armed with sticks and bars to be brought to the city in buses and lorries with the apparent acquiescence of the authorities, when private car drivers were prevented from reaching the town centre by the police? Organized violence was a feature of interwar Romanian political life, and just as it eroded the flimsy edifice of democracy in Romania then, so it is in danger of repeating the process today.

The threat of instability in Romania will also give greater impetus to calls for a return to constitutional monarchy. By standing above politics, the monarch can offer hope of reconciliation. In the person of King Michael the monarchy is represented by a courageous figure who overthrew the pro-German dictatorship of Marshal Antonescu in August 1944 and who, uniquely among East European royalty, attempted to save his country from Soviet domination. The exiled King Michael was due to make a private visit to his native country on 12 April 1990 in order to celebrate Easter and to see his grandparents' tombs, but at the last minute the provisional government clumsily withdrew the entry visa which they had granted him several weeks earlier on the grounds that his visit was politically motivated.

The landslide victory awarded to President Iliescu (85% of the vote) and the National Salvation Front (67%) in the May presidential and parliamentary elections led the opposition to claim that there had been wholesale fraud. While most foreign observers were unable to find evidence of a total theft of the election by the Front, some of them were concerned at irregularities in the voting process, particularly in village areas, where the opposition parties, either as a result of intimidation or of poor organization, were not represented at the polling stations. Among the malpractices reported were voting by persons not on the electoral list and failure to stamp identity cards as a safeguard against voting more than once. The scale of these malpractices in some districts led observers with the Helsinki Watch to call for the annulment of the result.

In assessing the fairness of the elections one must consider both the timing and the nature of the electoral campaign which preceded them. It is perhaps unrealistic to expect the same democratic standards from a country which had only just emerged from the worst dictatorship Europe has known since World War II. Having said that, the electoral process was flawed from the moment in January when the Front, behind the mask of the provisional government, declared itself player as well as umpire in the elections. By inheriting the propaganda machinery of the former Communist regime, including two mass-circulation newspapers, they gave themselves a great advantage in presenting their case. By contrast, the major opposition parties had to start from scratch in building up their party and media apparatus. Although the contestants were granted equal airtime on the television, the inevitable identification of interim government and Front ensured that the latter always remained in the forefront of viewers' consciousness. The difficulties which the National Liberal and National Peasant Parties, with their respective presidential candidates, encountered in making themselves known to the voters, particularly in provincial areas, arose from a combination of party mismanagement and intimidation. Claims that intimidation was stage-managed by the Front were difficult to substantiate. It was probably spontaneous, resulting from an inability on the part of many Front supporters to accept the opposition as adversaries rather than enemies. However, it is not without significance that there were virtually no reported incidents of intimidation and physical assault directed against Front candidates.

However, violence and dirty tricks alone will not explain the Front's victory. Essentially, the vested interests of several sectional groups converged to provide the Front's overwhelming support. The large Communist bureaucracy and the *securitate* regarded their future as safer with the Front, the peasants are content with the land which they have been given, and the industrialized working class consider their jobs more secure with the Front's platform of gradual economic reform. President Iliescu is widely seen as the St George who slew the Ceauşescu dragon and the populist measures which he introduced immediately after the revolution were sufficient to earn him a decisive victory.

Dismayed by the scale of its defeat, the opposition will try to regroup its forces in order to offer firm resistance to any attempt on the part of the Front to revert to totalitarian government. It is on the deed rather than the word of the Front that the rest of Europe will judge whether Romania deserves to be admitted into the democratic community of nations. In this respect, the new Constitution, which the new Parliament is charged with drafting, will be the crucial litmus test of the Front's intentions.

8 YUGOSLAVIA
First and (almost) last to change

The Yugoslav situation can be defined in three sentences: (1) a society without a state; (2) an economy without a market; (3) a people without freedom and democracy. It is further characterized by high unemployment, acute social misery and galloping inflation. Has a programme been established, in real and exact terms, to get out of this apocalyptic situation?

Such was the opening question of a well-publicized interview with the head of one of the eight regional leagues of Yugoslav Communists. In another set of interviews with leading economists, a professor from Titograd University said 'We have the last Bolshevik-type party in Europe'. When interrupted with 'You have forgotten Albania', he retorted: 'Don't mention Albania, please. Must we always compare ourselves with the worst?' (*Svet*, 1 November 1989; *Intervju*, 5 January 1990.) At the time of the first interview the pun was that Yugoslavia was in *RAJ* ('heaven' in Serbo-Croat, as well as being the initials for Romania–Albania–Yugoslavia). At the time of the second, in January, it had become *AJ* ('Ouch!').

Such is the bleak view from within, but in the West who remembers the days when Yugoslavia's special brand of socialism elicited admiration and envy beyond its eastern borders; when the claims of its Communist rulers about how they came to power, reunified the country and solved its problems were accepted at face value? Who remembers, now that the land of the South Slavs is the sick man of the Balkans, in danger of 'Balkanization'? (This ugly word is often used by people who know little about the Balkans, and who prefer not to have to pronounce Timişoara or look for Kurdzhali.)

The People's Liberation Struggle
On the eve of the German invasion in 1941 the Communist Party of Yugoslavia, ancestor of the present-day League of Communists (SKJ), was a Stalinist and revolutionary organization which Tito had rejuvenated since the Comintern had appointed him to take it over. With the war and liberation, it had acquired a good base of its own, and it stood out among the Communist parties that had taken power in east-central Europe as the one that had gone furthest on the way to copying the Soviet model before Stalin excommunicated it in 1948.

Finding itself rejected by its mentor, it was forced to look to its own base, and to adapt to a situation that would reflect the constraints of

YUGOSLAVIA

Official name	The Socialist Federal Republic of Yugoslavia
Area	255,804 sq. km (98,766 sq. miles)
Population	23,657,000 (1989) (annual growth rate 0.7%)
Capital	Belgrade (Beograd)
Language	73% Serbo-Croat, 7.8% Slovene, 6% Macedonian, 7.7% Albanian
Religion	40% Eastern Orthodox, 30% Roman Catholic, 12% Muslim
Currency	dinar

geography and mentality, while drawing from its Stalinism the strength to hold out against Stalin, before extracting from its Marxism–Leninism the ability to indulge in ambitious experiments. Without relinquishing its totalitarian origins and aspirations, Tito's regime acquired a specificity which it owed partly to historical circumstances. Titoism was to be characterized by the People's Liberation Struggle as its source and inspiration by workers' self-management and by non-alignment as principles of its domestic and foreign policies, respectively.

The People's Liberation Struggle was actually more of a civil war for the control of post-war Yugoslavia. As such, it did little to heal war wounds and to rally patriotic feelings in a country where memories are long. To support the claim that its monopoly of power is a defence against the threat of renewed strife between its domestic enemies, the Party has magnified and mythologized the partisan struggle. The recent interest in that period is a symptom of the dissatisfaction created by this policy.

A brilliant idea in terms of ideology and publicity, self-management could, arguably, have been a useful model for an economy of industrial take-off at the time when it was conceived if it had really been applied. Exploited as an all-purpose slogan, it was claimed as a substitute for political democracy but it turned into an economic disaster. As for non-alignment, it was but the latest in a series of 'grey-zone' situations for the Yugoslav lands. For a while, it was of marginal international importance, but for the leadership it was a way of satisfying its foreign-policy ambitions.

Serbs and Croats

Serbs and Croats make up the core of the Yugoslav population. They are intermingled, speak the same language, have the most ancient collective self-awareness, and feel different. Together they form an absolute majority of about 60%. Religion remains the symbol of the differences. Serbs, nominally Eastern Orthodox, are the most numerous, followed by Croats, nominally Roman Catholic. On the eve of the collapse of Austria–Hungary these two groups, along with their Catholic Slovene cousins to the north, had already fully developed such attributes as a modern language, a literature, a national ideology, political parties and an aspiration to greater unity. In the movement towards unification, differences were underrated, while all the emphasis was placed on common origins and affinities.

The diversity of historical experiences can be reduced to two major trends which met in 1918: Serbia's, unitary and centralist, and Croatia's, born of the institutional and ethnic complexity of Austria–Hungary. For the Serbs, their local Orthodox Church, the only surviving institution of the medieval kingdom, had continued the development of a conscious entity during the centuries of Turkish rule. In the nineteenth century the growing embryo of a principality, and later kingdom, of Serbia provided the framework within which nationalism and politics could blossom, and contemplated the liberation and integration of kindred populations. This tradition assimilated the emancipation from Austrian and Hungarian overlordship to the wars of liberation against the Turks, and viewed the Yugoslav state as the final stage in the long process of liberation and unification.

The experience of the Croats was that of the continued separate existence of the 'Crown of Croatia'. It fell to the nobility, and later to the bourgeoisie, to continue to give shape to a wider national feeling during the centuries when that crown belonged to foreign dynasties, and the struggle for its rights kept it as a legal framework in which nationalism and politics were able to develop under the Habsburgs. By 1918, Croatia's political class yearned for a Yugoslavia where an extended Serbia would have been balanced by a consolidated Croatia. The Serbian tradition, modelled on the French post-revolutionary ideal, led to Serbian (then Yugoslav) integration of a nation defined by the state. The Croatian, on the model of Hungary, perceived Yugoslavia as an improved dualistic system which would have strengthened Croatia's historic rights.

The outcome of the constitutional confrontation was influenced by several factors which lent support to the unitarist trend, not least the romantic view of the one Yugoslav nation-to-be with its triple Serb–Croat–Slovene name. The Serbian conception prevailed. The 1921 Constitution set up a centralized parliamentary government under the Serbian royal house. Serbs were satisfied with the framework of the new state of Yugoslavia, which they viewed as the natural extension of their father-land. Divided into regions and parties, far from seeing themselves as a domineering element, they thought themselves to be the ultimate rampart of a unified country for which they had given up their own identity.

The disappointed Croats immediately began to demand a revision of the Constitution. Not numerous enough to change it by regular parliamentary procedure, they increasingly coalesced into one large ethnic party, which went back and forth between opposition and government, while a fringe would turn to violence feeding on more general frustration. The tragedy of pre-war Yugoslavia was that parliament was closed down in 1929 by King Alexander. The Crown tried to foster 'Yugoslavism' from above, but in so doing it merely alienated the Croats, while it irritated many Serbs, and others too. Serbian and Croatian opposition coalesced in the 1930s, but it was with the Crown that the latter eventually struck a bargain which gave Croatia a special status. This divided the opposition and caused bitterness on both sides. The Axis then invaded and destroyed Yugoslavia, but the country was to come back to life, albeit in another form, in the wake of the collapse of Hitler's New Order.

Postwar Yugoslavia

Yugoslavia was restored after the war as a multinational state of related nations, united under the Communist Party. The new federal division made additions to the three original components of Serbs, Croats and Slovenes whom the monarchy had failed to blend into a single Yugoslav people. The Macedonians to the south were acknowledged as a distinct nation, and the Yugoslav part of Macedonia was set up as a separate republic. The same status was granted to Montenegro, whose inhabitants were encouraged to identify with the territory's historic identity rather than with the wider concept of Serbdom, and to Bosnia-Herzegovina, kept undivided because of its ethnic and religious compound of Orthodox Christians (Serbs), Catholic Christians (Croats) and Muslims (Serbo-Croat-speaking Slavs). This produced the six constituent republics of the Communist federation.

Furthermore, two autonomous regions were carved out of Serbia – Vojvodina to the north and Kosovo to the south, because of their mixed ethnic composition, according to the Soviet model. They had been the cradle of Serbdom, at the beginning of its medieval and of its modern development, respectively. But Serbia had to be cut down to a size not too large in comparison with Croatia. What many felt to be Serbia's dominant position had to be diminished, and satisfaction given to the differences that existed in these regions.

As internationalists, the Yugoslav Communists had not had a consistent record in national matters. They had started as unitarists, had dutifully turned disintegrationist to follow the Comintern line, before they were to convert to federalism. The Party had inserted itself into the resistance of Serbs during the war – mainly among Serbs outside Serbia – but it had also used the notion of Serbian hegemony to win support among other nationalities. It looked to the peripheral groups to weaken those at the core, Serbs and Croats, whom it wanted to equalize and neutralize. At first, federalism was no more than a form, for it was subordinated to a new political unitarism, that of the Party, and to a new ideology of integration, that of Communism. It did, however, immediately give birth to regional political elites, who were to prosper with the decentralization that expanded after the break with Moscow in 1948.

Federalism – and nationalism

By the late 1960s federalism was not only well established but was even turning to confederalism. The distribution of social goods had been one of the means initially used by the Party to acquire support. The creation of a new elite and Soviet-style industrialization had led to large-scale social mobility. After the chaos of the war years, people were more ready to accept rule from the centre, especially if backed by the lure of rapid economic progress. In the 1960s, however, these possibilities were no longer what they had been, and the Party gave up its control of certain areas of social life. Ideology became less significant, and the primary object of the political elite turned to enjoying the privileges of power rather than trying to change society. This was achieved by a combination of tactical concessions, selected repression, tolerance of particular interest representation within limits, and Western aid.

Having assumed more and more responsibilities, local Party leaderships took on the representation of territorial interests as a way of legitimizing their roles. Not able to satisfy the new post-revolutionary generations with more political or even economic freedom, the regime ignored the expression of nationalist feelings. To the extent that such a freedom weakened the more conservative wing of the Party, the decentralizing reformers encouraged it. No sooner had social and economic developments led to a pluralist reaction against ideological and political uniformity than the Party was faced with the same multiform nationalism it had hoped to eliminate. Meanwhile, it had prevented any attempt at Yugoslav integration by means other than those of official ideology. Driven by disappointment in the present, concern for the future and nostalgia for the past, feelings of nationalism flowed out again into old moulds.

Without the possibility of discussing openly the all-important problems the country had to face, national identity, because of its highly emotional character, was the question that tended to pervade all others. The craving for more freedom of expression was all too often reduced to a need to call oneself by the name of one's nationality. Faith in a supranational Communist ideology having failed, people fell back upon the collectivity to which they felt they belonged. Economic, social and even political grievances were increasingly seen as national grievances – in a state that had a minorities problem and no integrative national feeling. In the 1960s, it turned out that Yugoslavia's national question was much more serious than in the 1930s.

Before the war, the problem had been primarily seen in political and constitutional terms; 30 years later, it had become economic, social and cultural as well. More nationalities had been recognized, assisted in inverse proportion to their numerical importance and historic seniority, so as to divide the population into smaller categories and speed up their integration. Yugoslavia, which had been set up again as a federation of nations, was turned into a confederation of territories with the 1974 Constitution. That was the fourth of the Titoist regime's fundamental laws, the longest, most verbose and most confusing, bringing together what had become the twin evils of the SKJ – nationalism and *langue de bois*.

In principle and in rhetoric, it was made to appear as the final outcome of the country's socialist progress – a charter of the working class. In reality, it institutionalized the nationalism it could no longer oppose, by giving the parts – the federated units – greater rights than the whole – the federation. The autonomous regions, which had become autonomous provinces with increased prerogatives in the 1960s, were equated with the republics in all but name, while the domain of the federal government was reduced to defence, foreign affairs, certain limited prerogatives of economic and financial policy, and the overall maintenance of the constitutional system. Even in those areas, however, policies could only be adopted and implemented through the 'consensus' or unanimous consent of the federated units.

The trend towards identifying republics with ethnic groups thereafter increased the malaise of the Serbs, who were further hurt by developments in Kosovo. In what was theoretically still a part of the Republic of Serbia, Albanian demographic pressure was constantly reducing the Serbian proportion of the population, while local Albanian SK cadres were busy turning the province into an Albanian unit within Yugoslavia. In the 1960s Serbs had begun to ponder on the consequences of their dispersion. By 1981 there were 4.9 million of them in what had come to be called 'Inner Serbia' – Serbia without the provinces – as opposed to 3.3 million in other territories, with another 600,000 Montenegrin cousins, not to say brothers.

The territorial division of the country, which had been acceptable as an administrative structure, was no longer so as the framework for mini-nation-states in a 'Balkanized' Yugoslavia. Serbian public opinion resented that it had got nothing out of its leadership's identification with the federal leadership. Serbian national frustration began to resemble an opposition to the regime, culture and religion picking up what Party cadres had not dared handle.

Meanwhile in Croatia, the defenders of that republic's identity had been recruited from the local SK, making the Zagreb government fly in the face of the federal authorities in Belgrade, which were, once again, openly identified with Serbian influence. This heresy was brought to an end in 1971, along with other heresies elsewhere, notably that of the liberals in Serbia's SK, and in Croatia it led to a more orthodox, but weaker and unpopular, leadership. In exchange for losing a government that had become both populist and popular, Croatia would be appeased by the 1974 Constitution, which gave the new set in Zagreb a chance to legitimize itself.

In the more outlying regions, the then relatively level-headed nationalism of Slovenia and the still young nationalism of Macedonia simply carried on with the task of turning their territories into nation-republics. Whereas Slovenian particularism believed that a looser Yugoslav community would give greater scope for economic development to its republic on the borders with the Western world, Macedonian particularism felt the need for a strong South Slav federation in order to survive in the heart of the Balkans, unacknowledged outside Yugoslavia, caught between Albanian and Bulgarian aspirations.

Tito's legacy

Revolutionary turned conservative, Tito had harmonized all the contradictions of the Stanlinist system he had had to adapt to the isolation of his country's geography and mentality. He had eventually come to solve all the problems by ignoring or condemning them, by his hold over the Party cadres, by the cult of his personality which equalled that of the greatest dictators of our century, and by the propaganda which was one of the regime's greatest successes. He had become monarch, originally anointed by Stalin but inheriting the traditions of the sultans in Stambul and the emperors in Vienna, along with the authoritarianism of Serbia's Obrenović and Karadjordjević rulers.

Tito had more palaces and villas, hunting lodges and islands, yachts and custom-built cars, uniforms and suits, medals and titles than any of his royal predecessors (who actually had very few of these) or of his Communist counterparts. While still alive, he had installed not one heir, apparent or presumptive, but a set of *diadochi*, mediocre apparatchiks selected to take the place of the up-and-coming elite of the 1960s that had been purged of its more popular and able leaders. His advanced years were accompanied by increasing court intrigues, and when he died in 1980, the system was paralysed. Without him as supreme symbol and moderator, the Constitution could no longer function. Trapped between nonsensical rhetoric and rival nationalist power factions, it ground to a halt once it had put its anointed monarch to rest.

At a popular level, the legitimacy of the SKJ was founded on three facts: it had ended the civil war, and brought the various ethnic groups out of the blind alleys into which the Axis had pushed them; it had then stood up to Stalin; finally, it had introduced the Yugoslavs to the joys of consumerism, and put the country on the map. By the time Yugoslavia remembered that it was 70 years old, at the end of 1988, all that had evaporated. The country was but one instance of the tension between regime and society in Communist Europe. The difference between Yugoslavia and the others was that Yugoslavia had started it all. For 40 years, the ruling Party had looked for ways of legitimizing itself independently of the Soviet Union, and of making the economy more efficient while maintaining its monopoly of power.

To acquire that monopoly and to preserve it had been at the fore of the Yugoslav Communist leaders' preoccupations. This had been the case in the initial period, when Tito was anticipating and fomenting revolution outside Yugoslavia's borders, while still fearing the possible victory of anti-Communist forces within. It had been true of the middle period, when Tito approached the nationalities issue as a balancing act, if not actually with a divide-and-rule policy, which accentuated the difference between nationalities and regions. It was so of the final period, when he delegated power to his trusties in the republics who have since been drawing on nationalistic feelings and international credit to build up their separate bases.

Shaken by the loss of faith, the SKJ bureaucracy has clung tenaciously to those bases. Its fragmented nationalism, in search of a new make-up with which to restore its tarnished image, has managed to break the enormous potential of opposition, but at the cost of promoting the primacy of national identities, of threatening the state with disintegration, and its component nationalities with the loss of feeling for their common interests.

After Tito

Since Tito's death, a growing section of public opinion has aspired to more pluralism, more legality, more rationality, more reality. Its educated elite clamoured for it in the years 1985–7, particularly in Slovenia and in Serbia. Throughout these years, several hundred intellectuals were standing up to be counted. An all-Yugoslav opposition platform, however inchoate, was emerging, and the mood was spreading to the more educated rank and file of the Party, aiming at introducing into government and society some basic rules of generally accepted civilized behaviour. An atmosphere of *glasnost* produced a public debate in which everything was discussed with frankness and at length, while action based on these debates remained small, slow and disorganized.

By 1987 the failure to grapple with the economic crisis had removed the last shreds of credibility from the people in charge. There was widespread popular agreement with the intellectuals that the political system was responsible, and that radical change must come, to include the political leadership put together by Tito in his last decade. A workers' revolt, caused by the sharp fall in their standard of living, spread to all sectors and all republics from its source in Croatia's heavy industry. It was the prelude to the year 1988, which saw the resignation of the Mikulić government, which had been thought tougher than its predecessors, coming after six months of criticism, and mass demonstrations that swept away Party leaderships and governments in Vojvodina and Montenegro. Whole groups of high officials, selected by the tried and tested processes of the *nomenklatura*, suddenly found themselves at the mercy of the working class, in whose name they had been ruling for so long.

These events were linked to the explosion of Serbian nationalism, which brought to the leadership of that republic the only Yugoslav politician since Tito to have made an impact, even if a negative one, on the west – Slobodan Milošević, head of the Party hierarchy and genuinely popular hero. Mass demonstrations called for the sacking of corrupt officials, exploiters of the workers, and traitors to Serbian interests. They were the result of discontent pent up since the 1960s, especially since 1974. The constitutional arrangements of these years appeared as a feudalization of Party power at the expense of Serbian interests, with the approval of Serbia's leadership. At the same time, the prominent position of Serbs in the country's political elite, at federal and regional level, left only Slovenia north and Macedonia south without relatively strong Serb Communist influence, and made them resented in most other regions. The Serbs felt that their historical past and consciousness had been sacrificed for the sake of a common Communist Yugoslav cause.

The Kosovo situation had burst the abscess. Set up originally as an autonomous region within Serbia, adjoining Albania, to ease the latter's hoped-for entry into the federation, Kosovo had been moving towards the status of Yugoslavia's Albanian component. This had been institutionalized in all but name in 1974. The demographic thrust of Albanian Muslims, together with the affirmation of their ethnic consciousness by the regional government, had dramatically accelerated the reduction in the proportion of Serbs living there. Pressures and intimidations of all sorts had turned Serbian emigration into an exodus, without the government of Serbia being able to do anything about it.

While being a relative majority in Yugoslavia, Serbs saw themselves as having just one vote in eight, as being out of favour and without protection. It was becoming clear to them that the original division, which historians are discovering to have been established with some arbitrariness and opportunism, had been made to find an immediate and practical answer, not only to the question of ethnic minorities but also to that of the Serbs' relative majority.

Milošević had made use of these feelings of humiliation, frustration and fear among Serbs, and of their resentment at the lack of sympathy in other regions for their predicament. He did what other regional Communist leaders had done in the 1960s and 1970s, but he did it with added advantages – a more numerous and extended basis, and rampant de-Titoization. His was the latest and most successful attempt to try to save the power of the Party by jumping on the bandwagon of nationalism.

Stumbling into a grey and uncertain dawn from the long anaesthetized sleep of ideological rule and the surreal dream of Titoist charlatanry, people huddle together in groups that recognize each other by language, religion and common memories of the past. In their resistance to a radical restructuring of society imposed from the top, they had usually taken the side of what had been erased from the history books, of the names and stones that had been removed from their cities, and blamed their misfortunes on others. All thought of themselves as being unequal, exploited and oppressed.

Once particularism had been taken over by the regional bureaucracies, communities tended to blame one another, and one another's history, one another's foreign overlords, religious or ideological centres abroad. Poets and novelists moved to the forefront of a vacant political scene with their moral exhortations and literary visions, while bankrupt Communist apparatchiks were left to mismanage economic wars between their republics.

Eight different models of Yugoslav Communism thus appeared in the 1980s. In the 1960s and 1970s, Slovenia had developed an increasingly humanized version that provided space for various interests to interact, that gauged the public mood before acting, and acted more openly, thus obtaining much-improved economic results. This opening out was, however, done in very special circumstances, with an ethnically homogeneous population already endowed with a more prosperous environment.

In the 1980s, however, Slovenia's privileged position was translated into the highest rate of decline in real income, thus inciting the local leadership to oppose, often stridently, all attempts aimed at giving the centre the power to implement an all-Yugoslav economic policy. A smugly chauvinistic rhetoric has certainly not contributed to allaying Serbian sensitivity or the anti-reformist vested interests of most Communist caucuses.

In Croatia, a weak, unpopular and dogmatic leadership has, since 1974, been trying to acquire a doubtful legitimacy by adopting an all-too-often negative attitude to what came from Belgrade. Placed between Serbia and Slovenia, it increasingly tends to side with the latter against the former. The leaders who fell from power in Montenegro and Vojvodina did not do so because they were more incompetent than most of their opposite numbers elsewhere, or as a result of ethnic clashes, but because they were defending their positions without the backing of strong particularist feelings. Of the new governments there, one can only say that they have younger faces and cleaner hands, and that they stand by Serbia.

The return to that republic of certain prerogatives in matters of defence, the maintenance of order, international relations and taxation, that had previously been devolved to the autonomous provinces, although it does not affect their basic autonomy, especially in cultural affairs, nevertheless poses a long-term problem in Kosovo, whose non-Slav population feels more and more alienated.

Macedonia keeps quiet, concealing its own expanding Albanian minority. It is in need of Yugoslav solidarity to be able to stand economically and ethnically. Its neighbours outside Yugoslavia do not recognize the existence of a Macedonian nation, and all the richer republics – Serbia included – are unhappy about continuing to subsidize its economy. As for Bosnia-Herzegovina, that republic is barely emerging from a long reign of corruption, racketeering and arbitrary authoritarianism.

Yugoslav Communism has made compromises with forces hitherto perceived as hostile (such as the market, religion or nationalism) in order to remain somehow in power. A complex situation has arisen, all too often simplified by Western onlookers disappointed by the failure of a regime in which so many hopes, illusions and funds had been invested. Facile clichés present it as a North–South or West–East opposition, consolidated into NW–SE to make it even simpler, with Slovenia (replacing, to a certain extent, the Croatia of yesteryear) – Catholic, Austrian-like, central-European, liberal, mercantile, industrious and pluripartite – threatened by a Serbia that is Orthodox, Turkish-influenced, Balkan, authoritarian, peasant, militaristic, hegemonistic and neo-Stalinist. Yugoslavia's need for change is interpreted as an ethnic conflict, because it seems at present to take the form of a confrontation between the Communist leadership of

Slovenia and that of Serbia, whereas the ethnic conflict is the consequence, and not the cause, of the deadlock.

The 'agreed economy'

The leadership was still unified enough in 1985 to decide in principle to try to overcome existing constitutional obstacles to the further development of the market economy, and to extend federal powers over economic policy. It took time to obtain the necessary consensus on a scheme, which was limited to proposals for better guarantees to private small enterprises, a unified tax system, and rationalized planning as a way towards an integrated Yugoslav market. Finally submitted in 1987, it has been overtaken by events.

Serbia, which had so much wanted to change the Constitution of 1974, has since appeared to wish to defend it against Slovenia, which wants to loosen the links even more. The amendments of 1989 to Serbia's own constitution have changed little, and it is difficult to see why they gave rise to such euphoria in Serbia and to so virulent an anti-Serbian reaction in Slovenia. Slovenia, who insisted on the sanctity of the 1974 settlement in the face of Serbia's onslaught, has amended its own constitution to give itself the right to secede from Yugoslavia altogether.

In fact the Constitution of 1974 barely exists, as it is being amended piecemeal within the republics but cannot be altered at federal level. The only rationale for attitudes struck by various leaderships is their wish to hold on to the appearances and privileges of political power, but the only practical solution would be to move towards a totally new settlement through a transitional period when different parties with varying programmes would organize themselves into fully competitive politics.

In substance, this has been advocated for two decades or so by the Democratic Alternative forum of expatriates linked to the London- and Paris-based journal *Naša Reč*. Unfortunately, it has become difficult for most non-Serbs to regard any proposal of Serbian provenance as progressive if it implies the slightest interest for those Serbs living outside Serbia, or a minimum of real authority for the federal government. Likewise, it has become hard for Serbs to recognize that they could hold ideals or aims in common with people they suspect of camouflaging integrationist intentions towards Serbs living in their midst, even separatist thoughts, and certainly egoistical tendencies, under a Christian–Catholic–social-democratic discourse.

The latest stage of the 'Yugoslav road to socialism' as it took shape in the 1970s was the 'agreed economy', where political pressures were applied to ensure that market forces, such as had been released, produced the right decisions. These reflected local Party officials' perceptions of local interests, often at the expense of other local or all-Yugoslav interests. The pursuit of regional aims under political patronage led to each ruling hierarchy investing within the boundaries of its territory, whatever the cost, to retain control over its capital, thus aggravating regional differences.

The aim of the Yugoslav Communists had been to change society according to a given model, whatever its capacities, and because their essentially political project cost more than it produced, the deficit was at first made up by revolutionary zeal, which dampened consumer expectations in the immediate post-war period. The continued exploitation of natural resources and pressure on the peasants to produce cheap food were another phase, before the export of unemployment and the injection of foreign credits took over until the 1980s. Meanwhile, consumer appetites had been whetted as bureaucratic structures grew with foreign debts, feeding the system with make-believe money in the absence of real money.

Yugoslav economists have long been saying that the system had always been inefficient. Some are now claiming that it has never produced a profit. As inflation passed from a trot to a gallop, more institutions issued bills of exchange, thereby increasing the number of those who benefited from inflation. All economic reforms since the 1960s had always been more cosmetic than real – compromise solutions adopted by a hesitant and divided government, half-heartedly applied, forgotten and then taken up again. All anti-inflationary measures failed, as they did not attack the roots of the problem, and the huge bureaucratic structure was not keen to confront it.

After almost 20 years of operating under this convoluted system the Yugoslav economy is in a desperate state. As banks were made to inject more money into bankrupt enterprises, economic management was, more often than not, reduced to trying to pay salaries at the end of the month. 1989 ended up with an inflation rate officially said to be 1225%, but estimated by Western observers to be somewhere between 2000 and 3000% (it had been a mere 50% at the end of 1984). Living with inflation had become a part of the national culture.

Under pressure from foreign creditors, however, the present federal executive chaired by prime minister Ante Marković had, in 1989, managed to pass laws on the free circulation of goods, capital and labour, on foreign-exchange markets, and on foreign ownership rights, thereby reviving some decisions already taken in 1985 and not acted upon. On paper at least, that legislation was on a par with the best that was being achieved elsewhere in east-central Europe. Some progress had also been achieved in external accounts, the balance of payments being in surplus again by over $2 billion, hard currency reserves going up to $6.5 billion, and the foreign debt being reduced to $17 billion (from over $21 billion in 1981).

On that basis, the government – which Marković had tried to put together on the competence of its members rather than as a result of regional patronage – at last managed to cobble together an apparently more rigorous package aimed, perhaps too ambitiously, at bringing inflation down to 13% in a year. As from 1 January 1990 the dinar has been declared fully convertible, pegged to the West German mark for six months, and made to shed four zeros. Salary rises were severely curtailed but prices allowed to find their own level, except in the case of energy and infrastructural costs.

Economists in Yugoslavia argue that inflation is more political than economic, but an end to the political monopoly of the feuding components of the SKJ will not in itself produce a miraculous solution to the crisis of the country's economy, or to that of its national unity. An open debate between the legitimate and accountable representatives of different communities, interests and opinions is but a necessary condition. With the demise of Communist ideology, and fostered by the very disintegration of the ruling Party, nationalism has become the dominant ideology. To the extent that politics had for too long been appropriated by one ideology, resistance to it had turned to other dimensions – to the past and to religion, to feelings of wounded patriotism and to preoccupations with the survival of numerically small nations. As such, history, religion and the nation have moved in a basically anti-Western direction, and politics have become apolitical. A culture of resistance can, however, transform itself into one of democratic opposition, as has been seen elsewhere in east-central Europe. After all, most Yugoslavs, along with most east-central Europeans, are imaginary Westerners and aspire to Western 'civilizational' (a favourite Yugoslav neologism) values.

Moves towards a multi-party system

More and more calls have been made to repeal the legislation on verbal offences, on the slandering of the state and the official posthumous cult of Tito, but even more so for the introduction of a multi-party system as the only way to tackle the crisis. These calls come from various quarters, mostly, but not exclusively, from intellectuals who rarely see beyond the borders of their own republic. Public opinion around them is almost unanimous in thinking that the present system is at a dead end, and no more than 10% express any confidence in the SKJ. At the same time, people are still afraid of the cost of reforms, especially in the poorer regions and sectors, even though they have already been going through a difficult decade for no good reason and with no clear prospect of change.

It was in Slovenia, in January 1989, that east-central Europe's first independent political party since the Communist take-overs was launched. Since then a multitude of 'alternative' groups emerged, and, for a while, helped the local Party leadership to increase its regionalistic stance, but eventually they pressed it into accepting the principle of allowing others to compete with it in the April 1990 elections. 1989 ended with a new electoral law for Slovenia that legalized political parties. In Croatia, a dozen or so similar groups, although kept under closer surveillance, were able to obtain enough public support to force the SK of that republic to follow that of Slovenia in accepting the principle of competition at the next elections. The Zagreb-based Yugoslav United Democratic Initiative which, however small, does have branches in other republics was watched with particular dislike.

In Serbia, in the midst of the euphoria surrounding the secentenary of the Battle of Kosovo (1389) and the restoration of some control over the provinces, the dissident voices of intellectuals were no longer heard, but they have since campaigned again very strongly in favour of an end to the power monopoly of the SKJ. Of the independent political groups that have appeared (from the nationalist to the traditional), one stands out. A Democratic Party, Belgrade-based but devoid of an ethnic or regional attribute, has set itself up as a political party of individual representation, in opposition to, and in competition with, the SKJ. Its manifesto calls for a new constitution, to be drawn up through an agreement between the legitimate representatives of all communities, based on the equality of regions and citizens, on parliamentary government and on free enterprise tempered with social justice.

An affiliated group exists in Montenegro, and sympathizers have appeared in all republics. Three parties are being organized in Macedonia. Even the nationalist Albanian students of Kosovo, whose militants belonged to underground Marxist–Leninist groups in the early 1980s, demonstrated in favour of multiple parties in the wake of the failed Fourteenth Congress, as the situation in the province deteriorated yet again, while a Democratic Alliance of Kosovo was set up to demand a constructive and reasoned dialogue between communities. Most of these groups have held meetings and issued manifestos without hindrance.

Under such pressure, but also facing counter-pressure from conservatives, veteran partisans' organizations and generals, Party forums tried to show how democratic they were by accepting some degree of pluralism. Once again, the lead was taken by Slovenia, where public pressure was strongest. The declared concessions of the various leaderships were ambiguous. Political parties would have to be socialist, or should not be ethnic, or should conform to current legislation, or would be considered after the next elections. At best, initiatives were taken to turn the Socialist Alliance into a separate party, which would field candidates alongside those of the SK, and benefit from state support. The aim everywhere was to ensure the success of the SK in the forthcoming elections, and to delay the development of independent parties. Serbia had already held elections in November, in the wake of its nationalistic euphoria, according to the existing system, without independent candidates. The Party there had gained a respite, and could even afford to ban an ultra-nationalist alternative organization. In Slovenia, the Party still had to go to the polls and face competition.

The Fourteenth Congress

As far back as February 1989 it had been decided to call a Party congress to sort things out. By the time the Fourteenth Congress of the SKJ did meet in Belgrade, on 20 January 1990, the possibility of pluralism had been conceded in Moscow, and even in Ulan Bator. The Communist Party had been banned in Romania, and opinion polls had revealed that 80% of Yugoslavs thought their own SKJ incapable of pulling the country out of the crisis. The Congress had been summoned in an extraordinary capacity to launch a 'new democratic model of socialism', with tight financial constraints and no fraternal delegations. What remained of a federal leadership had just come round to accepting a draft declaration which pronounced in favour of the freedom of political association 'within the limits of the socialist democratic society and of the federal model', and in favour of the efforts being made by the government to integrate the Yugoslav market.

The Congress started off badly with a long wrangle over procedure, then accepted the draft document by an overwhelming majority, and eventually went to pieces over the rejection of amendments put by the delegates of Slovenia, to turn the League into an even looser 'League of leagues', with new forms to reflect its 'socialist' rather than 'Communist' nature. The tide which had initially gone in favour of the Slovene Communists' 'liberalizing' tendencies then turned against their 'disintegration-ist' demands. Insults were exchanged, the delegates from Slovenia marched out, and the Congress was adjourned on 23 January *sine die*. On that day, *Borba*, the one-time daily mouthpiece of the SKJ, and now the organ of the Socialist Alliance, still appearing under the slogan 'Proletarians of all countries unite', had a banner headline: 'The SKJ no longer exists.'

Historians of the Balkans know that the new Soviet concept of *perestroika* is but a literal translation of the old Ottoman *tanzimat*. Far from reforming itself into yet another 'democratic socialist project', the SKJ is disintegrating, and the false problem of how to restructure its regime is giving way to the real one of how to dismantle it. Its hesitating, contradictory and obfuscating policies manipulate the powerlessness of its apparatus. The abrupt interruption of the Fourteenth Congress has now made it obvious that clarity, with all its risks, is the only way to give Yugoslavia a chance to avoid a breakdown.

In a Communist polity paralysed by the deadlock of eight antagonistic regional Party elites, hard-line warnings against the dangers of party pluralism in a polyethnic country carry little weight, even, and perhaps especially, among those who think that it would be better to channel expressions of particularism in independent regional, ethnic and religious parties, rather than let (or encourage) it to spill out into the streets. The crisis of the Yugoslav federation is not a classical confrontation between a federal centre and federated components. The visible signs of disintegration are only the consequences of the malfunctioning of the whole system. Decentralization made little sense in economic terms as local bureaucrats took over the role of meddling decision-makers and unopposed rulers previously played by the central leadership. Redistribution of power, changes of personnel rather than of policies, watering down of Party rule, and recourse to crowd support are no substitute for political democracy, without which real economic reforms can hardly be made to take off.

Yugoslavia does have a point or two in common with Albania, which is why both countries, in spite of all the obvious differences, are the last of the Communist states of east-central Europe to confront the political monopoly of the ruling Party. Both regimes have had a smooth succession after the natural death of a long-ruling charismatic leader, both claimed that they were more truly socialist than the members of what used to be called the 'Eastern bloc', and since they were outside it, they were less prone to the 'domino effect'. 'We would have found it easier to get rid of the Communist legacy if it had been clearly imposed from the outside . . . Today maybe we would come out of this mess sooner if we were to join the Warsaw Pact,' a student remarked in January (Srdjan Trifković, 'When the center no longer holds', *US News and World Report*, 8 January 1990).

The Communist Party of Yugoslavia had acquired its own credentials by emerging victorious in a bloody four-year civil war, with help from both the USSR and the Western Allies. The length of Tito's reign and the cult of his personality identified him with the Party leadership, its cadres, the state and the nation. Because of its independence from Moscow after 1948, the Titoist regime was first saved, then supported, increasingly subsidized, and constantly flattered by the West into thinking that it was a model to be followed by the other Communist-ruled countries of Europe. Although the West was by far its best patron, it was not the only one, for the Soviet Union also sustained it against the West through the Non-Aligned Movement. Trading on the confrontation between blocs and superpowers, it was fêted by all.

If Western aid was meant to help produce a Communist system that could become economically viable and politically acceptable, it did no more than enable Titoism to live beyond its aims and eventually to stagnate. Intent as they were on salvaging what they could from the initial project by half-hearted concessions, Yugoslavia's Communist leaders have admittedly been resourceful in holding out.

Eventually the regime did both liberalize and decentralize. It diffused power within the SKJ, and it tolerated more and more personal freedom, but with little structural change. It institutionalized local interests in an elaborate system of checks and balances that achieved a decade or so of internal stability, at a cost which not only worsened economic problems but weakened the means available to the leadership. In Tito's lifetime the system still appeared to work, as it was propped up by the aging leader's personal authority and by heavy external borrowing. The simultaneous disappearance of both props was coincidental. When the Cold War was consigned to the archives, and left to historians, Tito's heirs realized that no-one was interested any longer in subsidizing their experiment, and the Titoist lobby in the West vanished almost overnight, leaving behind it a whiff of nostalgia, particularly in Britain.

The first and the last

The Communist regime that had been the first to set itself up outside the Soviet Union after World War II seems, for all these reasons, to be almost the last to disappear. Having come to power on the basis of its identification with the working class, it has ended up by hiding behind the primacy of national identity. Far from having resolved Yugoslavia's national question, it has given nationalism the chance to return to the fore with a vengeance. It has interrupted political traditions that were still in their youth, while freezing atavistic attitudes. Because of its bureaucratic, anti-cultural and anti-intellectual stance it has made it more difficult for people to distance themselves from instinctive reactions, and impaired their understanding not only of socialism but of democracy as well. On the one hand, it has formally replaced the concept of political citizenship by a system of indirect delegations. On the other, it has achieved the fusion of ethnic-religious communities in the Ottoman tradition with historic-territorial rights in the Habsburg tradition. All this appears to have blocked the possibility of a democratic evolution within the present constitution.

The Socialist Federal Republic of Yugoslavia is now a hybrid. In fact a confederation, it has not become that through the coming together of pre-existing states but through a process of degeneration, and it is so loose a confederation that it has either to break up completely or be turned back into a real federation as a third Yugoslavia, set up on deeper foundations than its monarchical and Communist predecessors. Yugoslavia exists for the time being, without a perceptible alternative. Today's stresses are, paradoxically, the result of common influences, moulds and mentalities, which gave birth to a Yugoslav idea and a Yugoslav movement even before these led to the formation of a Yugoslav state in 1918.

Initially unification went against the grain of 'Balkanization'. Yugoslavia had to prove itself before the West acknowledged its existence, and it had to stand up against the attempts of both Comintern and Axis to 're-Balkanize' it, before the country proved itself yet again under Communist leadership. The idea of survival helps to illuminate the way in which Yugoslavia seems to have spent 70 years lurching from crisis to crisis. Milorad Ekmečič, the author of *The Creation of Yugoslavia, 1790–1918*, says that the crisis of Yugoslavia has been going on for 200 years – a long historical process whose outcome is being decided now.

Both in 1918, when the united Kingdom of the Serbs, Croats and Slovenes (later Kingdom of Yugoslavia) was proclaimed, and in 1945, when it was formally reorganized as the Federal People's Republic of Yugoslavia (later Socialist Federal Republic of Yugoslavia), there was no real alternative to a Yugoslav solution, but the question was never directly put to the population. The self-determination of Serbs, Croats, Slovenes and others living there was somehow exercised through a relative parliamentary majority, or the force of arms and circumstances, or unsatisfactory bargains with the rulers. Although there has generally been interest in the common enterprise, no party to these outcomes has ever had full confidence in either its partners or the community as a whole, and each has always tried to safeguard its own position through a centralistic state structure, or a special status, or a confederal arrangement. The state itself has been identified with its rulers. Rarely has there been real compromise between Yugoslavia's component groups, ethnic or political, preceded by a real debate. Rarely have any means of promoting integration been allowed, let alone encouraged, other than those of the official ideology of the time. Yet Yugoslavia's communities have not been at each other's throats except when shamelessly exploited by invading powers in European wars, and there are precedents of active co-operation between the political parties of the various nationalities, especially in trying to restore parliamentary government to set the common state on a new course.

Public opinion does not seem to be particularly perturbed by the crisis of a ruling party that it has long ceased to consider as anything but secondary. If anybody has benefited by it, it is Marković's executive government and its programme of economic reforms. The government is keeping its calm, and it awaits the new political parties.

But is Yugoslavia worth keeping? Only Slovenia could secede without leaving many of its kin behind. For the rest, population transfers would be painful, as they always are. Nevertheless, they are a radical way of separating people when all rational arguments in favour of unity no longer carry weight. At best, the small successor states would find it difficult to pull their economic weight; at worst, to survive politically. Disintegration is not the road that leads to an integrated Europe, but self-determination has to be practised formally, if only for psychological reasons, to exorcise the demons that have come to inhabit Yugoslavia's nationalities. If Yugoslavs are to continue living together in a united country, and edge their way towards a united Europe, rather than become again the proverbial powder keg that is alleged to start European wars, it is essential that they should be able to participate fully in the development of their community. They must know what is implied by cohabitation and divorce. The rest is dialectic (tried for 40 years, and failed), Balkanization (regressive for the 1990s), or even Lebanonization.

Postscript: an open question

The first multi-party elections since 1938 took place between 16 April and 7 May 1990 for the local parliaments of two republics, Slovenia and Croatia, according to different systems. In Slovenia, Demos, a broad right-of-centre coalition of new parties, won just over half the votes, relegating the local SK (renamed Party of Democratic Renewal) to 18%, but the Communist leader was elected president with 52%. A hitherto relatively prosperous population now feeling the pinch of real economic reforms made the Communists take the blame, but rewarded their leader for apparently allowing a peaceful transition. In the tense nationalist climate that was created by the war of words between Slovenia's and Serbia's leaders, Demos spokesmen said that they plan a referendum on whether their republic should, or should not, stay in Yugoslavia. The Slovenian election could mark the beginning of disintegration (or of democratization) for Yugoslavia.

The voters of Croatia then went to the polls. The local SK, also renamed Party of Democratic Renewal, was resigned to defeat. Its competitors were, on the one hand, a broad coalition of a dozen or so new groups which had come together with former reformist Communists purged by Tito in 1971, which fared even worse than the Communists. On the other hand, the very right-wing and nationalist Croatian Democratic Alliance, led by an ex-Communist, the retired General Tudjman, endowed with personal leadership, mass appeal and fiery rhetoric, won an almost two-thirds majority, and immediately issued conciliatory statements towards Serbia and the Serbian minority in Croatia, to defuse growing concern over the rising tide of Croatian nationalism and memories of the horrors perpetrated by its fascist fringe during World War II.

There too, a relatively prosperous working class has been losing out, and blaming the Communists. The nationalism of Serbia's Communist President Milošević and the nationalism of Croatia's new right-wing leader Tudjman have been feeding one another, as the federal parliament – along with other regional legislatures – extended its mandate to enable it to agree on a new electoral law for multi-party general elections to be held before the end of 1990.

Yugoslavia is currently in transition from a monolithic Communist polity to a multi-party post-Communist regime, but it is uncertain which forces will come to power in individual republics, and whether Yugoslavia will survive as the united state of Serbs, Croats, Slovenes, Macedonians and South Slav Muslims. With the demise of Communist ideology, nationalism has become dominant, and it could be the first stage in the regeneration of political and social consciousness in a society long anaesthetized by authoritarian rule. With luck and goodwill, it could eventually be turned towards involving people in real decision-making processes related to everyday issues. An open debate between the legitimate and accountable representatives of Yugoslavia's different communities, interests and opinions is a necessary (though not a sufficient) condition to finding a solution to the crisis of the country's economy and identity. It could finally make Yugoslavia (at a third attempt) or it could finally break the country.

Part 2
The
Soviet
Union

9 AN OVERVIEW

From dogmatism to uncertainty

Historical background

The Soviet Union now appears an anachronism. Yet in the 1970s it was still commonly suggested that its social and economic system represented a successful model of modernization that other states might follow. It is now clear that despite the transfer of a large proportion of its workforce from subsistence agriculture to an urban, industrial environment and a rise in educational standards, the Soviet experiment has been a dead-end. It has isolated the country from a dynamic world economy and the spread of market consumerism. Despite a rise in living standards it has failed to establish a form of legitimacy to rival that enjoyed by representative democracies. Military superpower status masked the failures of the system. In the early 1980s one perceptive (if cynical) Western observer remarked that the Soviet Union resembled 'the Upper Volta with missiles'.

Whether the Tsarist regime was succeeding in breaking the cycle of Russian history in which a passive society was periodically modernized by the state, often in a bloody fashion, is a matter of historical controversy, but the seizure of power by the Bolshevik Party in October 1917 re-affirmed it. A totally new ruling elite was to be established to carry out a 'modernizing' project. Bolshevik rule was imposed after a bitter civil war in which, at first, it faced only the old Tsarist elite but later also a wave of popular protest, culminating in a revolt of sailors and workers in Petrograd and the Kronstadt naval base and peasant risings in early 1921. Many Russians finally accepted the Bolsheviks as the only force able to provide the country with a strong government, but in the non-Russian parts of the old empire even this limited form of support was diluted.

The Bolsheviks seized power with the intention of implementing a Marxist social and economic revolution. Until Lenin's death in 1924 the utopian aspect of the Party's programme was tempered by a degree of pragmatism. Thus, faced with popular discontent in early 1921 he persuaded the Party to accept the New Economic Policy (NEP). The NEP, which forced industrial enterprises to prove their financial viability, allowed the private sector to dominate internal trade and encouraged peasant agriculture, was a retreat from earlier attempts to create a Communist society by force and fanning class war. It was also an alternative Leninist model of socialism that would tantalize future reformers.

Stalin's emergence as the pre-eminent Bolshevik leader at the end of the 1920s saw a return to policies of mass coercion in the shape of the

UNION OF SOVIET SOCIALIST REPUBLICS (USSR)

Official name	The Union of Soviet Socialist Republics
Area	72,400,000 sq. km (8,646,400 sq. miles)
Population	286,717,000 (1989) (annual growth rate 0.9%)
Capital	Moscow (Moskva)
Language	Russian, many regional languages
Religion	Russian Orthodox with Catholic, Jewish, Muslim minorities
Currency	rouble

Autonomous Soviet Socialist Republics (ASSRs) were created for important nationalities within Union Republics (SSRs). Since 1941 the Karelo-Finnish Republic has become an ASSR, the Crimean ASSR has been incorporated in the Ukrainian SSR and the Volga-German ASSR has been dissolved. In addition to the ASSR system, there are also Autonomous Okrugs and Autonomous Districts, similar attempts to resolve the multinational problems of the Soviet Union. Geographically, these subdivisions are often at odds with political expediency: the core Russian Soviet Federal Republic has numerous enclaves – often incorporating sensitive defensive zones (southern Kamchalka, Sakhalin and the northern Kuriles, Novaya Zemlya, the Kola Peninsula and, notably, Kaliningrad). Further, the existence of isolated national enclaves has recently caused ethnic problems (notably the Armenian autonomous district of Nagorno Karabakh, within the Azerbaijan SSR). In 1990 the Supreme Soviets in Lithuania, Latvia and Estonia all declared independent republican status.

collectivization of agriculture and Communist enthusiasm in a five-year plan to carry out a rapid industrialization programme. By the mid-1930s a massive industrial base had been built which was to give the Red Army victory in World War II and the country superpower status after 1945.

The 'centrally planned economy' was a myth that masked a system based on coercion and improvization. The belief that every aspect of the economy of a vast country like the Soviet Union could be run from Moscow led to the proliferation of a stifling bureaucracy of ministries, the creation of twentieth-century 'Potemkin villages' as managers made exaggerated reports of broken production records to satisfy the centre and the squandering of the country's natural resources. Considerable increases in the production of steel, coal and electricity were achieved by savagely cutting the living standards of peasants and workers to the point of famine. Agriculture, industries serving the needs of the consumer and the service sector were permanently neglected. Soviet women suffered particularly badly from the backwardness of these sectors. Women were drawn into the urban workforce but continued to perform the bulk of the domestic duties – what came to be known as 'the double burden'. This position was reinforced by Soviet propaganda, which, after stressing sexual equality in the early days of the Revolution, later created a cult of motherhood, with the attendant reward of 'hero-mother' status for those who produce large families.

Appalling living conditions were only one side of the Stalinist nightmare. Against the background of social upheaval, extravagant visions of a Communist utopia and Stalin's pathological suspiciousness, many Soviet citizens were physically eliminated. Millions of peasants who resisted being herded into the new collective farms were labelled *kulaks* (rich peasants) and deported. Between 1936 and 1938 former political opponents of the regime and ordinary citizens were joined in the labour camps by millions of loyal Party and government officials arrested on trumped-up charges. Those who avoided execution found that camp conditions were often no better than a death sentence. During the Civil War the pre-revolutionary elite had been largely chased from their jobs into death or exile. The post-revolutionary elite of politicians such as Trotsky, Bukharin and Zinoviev, cultural figures such as the theatre producer Meyerhold and the poet Mandelshtam and, most absurdly of all on the eve of World War II, the cream of the Red Army such as Marshals Tukhachevskii and Blyukher were liquidated.

Stalin died in 1953, and the new leadership was determined to avoid the fate of its predecessors. After Khrushchev's 'secret speech' to the Twentieth Party Congress in 1956 the labour camps were opened and the inmates, many of whom had been re-sentenced on the expiry of their term, were released. The relatives of those who had not survived could apply for their rehabilitation. Greater intellectual freedom was permitted. Solzhenitsyn's *One Day in the Life of Ivan Denisovich*, which vividly described camp life, was published. However, disturbed by his unpredictable behaviour, his so-called 'hare-brained schemes', Khrushchev was deposed by his fellow Party leaders in 1964. Liberalization had not been indiscriminate even under Khrushchev. The cultural 'thaw' coincided with an intense campaign against the Orthodox Church, which had escaped annihilation by helping to rally the population during the war. But as Leonid Brezhnev gradually emerged as the pre-eminent leader in the 1960s, criticism of Stalin halted.

After the death of Stalin the apparatus of state repression continued to be employed against anyone who questioned the regime, but terror was no longer applied on a mass scale. The co-operation of the mass of the population was sought by the promise of rising living standards. Economic growth stagnated by the 1970s and Soviet GNP was later overtaken by that of Japan, a much smaller country, and West Germany was not far behind. This not only threatened rising living standards, it also jeopardized the country's status as a military superpower. By the early 1980s the economic slow-down was reflected in growing social problems, such as an epidemic of alcoholism, a deeply alienated youth, and corruption. The SDI (America's 'Star Wars' programme) presented the Soviet Union with new, insurmountable technological challenges.

The social stability of the Brezhnev period saw an increasingly well-educated population gaining in confidence. By and large, the new intelligentsia rejected the values of the Party and frequently turned to the West for inspiration or to national or religious traditions. However, the skills of the intelligentsia were vital if the Party was to maintain rising living standards and the country's superpower status. The problem of overcoming the scepticism of this alienated class and persuading it to collaborate in achieving the leadership's policies, even though the goal of Communism was put more and more feebly, lay at the heart of the dilemma of political legitimacy posed by destalinization.

Gorbachev's *perestroika*

When Mikhail Gorbachev became General Secretary of the Communist Party in March 1985 he was not alone in underestimating the malaise that afflicted the Soviet Union. For the best part of his first two years as leader Gorbachev believed that the system could be made to work better by a mixture of greater discipline and technocratic reform. The slogan then was *uskorenie* (speeding up), not *perestroika* (reconstruction). Many people have forgotten that Gorbachev was best-known at first for his anti-alcohol campaign. More substantially, he set up now half-forgotten bodies to improve the quality of goods produced (*Gospriyomka*) and agricultural production (*Gosagroprom*) by the traditional method of central directive.

Then towards the end of 1986 his reforms began to change character, and *perestroika* began. In one respect this was a response to reverses in foreign policy. Soviet diplomacy had failed to break European support for the SDI programme and the explosion of the nuclear reactor at Chernobyl in April 1986, and the subsequent delay in informing its international neighbours, undermined the international reputation of the Soviet Union. The return of Andrei Sakharov from exile in December 1986 was as much a gesture to world opinion as domestic. At home, technocratic reform had failed to make an impact against the resistance of the bureaucrats. Firmer discipline was not enough to make the system work. There had to be a much greater degree of commitment to reform by those who were supposed to implement it.

Over the next three years there was a turnover in government and Party personnel greater than at any time since Stalin. To remove the people whom he saw as the opponents of his reform, without resorting to Stalinist methods, Gorbachev had to break down the fear that was the legacy of the Terror. Under the slogan of *glasnost*, Stalin and his policies were subjected to fierce criticism, and as a sign of good faith many books and films which had been banned under Brezhnev were published. Almost all political prisoners were released and religious freedoms were greatly extended.

This stage of *perestroika* reached its apogee with the elections to the Congress of People's Deputies in the spring of 1989. Although single-candidate elections persisted in many places and almost everywhere else special commissions weeded out unacceptable people, Soviet citizens used the choices they now enjoyed to throw out local bureaucrats. In the Baltic states candidates with the endorsement of the nationalist popular fronts were triumphant, and in Moscow Boris Yeltsin, who had been forced out of the Politburo at the end of 1987 for criticizing the slow pace of reform, was elected by an overwhelming majority. The unprecedented outspokenness of the Congress debates attracted avid television audiences.

At the end of 1989 a new third stage in Gorbachev's reforms could be detected. While economic reforms had lagged, the supply of food to the population had deteriorated. In the summer of 1989 the Soviet mining industry was hit by a serious strike wave. Furthermore, miners not only protested against their appalling working and living conditions (which even included a shortage of soap) but they also demanded that the Party give up its legalized monopoly of political power. In the autumn and winter, in an amazing series of revolutions, the Communist governments in all the Soviet East European satellites were overthrown. It was clear that Soviet regimes were not capable of reform. Gorbachev recognized this at an historic plenum of the Communist Party Central Committee in January 1990, when, he appeared to concede the right of republics to secede from the Union and accept the principle of a multi-party system.

The Soviet regime was established by force, and the social and economic transformation of the 1930s was also achieved by force. It is this fact that makes the Soviet system so inflexible. Gorbachev is a representative of a generation that has grown up since the death of Stalin, a generation that both rejects mass terror and, more quietly, Communist utopianism. It is greatly to Gorbachev's credit that he has pursued this very necessary corrective, but his reforms have had an increasingly reactive nature. Although Gorbachev has shown exceptional skill in keeping up with the changing environment in which he operates he is no longer setting the agenda and even risks becoming a brake on further reform.

The economy

There is broad agreement on the nature of the problems that afflict the Soviet economy and the necessary remedy. The first attempts to decentralize decision-making and increase incentives were made in the 1950s and were repeated in the 1960s. Little progress was made, and now leading Soviet economists, such as Leonid Abalkin, Gavriil Popov and Oleg Bogomolov, agree on the need to replace centrally laid-down plans with market mechanisms. In practice, it has proved difficult to introduce elements of a market into a system where, as a result of the setting of arbitrary prices, all goods for which there might be a demand are in short supply.

Shortages of basic foodstuffs are endemic, and time spent in queues acts as a serious brake on labour productivity. Raising agricultural production is a priority on the reform agenda. Most hopes have been pinned on the idea of leasing plots of land or livestock herds from the collective farms to small groups of peasants, usually families. After making deliveries to the state the lessees are free to dispose of their surplus on the market. Although highly successful individual cases have been given wide publicity in the media, leasing arrangements have not yet been taken up on a wide scale. To increase incentives, in the summer of 1989, farmers were promised bonuses in hard currency in return for improvements in output. At the beginning of March 1990 state ownership of land was abolished but the new law fell short of introducing full private ownership and a market.

The leasing of land is often justified by reference to the NEP, but 60 years have passed since the demise of the peasant agriculture that was at its base. The contemporary Soviet agricultural workforce tends to be elderly and younger workers no longer feel any real interest in the land. There have been institutional obstacles to agricultural reform as well. Peasant scepticism is not allayed by the relatively short term of most leasing agreements. Local bureaucrats, fearing the loss of their authority, hinder leasing by insisting on high deliveries to the state or, for example, refusing to supply fertilizers or animal feeds. The situation has not been helped by Gorbachev's decision, for reasons of political expediency, to appoint Yegor Ligachev, a leading opponent of radical reform, to oversee agriculture for the Party. Grain output has not improved over the past five years and the harvests in 1985 and 1988 were particularly bad.

Reform of industry has not been much more successful. A new law on enterprises, again drawing on the NEP model, which came into force in January 1988, transferred the bulk of industrial concerns to self-financing (*khozraschet*). In theory, this meant that they would no longer have to deliver their production to the state according to centrally laid-down plans, and instead managers would be forced to seek out the most profitable buyer. This measure should also have removed the massive state subsidies to unviable factories and given greater scope for the introduction of incentives. In practice, state production targets were replaced by priority orders from the centre.

There have been other more radical initiatives which have conflicted with Communist taboos on private property. First, some enterprises, particularly in the light industrial sector, have been leased to their managers and workers. Second, and best known, a policy of encouraging co-operative enterprises has been begun. In theory, co-operatives are not allowed to employ hired labour, and people are only supposed to work in co-operatives in their spare time. In practice, local authorities display considerable discretion either to further restrict co-operatives or sometimes to turn a blind eye to breaches of regulations. Where co-operatives operate, they are, to all intents and purposes, small private firms. By the middle of 1989 over 100,000 co-operatives had been set up, employing over 2 million people producing 12 billion roubles of goods and services annually. A small number of co-operatives are in light industry but the great majority are involved in retail and wholesale trade, supplying goods and services to the ordinary consumer and sometimes to other co-operatives or even state organizations.

Great emphasis has been put on the need for the Soviet Union to re-enter the world economy. At present, foreign trade is a small part of the GNP. In the West the most important Soviet trade partner is West Germany. Britain comes low down on the list and runs a regular deficit with the Soviet Union. Despite the number of Lada cars on Britain's roads, the bulk of Soviet exports are raw materials, oil, gas and timber, and most of its imports, apart from grain, consist of machinery. Until recently these were mostly made up of industrial goods but the emphasis has switched to consumer goods; most economists agree on the need to increase such imports to provide incentives for the workforce. The Soviet Union usually runs a foreign trade deficit, but the foreign debt rose from $27 billion in 1985 to an estimated $40 billion in 1988, and this will probably limit future growth. More importantly, the unconvertibility of the rouble is also an important obstacle to the development of trade, much of which has to be conducted under barter arrangements.

There is also a strong desire on the part of the Soviets to import foreign capital, management skills and technology. Most significantly, in the spring of 1989 the possibility of establishing 'Special Economic Zones' on the Chinese model was mooted. Despite enthusiasm from some local authorities, such as Odessa, there have yet to be any concrete proposals. The most widespread initiative in this area has been the encouragement of joint ventures. A substantial number of agreements, 1300 at the beginning of 1990, have been negotiated with foreign companies but only 200 are up and working. Only 5% of the ventures are in engineering and even fewer have been established in agriculture. Meanwhile, fully one third of them are in 'trade', tourism and light industry, and another third are categorized as consultants or research development. The Soviet authorities regard this as speculative, and are responding by imposing restrictions.

Economic reform has failed to have a positive effect on performance so far. In the first nine months of 1989 national income rose by 2.4%, an increase that was wiped out by inflation. Over the same period almost every key indicator fell behind target, partly due to strikes which cost 700 million roubles in lost output. This was despite the much-trumpeted conversion of some military enterprises to peaceful production. Crucially, output of food products was only 3% higher against a planned 11%. The food supply situation has deteriorated badly. In the autumn of 1989 meat was rationed in 33 regions of the country, butter in 20 and tea in 16. At this time, crowds broke into railway wagons waiting to unload foodstuffs in Leningrad, where supplies are better than in many of the more isolated provincial centres.

It is common in the Soviet Union to hear these problems attributed to deliberate sabotage by bureaucrats. A failure to satisfy rising expectations may also be important. While these factors cannot be ruled out in all cases, economic difficulties are much more a consequence of the half-hearted nature of reform. The service sector is still in a terrible state. Partly this is a problem of physical infrastructure (for example, the railways lack necessary rolling stock), but restrictions on co-operatives prevent them developing into a flexible consumer-orientated distribution system. As a result, tons of foodstuffs rot in railway marshalling yards and consumer goods purchased with precious hard currency lie in foreign warehouses because of a shortage of containers.

The introduction of small oases of private enterprise into the desert of a state economy where everything is in short supply inevitably creates a threat of inflation, and without real incentives production will not increase. Many politicians now accept that the old centralized system will have to be discarded in its entirety. In the middle of December 1989 the prime minister, Nikolai Ryzhkov, proposed an economic programme to the Supreme Soviet whereby the market would be introduced over an extended period. In the meantime, the collective farms would continue to dominate agriculture and state enterprises would rule industry. This programme was greeted with dismay by reformers, and as an indicator of the fast pace of change, at the January 1990 Central Committee plenum Gorbachev was already saying that private ownership of the means of production would be permitted. Nonetheless, reforms which are generally agreed to be necessary, and which would allow citizens to employ hired labour, introduce a pricing system based on the market, and a convertible currency would face serious ideological and social opposition. In March

1990 Gorbachev was elected to the new post of Soviet president with wide executive powers in what was interpreted as an attempt to overcome the impasse. However, a new programme of economic reform put to the Supreme Soviet in May did not represent much of an advance on the December proposals. Clearly, Gorbachev himself has Marxist qualms about radical economic reform.

The nationalities

Nothing has illustrated the fundamental nature of the difficulties facing the Soviet Union more than the re-emergence of the nationalities question. In every part of the country national groups are calling for a relaxation of control from Moscow, and sometimes for complete secession from the union. Nationalist unrest has considerably hampered Gorbachev's reform programme. At the most basic level, strikes and conflict in Azerbaijan and Armenia have cost millions of roubles of lost production. The centralized economic system in the Soviet Union means that the consequences of such interruption are magnified. For example, most cigarette paper is produced in Armenia, and strikes in that republic caused shortages throughout the country. More seriously, in the long term, nationalist unrest is an issue on which opponents of reform can capitalize by stirring up a Russian backlash and strengthening demands for force to be used to ensure the territorial integrity of the country.

The rise of nationalist feeling in Russia, Ukraine, Byelorussia, Moldavia and the Baltic states are covered later in this book and will only be touched on in passing here. Nationalist tensions in the Transcaucasus have been in the world's headlines in a particularly tragic fashion. This region has great economic potential. It is strategically situated at a cross-roads between Europe, Asia and the Middle East. Its jumble of ethnic groups and ancient Christian and Islamic cultures are not just a source of conflict, they are also a symbol of its richness. The strategic importance of the Transcaucasus has made it a perennial target for outside conquerors. The Russian Empire did not really establish its power here until the middle of the last century. None of the three main Transcaucasian nationalities, the Georgians, Armenians and Azerbaijanis, are Slav, and all briefly established independent republics in the aftermath of the Revolution.

Nationalist feeling in Georgia is intense and support for total independence is strong. At the end of 1988 the nationalist movement took on a mass character as tens of thousands of Georgians demonstrated in the streets of the capital, Tbilisi. The early mood of celebration turned sour after a peaceful demonstration was brutally broken up by special Soviet troops on 9 April 1989, killing at least twenty people. Ominously, this seems to have represented an attempt by anti-reform leaders in Moscow to rehearse a Tiananmen-style solution to the country's problems. The local Party leadership was also implicated and replaced. Subsequently, nationalist sentiment has intensified, if it is not so visible on the streets.

Unfortunately, the leadership of the Georgian nationalist movement has not always deserved the confidence it undoubtedly enjoys. Insensitivity on their part has inflamed anti-Georgian feeling among the Abkhazian and Ossetian minorities. Prolonged wrangling meant that the formation of a popular front on the Baltic model was delayed in Georgia until July 1989.

If Georgia were to become independent it would face many problems as a small country, with a population of under 6 million, whose economy has been closely tied in with that of the Soviet Union as a whole. Conceivably, it might also come under pressure from Turkey as well as facing serious internal ethnic problems. As elsewhere in the Soviet Union, central planning has had a deleterious effect on the local agriculture. But the country is proverbially fertile, and Georgian wine and, with some effort, tea and citrus fruit could be valuable exports. The tourist industry has considerable potential and the Caucasus mountains contain valuable minerals. Georgian entrepreneurial skills are well known, although under the planned economy they have mostly frequently found an outlet in the black economy, which does not suit them immediately for modern business. However, reflecting its key position in Transcaucasia, there has already been a certain amount of foreign investment in Georgia and co-operative enterprises are well-developed.

Conflict between the republics of Azerbaijan and Armenia began in early 1988. Armenians took advantage of *glasnost* to restate a long-standing demand that the Armenian enclave of Nagorno-Karabakh in Azerbaijan be joined to their republic. A mass movement quickly grew up around this issue led by a Karabakh Committee, whose prestige rapidly overtook that of the local Party. Gorbachev refused to countenance any change in republican boundaries and took advantage of the disastrous Armenian earthquake in December 1988 to arrest most of the Karabakh Committee. Meanwhile, inter-ethnic conflict was rapidly growing worse, beginning with the murder of 31 Armenians in the Azerbaijani city of Sumgait in February 1988. A flow of refugees began, which eventually created a population of 300,000 displaced persons in the two republics and a permanent cause of instability. To force the Armenians to withdraw their claims, the Azerbaijani Popular Front imposed a blockade which not only put a stranglehold on the Armenian economy but was also an overt challenge to the authority of Moscow. After an upsurge of inter-ethnic violence, a state of emergency was declared in Azerbaijan in January 1990 and the Soviet army could wrest Baku, the capital, from the control of local nationalists, only after great loss of life.

Azerbaijan is the largest of the Transcaucasian republics in terms of territory and population. By the end of the 1980s there were nearly 7 million Azerbaijanis, the great majority of whom live in their native republic. Azerbaijani national identity is shaped and reinforced by the Muslim religion. Ethnic proximity to the Turkic peoples of Central Asia and Turkey and their national movement, which is dominated by the Popular Front, has shown great self-confidence. The Popular Front arose to articulate the Azerbaijani opposition to the Armenian claim on Nagornyi-Karabakh and the discontent of local workers, but quickly made independence its main goal. Azerbaijani self-confidence also stems from the mineral wealth of its republic. Although reserves have greatly diminished, Azerbaijan is still an important oil producer and, like Georgia, it enjoys a fertile soil and a good climate.

The Armenian national movement has been much more ambivalent in its attitude to Moscow because most Armenians recognize that independence is not a viable option. The massacres of over a million Armenians by the Turks at the beginning of the century have left a permanent scar on the national psyche. However, they continue to press their claims for Nagornyi-Karabakh without expecting any support from Moscow. Armenians are skilled traders, and through their diaspora they have unrivalled international contacts. But Soviet Armenia is not agriculturally rich, and pressure from its neighbours means that the land is heavily populated. The earthquake of December 1988 dealt the country's economy a cruel blow from which it has still not recovered. An independent Armenia would be a small (its population is around 4 million), crowded, landlocked Christian territory surrounded by traditionally hostile Muslim Turks and Azerbaijanis.

The extent and nature of nationalist feeling in the five Central Asian republics, Uzbekistan, Kazakhstan, Kirgizia, Tadzhikistan (Tajik) and Turkmenia, is difficult to gauge. This not just because the local Party leaderships are hostile to *glasnost* but also because the population has determinedly maintained its culture, language and Muslim religion by carefully presenting a picture of outward conformity to Soviet norms. In the past five years organizations with the aim of promoting the local language and culture and supporting democratization, such as the Uzbek Popular Front (Birlik), have appeared. In practice, clan and ethnic identities (and possibly Muslim brotherhoods) have been more important in mobilizing the populace. Violent conflict has broken out on a number of occasions. In Alma Ata, the capital of Kazakhstan, in December 1986 mass demonstrations turned violent after the local Kazakh Party's first secretary was replaced by a Russian. In July 1989 the Uzbek population in the Fergana valley attacked Meskhetian Turks who had been transported there from Georgia by Stalin. In February 1990 in Dushanbe, the capital of Tadzhikistan, there were violent demonstrations by the local population who have close ethnic relatives in Afghanistan.

Agriculturally, these are potentially rich territories, but the local environment is in a terrible state. The economy of Central Asia has been geared to produce raw materials for factories which are mostly situated elsewhere in the Soviet Union. The profligate application of chemical fertilizers and pesticides and the diversion of local rivers has created an ecological disaster in the Aral Sea, which has shrunk to a toxic puddle. These are already sizeable republics. Uzbekistan, which is the largest, has a population of nearly 15 million, and the high local birth rate means that they will become even more important. The combination of a rapidly rising population with a ruined economy creating unemployment and land hunger and a strong identification with Islam has created a potentially explosive mixture in Central Asia.

This upsurge in nationalist feeling is the single largest problem facing the peoples of the Soviet Union. Gorbachev, with his Russian background and training in Marxism–Leninism, is not well equipped to deal with it. On a visit to Lithuania in January 1990 he asked a protester holding up a banner calling for independence who had told him to do so, apparently unable to believe that anyone would do this voluntarily. In his handling of the conflict between Armenia and Azerbaijan he has consistently under-estimated the strength of local feeling, and has taken decisive action too late and in such a way that only exacerbates the situation. The unity of the Soviet Union is a principle that Gorbachev is unwilling to see breached. At the end of 1988 amendments to the constitution that he proposed would have put new restrictions on republican sovereignty, but after strong protests some of the new provisions were relaxed. Then, after his visit to Lithuania in January 1990, he finally agreed that arrangements would have to be drawn up to allow republics to secede from the union. However, when his proposals became known, the procedures they laid down were so complex that they were a factor which caused Lithuania to declare independence in early March before they became law.

The dilemmas of reform

Between 1985 and 1990 the main dilemma of reform in the Soviet Union concerned the contradictions implicit in the attempts of an authoritarian regime to implement change without weakening its own legitimacy. In the Soviet case these did not merely stem from the relaxation of coercion but also from the weak hold of its Marxist–Leninist ideology. With the entry of the people of the Soviet Union onto the political stage, new dilemmas arise. In the past, radical Soviet reformers have sought merely to mobilize popular support for their programmes, but now the population is being asked to decide between different alternatives. Are Soviet citizens, who have never really experienced pluralist democracy and a market economy, capable of responding to the new challenges? What happens if reforms which are generally recognized to be necessary conflict with the interests of important social groups?

The introduction of the market economy in the Soviet Union will mean that many of its citizens will experience a drop in living standards. For some, this will entail merely a relative decrease as social inequalities increase, but for many, those on fixed incomes and workers in loss-making enterprises who face redundancy, the decline will be absolute. Despite occasional campaigns against 'petty bourgeois levelling', the official ideology in the Soviet Union has reinforced popular egalitarianism. This is now backfiring in the shape of popular resentment against Party privileges. Fear of widespread unrest consequent upon the introduction of policies which will raise prices, increase inequalities and create unemployment (Poland in the early 1980s is an example of what might happen) has been a considerable brake on reform.

The nationalities question poses seemingly intractable problems. Nationalist movements have been given great impetus by the adverse economic situation, but they have their own momentum. Pro-independence sentiment in the Baltic republics and Georgia would have been strong, whatever the economic outlook. Political liberalization has simply raised expectations rather than satisfying them. More seriously, the rise of nationalist feeling in one republic is met with suspicion both by Russians and minorities in the republic, who are often Russian as well. Inter-ethnic conflict has caused the loss of many lives over the past few years, and left the country with over half a million refugees. Complaints of discrimination by Russian minorities in the Baltic republics or Moldavia could provoke an authoritarian backlash.

Gorbachev's acceptance of the principle of a multi-party system is severely qualified. He may have abandoned the Party's 'leading role' but, in its place, asserted its position as a 'vanguard party'. Gorbachev has realized that the Communist Party is the bond that holds together the Soviet Union and has stressed the need for unity. Despite this, faced with the rejection of its ideology by the population, it seems clear that the Communist Party will split, probably as early as the next Party Congress in July 1990. A 'Democratic Platform' faction has already been formed, ostensibly to press for greater democracy within the Party, but it may well follow the path of the reform Communists in Eastern Europe, reject Marxism–Leninism and divide off to form some sort of democratic socialist or social democratic party.

Furthermore, all over the Soviet Union political organizations are emerging to articulate the aspirations of the population. Sometimes they are tempted to play on the raw nerves of wounded national pride and the desire for scapegoats, but they have also displayed remarkable political skill. This is particularly so for the Baltic popular fronts, which have outmanoeuvred Moscow with a steady stream of small symbolic victories and the occasional tactical retreat. In Russia itself various groupings have sprung up covering the political spectrum, from monarchists to anarchists, reflecting an exceptionally rich political tradition. So far, despite their headline-grabbing demonstrations and an undoubted increase in the number of attacks on Jews, Russian chauvinist organizations like *Pamyat* have failed to attract a mass following. In the elections to the Congress of People's Deputies in March 1989 anti-reform and Russian nationalist candidates, even where they were not associated with the Party apparatus, did badly, and then did not do any better in the republican and other elections in March 1990. An often painful learning process is going on over the whole of the Soviet Union, and there is good reason to think that the great majority of its citizens do not want to return to international isolation and rule by coercion in the name of a failed ideology.

Prognoses

The future of the Soviet Union can appear very uncertain. This sense of uncertainty in a society which has always been assured that it is travelling towards the creation of the perfect human community (Communism) explains the apocalyptic prognoses that one sometimes hears in the Soviet Union. All the same, pessimism is widespread. An opinion survey carried out at the beginning of 1989 showed that 37% of Muscovites considered that their lives had improved over the past three years and 24% thought that their lives had got worse. When asked the same question at the beginning of 1990 only 24% considered that their lives had got better over the past four years while 33% said that their lives had got worse. It is often pointed out that political reform (*glasnost*) has gone ahead much faster than reform of the economy (*perestroika*) and there must be a real danger that economic failure will undermine popular support for political liberalization.

Over the past five years Gorbachev has shown himself to be a consummate politician. He has a knack of just keeping ahead of his critics by brilliantly timed concessions or purges. The failure of *perestroika* to improve the living conditions of ordinary Soviet citizens has critically undermined Gorbachev's personal popularity and hence his room to manoeuvre. The contrast between his popularity abroad and his unpopularity at home has become obvious. His assumption of the post of president has left him even more exposed. Gorbachev promised to use his presidential powers to implement radical reform in a consistent way, but in fact they have tended to reveal his ideological limitations. As a result, it is possible that the discrediting of political liberalization will play into the hands of the 'conservative' Party apparat who want to slow down or even halt all reform.

This final variant seems the least likely of all. Despite attempts by some opponents of reform in the apparat, most notably the Leningrad Party leader, Boris Gidaspov, to mobilize discontent with falling living standards, they lack any coherent programme to deal with the country's all too visible problems. A more moderate, technocratic approach, symbolized for most observers by the prime minister, Nikolai Ryzhkov, is also an unlikely variant. If the experience of the past five years has shown one thing it is the inseparability of political and economic reform. Furthermore, the movement for change has gathered a momentum of its own which makes a return to the old style of rule impossible. New forms of government will emerge which will reflect better the aspirations of the people. For good or ill, the Soviet Union has begun a process which will completely transform the lives of all its citizens.

10 RUSSIA

The elder brother

Geography and economy

The Russian Soviet Federated Socialist Republic (RSFSR) is the largest of the fifteen Union republics that make up the Soviet Union. Its population in January 1987 stood at 147.4 million. For such a large territory it is remarkably ethnically homogeneous. The RSFSR stretches from Vladivostok on the Pacific Ocean in the east (nearly 10,000 kilometres and eleven time zones) to the border of Byelorussia in the west. Even further to the west is the Baltic enclave of Kaliningrad, which is cut off from the rest of the RSFSR by Lithuania. This territory was originally part of German East Prussia, annexed to the Soviet Union after World War II, and is now settled by Russians. Then, the RSFSR extends from Murmansk on the Arctic Ocean in the north (2,800 kilometres) to Pyatigorsk in the Caucasus mountains in the south.

The republic's eponymous ethnic group makes up the overwhelming majority of its population (82.6% in 1979). There are many minority peoples, sometimes grouped in their own autonomous republics or national areas. The largest of these minorities are the 6 million Tartars, who have an autonomous republic on the Volga with Kazan as its capital. Nearby are the closely related 1.5 million Bashkirs. Apart from the other small Volga peoples such as the Mordvinians and the Chuvashes, there is also a patchwork of autonomous republics in the north Caucasus; Dagestan, North Ossetia, Chechen-Ingushia and others. There are two other minorities who do not have a national area: the Jews and Germans. (The Jewish national area of Birobijan in the far east was an artificial creation, and few Jews actually live there.)

The European Russian heartland was not well endowed by nature. The rigours of the Russian climate are proverbial. It is continental in pattern with harsh winters (Moscow's average winter temperature is −8°C) and relatively warm summers (July temperatures of 20°C are typical). The growing season is short and, for the most part, the soils are poor except for the fertile black earth region in south-central Russia and the steppe that extends eastwards. Despite the unpropitious environment in some parts of north European Russia, dairying is successfully practised. For most of central Russia mixed farming is the norm, with potatoes and hardy grains the typical crops. Further south, however, are rich grain belts with sugar beet and maize also grown on a wide scale.

European Russia lacks natural resources. There are no major coal fields

RUSSIA

Official name	Russian Soviet Federal Socialist Republic (RSFSR)
Area	17,078,005 sq. km (6,592,100 sq. miles)
Population	147,386,000 (1989)
Capital	Moscow (Moskva)
Language	Russian, many minority languages
Religion	Russian Orthodox, Roman Catholic
Currency	rouble

or oil deposits and few minerals except in the Urals mountains, where there is copper, iron, nickel, zinc, aluminium and magnesium. The climate compounds with distance to make communications difficult. So although Russia does have extensive timber reserves, they have proved difficult to exploit. Russia is also constricted by a lack of ice-free outlets to the sea, thus hampering foreign trade. Murmansk, although it is in the far north, is navigable throughout the year, but its distance from the main population centres limits its importance. Leningrad, which is further south and the centre of a major industrial region, is closed for three months of the year. In contrast, Siberia is rich in minerals. It has extremely large oil deposits in west Siberia around the city of Tyumen, and coal reserves for several thousand years in the Kuzbass and east Siberia, at the present rate of extraction. There are extensive deposits of all kinds of ferrous and non-ferrous metals, including gold, aluminium, molybdenum, manganese and iron. There are also large diamond workings. West Siberia has consider-able reserves of natural gas and east Siberia a large surplus of hydro-electric power.

Russia's economic strength has stemmed from its agriculture and the creativeness and hard work of its people. It is a potentially rich country, but realizing that potential requires an immense input of human effort, and for most of its history it is the peasants who have made the country productive. In the pre-revolutionary period the productivity of Russian agriculture was low compared with West European countries, but the gradual penetration of the market into the countryside began to transform subsistence agriculture. In the south large estates were producing grain for export and the Siberian diary herds did the same with butter. One of Tsarist Russia's last prime ministers, Pyotr Stolypin, introduced measures to encourage the development of individual peasant farms out of the old semi-feudal structures based on the peasant commune, the *mir*. Fast industrial growth was also achieved.

The introduction of the market into the countryside and the inequalities that went with it caused social tensions. During the Revolution the peasants seized the large estates and divided them up. Individual peasant farmers were forced back into the *mir*, which was a major setback in the development of Russian agriculture. In 1917 the Bolsheviks had been able to secure the passive support of the peasants by calling for the division of the landlords' land, but gradually alienated them during the Civil War, until they rose in rebellion. The Bolsheviks abandoned their policy of grain requisitioning and their plans to introduce collective farms, and in early 1921 introduced the New Economic Policy (NEP). Under the NEP the problem of grain production was approached by offering peasants incen-tives, and recovery from the famine of 1921–2 was remarkably quick. The peasants showed that they were able to respond to these incentives, despite the restrictions placed on them by both the *mir* and the Soviet state. Under NEP, grain deliveries to the cities were dependent on the market, and if prices were not good enough the peasants would not and frequently did not sell. At the end of the 1920s, under pressure to get grain into the cities to support the industrialization programme, requisitioning was reintroduced and systemized under the collective farms. In its collectivization campaign the Communist Party tried to exploit the resentment that the more successful peasants, the *kulaks*, aroused.

Russia's lack of natural resources and poor communications has encouraged the state to play an important role in the development of the country's economy. Both under Peter the Great at the beginning of the eighteenth century, when industry was built up with serf labour, and the much more grandiose project of Stalin in the 1930s the state was used to pull the country up by its bootstraps. It is the negative consequences of this last 'revolution from above' which are now being tackled by Soviet economic reformers.

From the beginning of the 1930s a rapid process of industrialization was carried out in Russia, as elsewhere in the Soviet Union, and, as elsewhere, it transformed the traditional life-style and economy of the bulk of the population. In less than ten years Russia's traditional peasant agriculture was replaced by collective farms. This was a disaster. Many peasants regarded collectivization as a return to serfdom, with the forced labour for noble serf-owners (*barshchina*) being replaced with forced labour for the state. Production of most agricultural commodities fell, but the number of peasants needed to produce them fell faster. Although there was thus an apparent rise in productivity, Russian agriculture was now permanently depressed. This was partly due to the centre's persistent neglect, compounded by its failure to take account of local conditions and also because of the lack of incentives given to individual peasants. Some Russian intellectuals now argue that collectivization permanently destroyed the peasants' interest in the soil, but this is belied by the success of their private plots, which make a contribution to Russian food production, and one much larger than their area would suggest.

Russia's rapid urbanization and the development of heavy industry gave the impression of modernization. The population of old-established cities grew rapidly and new ones were built from scratch. From being an overwhelmingly peasant country in 1928, by 1941 Russia was becoming a nation of city dwellers. During the 1930s the output figures for iron, electricity, coal and machinery shot up, and by 1941 a massive industrial potential had been created which was the basis of the Soviet war effort. The structural bias towards heavy industry was established in the early five-year plans, and Russia's economic geography was transformed by the establishment of large new metallurgical combines at Magnitogorsk in the Urals and Kuznetsk in west Siberia.

It has been particularly profligate with the country's two most precious assets, its natural resources and its people. Cheap natural materials have been made to substitute for the absence of capital and technology and waste has been compounded by the lack of proper controls on costs. As a result, it now takes three times as much energy to produce a tonne of copper in the Soviet Union as in West Germany. Industrialization was wasteful in people not only because of the physical destruction of millions as *kulaks* and in famine. Low productivity is structural to the Soviet economic system. Western social scientists have described a sort of 'social contract', whereby the regime bought political quiescence with gradually rising living standards to be enjoyed roughly by all citizens, no matter what contribution they made to society. Wage differentials were small, job security almost total and pressure to increase productivity minimal. Russian workers called this the system of 'we pretend to work and they pretend to pay us'. The Soviet system has created a highly educated but greatly under-utilized workforce. Typically, across the Soviet Union today there are thousands of research institutes where highly educated graduates 'pretend to work'.

What is Russia?

Formally at least, it would be no exaggeration to say that 70 years of Soviet rule reduced Russia to the status of an administrative concept. Indeed, for many foreigners Russia is synonymous with the Soviet Union. In recent years, however, the fundamental questions that are being asked about the future of the Soviet Union are encouraging Russians to think about their own national identity. Russia's history, in many ways, separates it from the other nations that make up the Soviet Union and from those of Eastern Europe. In the past, both Russians and foreigners have tried to define Russia in terms of either its European or its Asiatic heritage. In practice, Russian culture has been European for over two centuries, and the Russian state and its relationship to society makes this a nation *sui generis*.

Modern Russian history began in the fifteenth and sixteenth centuries, with the campaigns of Ivan III and Ivan IV, the Terrible, to free Russians from Mongol and Tartar rule. To stave off its enemies in the east and later in the west (at first, Poland and Sweden, and later, France, Britain, Austria and Germany), the need for a powerful state to mobilize all available resources developed. However, the Russian autocracy was not merely a strong state: it was a very personal form of absolutism in which there were no intermediate institutions, such as an independent church, an aristocracy (as opposed to a service nobility) and rule of law. There were attempts to replace the 'bootstrap-pulling' convulsions to catch up with rivals who were always ahead and create a self-sustaining process of development by releasing the creative forces in society. Catherine II, the Great, tried to raise the prestige of the nobility, for example. In 1861 Alexander II abolished serfdom, and subsequently set up a judiciary and a representative form of local government, the *zemstva*. After the 1905 Revolution Nicholas II granted a limited representative assembly, the *Duma*. However, the

Bolshevik determination to industrialize the country through state planning represented a resumption of the state tradition.

The Communists have exploited aspects of Russia's political culture to maintain their rule, in particular peasant egalitarianism, and this is one reason for the ambivalence with which Russians have sometimes regarded the Soviet regime. However, Communist rule has destroyed a great deal more than it borrowed from Russia's traditions, and not just those of the Europeanized elite. Collectivization did not entail just the destruction of an economy, it also meant the elimination of a way of life. The *mir*, for example, restricted individual freedom in some respects but it did provide a basic form of mutual aid and even collective decision-making. The highly developed village handicrafts industry (*kustar*), which provided the bulk of the peasants' consumer goods and work tools, was destroyed during industrialization. The *artel* was a peasant-based form of co-operative work that had great social and economic potential, and it persists in various forms to this day, both sanctioned by the state (*brigady*) and unofficially (*shabashniki*).

The Soviet Union is, at least, the territorial heir to the Russian Empire, and for many in the non-Russian republics they merge into one. While many Russians feel a sense of patriotism about the Soviet Union, it is usually not without reservations. Professor Geoffrey Hosking, the 1988 Reith Lecturer, put it very well:

One nation in the Soviet confraternity is in a very singular position, and that is the Russians. They are to all appearances the imperial nation, the 'elder brother', in Stalin's words. They have no worries about their territory, or language, or alien immigration: in fact other nations feel threatened by *them*. Yet, curiously enough, in some respects the Russians feel like a national minority discriminated against in their own country. They know that the non-Russians are often more prosperous. And they can see that since 1917 their church has been undermined, their rural way of life mortally enfeebled, their finest writers, artists and thinkers banned, driven into the underground and emigration.

This discontent manifested itself in a search for roots among Russians that began long before *perestroika*. The best recent Russian prose writers, such as Valentin Rasputin and Viktor Astafev, eulogized the disappearing village way of life. Among many Russians there was a growing interest in and respect for religion. The Soviet regime reduced the Russian Orthodox Church to a state of complete subservience, and it was in no position to play a role similar to that of the Roman Catholic Church in Communist Poland. Nonetheless, in recent years Russians have increasingly turned to the Church both to express their rejection of Communist ideology and to affirm their national identity. Gorbachev attempted to capitalize on this when the marking of the millennium of the Russian Orthodox Church in 1988 was made the occasion for unprecedented offical celebrations.

At a time when politics could not be openly articulated, Russian national feeling also was expressed in opposition to the Siberian rivers project, whereby water from the north-flowing Siberian rivers would be diverted to irrigate the arid lands of Central Asia, with potentially serious ecological consequences, and occasional complaints that, alone of the Union republics, the RSFSR did not have its own capital (Moscow was better known as the capital of the Soviet Union) and did not have its own Academy of Sciences or even Party organization. When *glasnost* revealed the extent of national feelings in the non-Russian republics, Russians were forced to examine even further their own national identity.

As the tightly centralized Soviet state gives way to a much looser federation or even breaks up entirely, Russia will be forced to review its relationship with its Slav neighbours and the many minorities within the RSFSR. Before the imposition of the 'Mongol–Tartar yoke' in the middle of the thirteenth century Russian culture had been centred in Kiev. The Ukraine, of which Kiev is now the capital, and Byelorussia were not incorporated into the Russian Empire until the seventeenth and eighteenth centuries. The Ukrainians and Byelorussians have their own languages, but their historical links and common ethnic roots with the Russians (collectively, the East Slavs) make it difficult to imagine that they will not continue to be closely associated politically in the future. Siberia was claimed for the Russian Empire in the sixteenth and seventeenth centuries, and Russia became an Asian Empire as well as a European. An immigration of Russians began, and they now constitute the great majority of the population, although native peoples such as the Yakuts and Buryat-Mongols have their own national areas. There are regionalist tendencies in Siberia but, as a whole, its future is closely tied in with European Russia. The largest of the national minorities in the RSFSR, the Tartars, have formed a popular front, but its claims appear modest. Unfortunately, anti-semitism is a persistent tendency in Russian political culture, and some Russians try to present the Jews as a scapegoat.

The rise of nationalism in the Soviet Union has made the way that Russians regard the Soviet Union, either as a genuine expression of their own statehood or as a system alien to their traditions, one of the crucial factors affecting the outcome of the present period of rapid change in the Soviet Union.

The prospects for economic reform

At various times the Communist regime has attempted to mobilize popular Russian hostility to social inequality. The campaign against the *kulaks* is a prime example, and has reinforced negative attitudes towards private enterprise. The problems encountered by the present reforms which call for greater incentives and a larger role for the market indicate that such attitudes are indeed commonly held by Russians. Mostly impressionistic evidence suggests that they are less common among the Baltic and Transcaucasian peoples. If *perestroika* is to avoid the fate of NEP it will be important to investigate the real extent of such attitudes. Opinion polling in the Soviet Union is not very sophisticated, but some polls have given interesting results.

During the present reforms the question of reducing the massive Soviet budget deficit, which stood at 36 billion roubles at the beginning of 1989, by closing unprofitable state enterprises has frequently been raised, but the government has always failed to take action in the face of the spectre of mass unemployment. Another way of reducing the deficit would be to cut subsidies on basic foodstuffs and utilities, such as electricity and rents, and to introduce market prices. Once again, the government has backed away from this measure, and the number of rationed goods has risen inexorably. There is some popular support for this. A poll conducted at the end of 1988 showed that 83.7% of those questioned were against the prices for shortage goods being raised with 4.4% in favour, while 54.1% were against their being put on ration and 28.8% were in favour.

The co-operatives have been a particular butt for popular hostility to private enterprise. A poll carried out in Moscow, one of the most liberal parts of Russia, at the beginning of 1989 found that 23% of men and 8% of women thought that people who worked in co-operatives 'were businesslike people full of initiative' and that they merited respect and support. Almost half of the men and about a third of the women had reservations about the co-operative movement and about a quarter of the men and 38% of the women thought that people who worked in co-operatives were 'swindlers and businessmen who make a lot of money at the expense of honest working people'. At the end of September 1989 an attempt by a group of deputies in the Supreme Soviet to ban all commercial co-operatives as opposed to production co-operatives was narrowly defeated, but in the middle of October the Soviet bowed to popular pressure and gave local authorities the right to set 'maximum price levels' on 'essential public goods' for sale in co-operatives. Such popular hostility and the activity of protection rackets run by organized crime, the so-called 'mafia', make the position of Soviet co-operatives unenviable.

There are more optimistic signs for reformers, though. A poll conducted in Moscow at the end of 1989 found that 57% of those asked agreed that the private ownership of the means of production should be allowed. Positive responses were much more common among the young. Many people seem to be prepared to give the co-operatives a chance. When asked whether the development of co-operatives would help to ease shortages, 39.4% of those questioned agreed, 37.9% disagreed and 22.7% did not know. A particularly bad sign for the co-operative movement was the demand of many of the strikers in the summer of 1989 for their closure, but by the end of the year a degree of understanding between the two sides seems to have been established when the co-operative union agreed to provide financial and material help to the strike committees.

In general, the old 'social contract' has broken down, and there does seem to be widespread acceptance of the need for greater incentives or, as it is put sometimes more hesitantly, payment by results. Many Russians feel that the present economic system does not give them the opportunity to realize their potential. Many co-operatives and joint ventures are attempts to exploit this wasted talent. For example, Rolls-Royce have entered into an agreement with a Soviet company Sukhoi to develop a new aero engine.

Political choices

Perestroika is presenting the Soviet citizen, for the first time, with political choices. This is so no less for Russia than elsewhere in the Soviet Union. As Marxist–Leninist ideology dissolves and the Communist Party fractures, groupings within the apparat are seeking new bases of support among the many informal organizations that are springing up. On the face of it, the Communist Party in Russia, untainted by deference to a foreign power, might expect to receive considerable support. Moves have been made to form a Russian Communist Party. However, the initiative has been taken by 'conservatives', some connected with the OFT (see below), and as long as Russians continue to support further radical reform its appeal will be limited. The contours of the new politics became clearer after the elections to the RSFSR Supreme Soviet in March 1990 and the main trends can already be distinguished.

On the extreme nationalist right are organizations like *Pamyat* (Memory). *Pamyat*'s roots go back to officially sponsored organizations set up in the 1960s and 1970s to channel popular demands for action to preserve Russia's national monuments, especially its devastated churches. When the organization, as such, surfaced in 1986 its ideology had clearly been formed under the influence of anti-semitic *samizdat* literature, such as that hoary old fake *The Protocols of the Elders of Zion*, which had been circulating in the 1970s. Gauging the support *Pamyat* really enjoys is very difficult, not least because the organization (if it was ever a single organization) has split into up to a dozen little *Pamyats*, the largest led by Dmitrii Vassiliev. *Pamyat* does not enjoy mass support, but it does have determined groups of activists in many Russian cities. More seriously, certain figures in the cultural intelligentsia give it their tacit support, and there is some evidence that elements in the KGB and the militia are sympathetic or even use it for their own ends.

The United Front of Workers (OFT) also has Russian nationalist tendencies, especially through its links with the Interfronts in the Baltic republics, but the OFT is more properly a child of 'conservative' elements in the apparat. In the search for a new base, some Communist politicians, most notably the Leningrad First Secretary, Boris Gidaspov, are trying to make capital out of the concerns of workers that the introduction of market mechanisms will lead to a fall in their living standards. The OFT undoubtedly has a resonance with popular anxieties, and has organized branches in different parts of the country. However, it has not been able to overcome workers' suspicions of the Communist Party and attract a mass following. Gidaspov's refusal to stand as a candidate in the elections to the RSFSR Supreme Soviet speaks volumes in this respect.

There are other radical political groupings which do not take part in electoral politics. Perhaps the most prominent is the Democratic Union (DS). With strong dissident roots a political party in opposition to totalitarianism was formed in Moscow in August 1988. Since then, they have been active in street demonstrations, with a radical programme for dismantling Soviet power. The DS is a small grouping. It has about 1000 members over the Soviet Union and does not have mass support – its attempts to link up with striking miners were rebuffed. On the other hand, it is well organized, with a strictly defined form of membership, in contrast to other informal organizations, and it produces a large number of publications. Anarchists have also made themselves visible but also (not surprisingly) do not participate in elections.

The strongest political force at present is represented by a coalition of radical Communists with liberal Russian nationalists, social democrats, Christian democrats and non-party radicals, particularly in the Russian popular fronts, which came together in January 1990 to form an electoral bloc, Democratic Russia, for the RSFSR Supreme Soviet elections in March. Democratic Russia draws its inspiration from the moral authority of the late Andrei Sakharov, includes members of the Inter-Regional Group of deputies, whose most well-known member is Boris Yeltsin, and has the grassroots support of some of the most active informal political associations. The elections gave radical reformers control of both Moscow and Leningrad; roughly 35% of the delegates to the new RSFSR Supreme Soviet were supporters of Democratic Russia. Sensationally, at the end of May, Boris Yeltsin was elected president of the RSFSR. This could put Gorbachev in direct conflict with the largest republic in the Union.

In view of the popularity of Democratic Russia, the programme that it put forward for the RSFSR Supreme Soviet elections deserves closer scrutiny. Its political demands centre on the introduction of a multi-party parliamentary system with legal safeguards for basic civil rights, and in the area of national policy it stresses that Russia has suffered as much from totalitarianism as any nationality in the Soviet Union and calls for the RSFSR to be granted full sovereignty. However, it fails to affirm the right of individual republics to secession from the Soviet Union, only calling for a renegotiation of the terms of union. Its economic programme displays parallel contradictions. On the one hand, it calls for the introduction of the market as 'the locomotive of the development and transformation of the economy', the transfer of a significant number of state enterprises to different forms of ownership and accepts the principle of private owner-ship of land. On the other, it proposes a sophisticated and unrealistically expensive system of social security which would guarantee all citizens a minimum income, freeze prices and maintain state subsidies and index pensions to wages. This programme encapsulates the dilemmas facing reform in Russia: the desire to Westernize the political and economic system and, at the same time, the need to defer to popular conceptions of social justice.

Many observers argue that Russia is, at last, experiencing the emer-gence of a 'civil society'. By this they mean that institutions and a political culture are being created which will allow forces in society to advance their aspirations, even against the state, in a coherent way. While great progress has been made in terms of political education, however, it is not clear that such institutions have really established themselves, and the Russian political scene continues to be dominated by a process of fragmentation. The contours of the new Russia are still obscure.

Conclusions

Russia is now going through a very painful transition process, a transition that has been made more difficult by 70 years of Communist rule. There is a risk of a backlash against political and economic liberalization: the treat-ment of minorities such as the Jews and Tartars will be a touchstone for this. In the nineteenth century intellectuals divided into those who saw Russia as having its own particular path of development (the Slavophiles) and those who saw its future in representative democracy and in the development of a Western-style economy (the Westernizers). The isola-tion that Slavophilism implied and that the Bolsheviks imposed are not an option for Russia at the end of the twentieth century. The overwhelming majority of Russians appreciate the opening of links with the outside world. Polls have shown consistently that the most popular way of improving incentives is increasing the imports of foreign consumer goods.

The Slavophile/Westernizer controversy hinged not only on the re-lationship of Russia to the rest of the world but also on attitudes to private property. The sort of hostility to private property that the Slavophiles showed is not as strong a force now as it was at the beginning of the century. This is so first, for good or ill, because of the disappearance of the peasantry and second, because of the discrediting of Marxist–Leninist ideology. The experience of 70 years of authoritarian rule has also raised popular consciousness of the need for civil rights to be guaranteed. Despite these Westernizing tendencies, the political system of a sovereign Russia would probably differ in many ways from those prevailing in West Europe. Popular ecological concerns, which border on anti-industrialism, and decentralizing tendencies will be prominent. The main question facing Russians now (and the rise of nationalism in the Soviet republics has been shown in other chapters in this book) is the attitude they take towards the empire. If they refuse to accept demands for greater autonomy they will be forced to return to authoritarian styles of government. The indications at present are that as long as the process of liberalization is not discredited, Russians will become reconciled to this.

11 THE BALTIC STATES
Struggles for sovereignty

Introduction

Since 1940, when the independent Baltic states of Estonia, Latvia and Lithuania were annexed by the USSR and disappeared from the political map of the world, they have often been considered as a single entity. In fact they comprise three nations with different linguistic and historical backgrounds. For that reason, each is here given a separate analysis. Yet there are similarities in their recent historical developments. All three provinces of Tsarist Russia gained independence as a result of the simultaneous collapse of the Russian and German empires before the end of World War I. Lithuania declared its independence on 16 February, Estonia on 24 February and Latvia on 18 November 1918. Soviet Russia renounced all former rights of sovereignty 'voluntarily and for ever' in the 1920 peace treaties signed with Estonia on 2 February in Tartu, with Lithuania on 12 July in Moscow and with Latvia on 11 August in Riga. The Baltic states entered the League of Nations during the period 1921–2.

The states lost their independence as a consequence of the Molotov–Ribbentrop Pact (MRP) signed on 23 August 1939 between Germany and the USSR. Its secret 'additional protocol' assigned Estonia and Latvia to the Soviet 'sphere of interest' and Lithuania to Germany. A further secret protocol on 28 September also transferred Lithuania to the USSR. The Baltic states were forced to conclude Pacts of Mutual Defence and Assistance with the USSR in September and October, after which Soviet troops entered their territories. Although the treaties guaranteed independence, the total occupation of the Baltic states was completed between 15 and 18 June 1940, at the time when Germany invaded France. The incorporation took place behind a facade of legitimacy. Workers' demonstrations occurred on 21 June and the Communist parties became the only legal parties. Elections on 14–15 July were in clear violation of the electoral laws of the three states. Before the elections, non-Communist leaders and activists were arrested. Voting was according to a single Soviet-assigned candidates' list. The new assemblies requested entry into the Soviet Union and their requests were accepted on 3 August (Lithuania) and on 6 August 1940 (Estonia and Latvia). Most Western countries to this day do not recognize *de jure* the annexation of the Baltic states by the USSR.

During the first year of Soviet rule, Estonia lost around 60,000 people (4% of its pre-war population), Latvia 35,000 and Lithuania 34,000 (1.5–2% each) through deportations, mobilizations and massacres. The deportations of June 1941, coming on the eve of the German–Soviet war, served as a shock to the people, which explains their passive welcome of the German armies. They hoped that the Germans would restore their independence, but German actions did nothing to encourage such feelings. Before the return of the Soviets in the autumn of 1944 there was large-scale emigration of the Baltic peoples to the West (6% of the Estonian, 8% of the Latvian and 3% of the Lithuanian populations). Nearly half of these had benefited from higher education. Guerrilla resistance continued until 1952. At their most numerous, the guerrillas constituted up to 1% of the total population.

Collectivization of agriculture was accompanied by mass deportations of farmers to Siberia. In the month of March 1949 the Baltic nations lost about 3% of their populations.

Large numbers of Russian workers were brought into the republics to man new heavy industrial plants. Whereas in 1939 there were 8% non-Estonians, 23% non-Latvians and 20% non-Lithuanians living in the republics, by 1989 the figures had risen to 39%, 48% and 20% respectively. Large-scale industrialization has considerably damaged the local environment, and the ecological crisis has come to symbolize the colonial system under which the countries have no control over their natural resources or environmental protection. Ninety per cent of their industries are directly under all-union control through Moscow ministries.

The deterioration of the standard of living, the destruction of the environment, the demographic situation, and the suppression of national cultures have contributed to the disillusionment of the Baltic peoples with the occupying power. The tradition of dissent, the existence of strong, locally educated elites capable of articulating the needs of their people and mobilizing them into movements, the memory of their independent democratic statehood are all factors motivating them for a change.

In the Baltic context, Gorbachev's policy of *perestroika* has become a movement for national liberation. Moscow reformers failed to understand that, by promoting social initiatives and creativity from below, they strengthened the national identity of the Baltic peoples. The policy of *glasnost* has endangered the Communist Party's prestige and has burdened it with responsibility for the past repressive policies. Being a symbol of occupation, the Party has no chance of survival. When Soviet reformers criticize the central bureaucracy, in the Baltic context this means Moscow's colonial rule over the republics. When Moscow radicals attack Stalinist policies, the Baltic peoples include Stalinist foreign policies, as a result of which they were occupied. When Moscow promotes democratic elections, Estonians, Latvians and Lithuanians vote for their political independence.

Estonia

The Estonians are a Finno-Ugric people, related to the Finns and, more distantly, to the Hungarians. They were subjugated by German and

Danish invaders in the thirteenth century and later ruled by Sweden from 1561 to 1721, after which the Estonian lands became part of Tsarist Russia. Economic development between the wars was similar to that of Finland. The gradual deterioration of Soviet Estonia's living standards when compared to those of Finland (and the ability to see this on Finnish television) has always reminded Estonians of what might have been an alternative path of development had they not been occupied in 1940.

The tradition of dissent has ranged from small symbolic acts (such as laying flowers at places connected with independence or hoisting the prohibited national flag in public places) to large student demonstrations (1980) and to the existence of small dissident groups (the Association of Concerned Estonians, the Estonian Democratic Movement). In 1980 40 prominent intellectuals signed an open letter to *Pravda* objecting to the Russification of the republic. By 1983 nearly all open dissidents were arrested and protests became even more muted.

When Mikhail Gorbachev came to power in 1985 and launched his campaign against ageing Brezhnevite officials to secure his position, nothing changed in Estonia. The conservative leadership of the Communist Party of Estonia (CPE) remained intact and it launched a campaign against Estonian nationalism. Under these circumstances people became even more frustrated, expecting relaxation but seeing the opposite. This was the background of the anti-phosphorite campaign.

The environmental protests of 1985–7 started after the decision of the Soviet Ministry of Fertilizer Production to increase open-pit phosphorite mining in the already highly polluted region of north-east Estonia. The most polluting industries of Estonia are subordinate to all-union ministries. Although Estonia was first in the USSR to pass a Nature Protection Act (1957), this legislation does not apply to Moscow-controlled industries (90% of Estonian industries). Estonian youth organized small protest demonstrations in April–May 1987 and public discussions took place in the media. As a result of public pressure, the planned mining of phosphorite was postponed. The success increased the confidence of the people and prepared the ground for further protest actions.

The anniversary of the Molotov–Ribbentrop Pact was for the first time commemorated at Tallinn's Hirvepark on 23 August 1987 with 2000 participants. The demonstration's organizers (ex-prisoners and dissidents) knew that they were supported by the instincts of most Estonians. After the meeting, the Estonian Group for Publication of the Molotov–Ribbentrop Pact (MRP-AEG) was formed.

The Economic Self-Management proposal (IME in Estonian) was published on 26 September 1987. Closet reformers within the establishment were afraid to lose the initiative to the openly pro-independence dissident movement. It was also a logical solution to the ongoing anti-phosphorite campaign. IME proposed that the republic should be granted jurisdiction over its economy, the establishment of a convertible currency and

ESTONIA

Official name	Estonian Soviet Socialist Republic (8 May 1990 Republic of Estonia declared)
Area	45,100 sq. km (17,413 sq. miles)
Population	1,573,000 (1989)
Capital	Tallinn
Language	Estonian, Russian
Religion	Lutheran
Currency	rouble

complete autonomy in trade relations with other countries. Throughout 1987 the proposal was criticized by the Communist Party leadership, but it gained growing public support.

Freedom of the press reached Estonia by 1988, when formerly prohibited subjects (Russification and destruction of the environment) were widely discussed. Since then it has played a major role in mobilizing people for change.

The Estonian Heritage Society (EHS) was formed on 12 December 1987, becoming the first grassroots organization. Its membership grew from 3000 to 10,000 during 1988. The EHS collected personal testimonies from victims of the occupation years, restored monuments destroyed by the Soviets, and organized collections of money for the restoration of the Estonian People's Museum.

A demonstration on 2 February 1988 to commemorate the Estonian–Soviet Peace Treaty of 1920 in Tartu was attacked by the police (the last such case). It brought about a sharp disagreement about tactics between MRP-AEG, standing for confrontational measures, and reformers within the establishment, who, fearing a backlash, were more moderate.

The Independence Day demonstration in Tallinn on 24 February 1988 was organized by the MRP-AEG with 10,000 people participating.

The Popular Front (PF) was unofficially established on 13 April, the Estonian Green Movement (EGM) on 23 May. The national flag colours of blue, black and white were first displayed at a meeting of the EHS in Tartu on 14–17 April 1988.

Spring was the beginning of the 'Singing Revolution' of 1988, which continued into September, when tens of thousands of Estonians waved flags and sang. The summer of 1988 was important because people lost their fear and became active participants in the movements. This frightened the non-Estonian population of the republic, and on 12 July the Internationalist Front (later Intermovement) was formed (formally constituted on 6 March 1989).

After the publication of the secret protocol of the MRP in a party daily newspaper, the MRP-AEG had achieved its short-term goal and re-emerged on 20 August as the Estonian National Independence Party (ENIP), the first opposition party to the CPE. On 2 October 1988 the Popular Front (PF) was formerly constituted when it held its first Congress. It included both Communist and non-Communist Party members and was formed as an umbrella organization to support *perestroika* in Estonia. Its programme called for political changes, including a 'transformation of the USSR from a federal state into a confederation of states' with juridical guarantees and the establishment of a political mechanism for leaving the union. The Communist Party of Estonia had lost its leading role in practical terms, but it tried to rehabilitate itself. The new CPE First Secretary, Vaino Väljas, told the republican party organization in September that there was little to distinguish the new-look party from the Popular

Front. Demands for future sovereign rights were met by the formal granting of symbolically important demands: the restoration of the tri-colour and of local rather than Moscow time, the adoption of Estonian as the state language (January 1989), and the celebration of Christmas as a public holiday.

When the Estonian Supreme Soviet adopted the Declaration of Sovereignty on 16 November, giving the republic the right to veto all-union laws, Vaino Väljas declared that the decision was consistent with the policy of the CPE to encourage local autonomy. Although the Presidium of the USSR Supreme Soviet declared the Estonian sovereignty legislation unconstitutional, the Estonian Supreme Soviet affirmed its decision on 7 December 1988. As a result of all these measures, the CPE was split along national lines.

At dawn on 24 February 1989 when the Estonian tricolour was hoisted in Tallinn by the leaders of the Communist Party and the Popular Front, the Estonian National Independence Party (ENIP), the Estonian Heritage Society (EHS) and the Estonian Christian Union called on the Estonian people to form local committees to register citizens of the interwar Estonian Republic, their descendants and post-1940 immigrants as applicants for Estonian citizenship. After registration a congress of Estonian citizens would be called to discuss the future of Estonia. The Greens declared their support within weeks, the PF withheld total backing, perceiving the Committee as a political challenge.

Further political confrontation developed over elections to the USSR Congress of People's Deputies in March 1989. This was between the ENIP and EHS on the one hand, who stood for the re-establishment of the Republic of Estonia and considered sending Estonian delegates 'to the parliament of a neighbouring state' absurd, and the Popular Front, who supported the elections. About 95% of Estonians and 75% of non-Estonians voted. The supporters of the PF won 27 out of the 36 seats and Interfront won five.

By August the Communist Party of Estonia had come to support the Popular Front's demand for a treaty of confederation between Estonia and the Soviet Union but delivered several attacks on the Citizens' Committees, equating them with the conservative Russian Interfront. Their primary fear was that the Citizens' Committees would create an alternative state power structure.

From 11 to 16 August 1989 Interfront organized strikes and lock-outs, with 30,000 non-Estonian workers protesting against the new electoral law. The week was the highpoint of inter-ethnic tension in Estonia.

By September, some 300,000 people had registered as citizens. Faced with this competition, the Popular Front in October set an independent Estonian Republic as its final goal. This programme coincided with that of the Citizens' Committees (even in calling for the convocation of the Estonian Congress), in all but one crucial point. The PF requested a referendum on independence and on a new Constitution. The ECC denied the need for a referendum because under international law, the Republic still exists *de jure*, a position supported by the Western nations' policy of non-recognition.

The end of 1989 and the beginning of 1990 was a time for forming new political parties, blocs and organizations, on the one hand, and on the other, for the already existing movements to further define and consolidate their strategies. During 1989 the role of the Communist Party diminished very sharply. The cessation of Party activity in the Writers' Union was followed by the dissolution of Komsomol in November. A poll in December showed that no more than 2% of Estonians and 19% of non-Estonians supported the CPE.

By 24 February, the first day of the elections to the Congress of Estonia, 700,000 citizens and applicants had been registered. It was not until 28 January that the Popular Front announced its formal backing to the Congress. By delaying its endorsement the PF could no longer claim to be the leading force among the popular movements. In consequence, the leaders of the PF began to form parties, mainly of a social-democratic type.

The Congress of Estonia was convened on 11 March 1990. It was not organized along ethnic lines but was based on citizenship of the Republic of Estonia. Of the non-Estonian population, 5% had petitioned for citizenship and were represented by 43 non-voting delegates. The Congress created a further structure, a 71-member Council of Estonia (including ten members from the exile communities), who elected from among themselves an 11-member Executive Committee, with Tunne Kelam as chairman. The Congress claimed it was prepared 'to accept parliamentary responsibility should the need arise'. The Supreme Soviet of Estonia, as an organ of the occupation authorities, was to maintain public order and the normal functioning of everyday life, while the Congress was to exercise sole authority over the questions of Estonia's status and its international relations. The majority view at the Congress and in Estonia at large was that there need not be a proclamation of independence, since this was done in 1918.

Three quarters of the members of the newly elected Supreme Soviet support Estonian independence. A number of the Supreme Soviet delegates are also members of the Council of Estonia. At its first session, the newly elected Supreme Soviet stated that the Estonian Soviet Socialist Republic was an occupied country, and gave notice of a period of transition towards full independence. The main task of the two bodies is to prepare economic and political conditions for restoring the Republic of Estonia.

The Estonian Supreme Soviet also passed a law on 8 May on state symbols, restoring the name of the pre-war Estonian state – 'the Republic of Estonia' – and abandoning the state emblem, anthem and flag of the Estonian SSR.

On 26 May about 200 local and Supreme Soviet Russian deputies set up the Inter-Regional Soviet of People's Deputies and Workers of the ESSR in Kohtla-Järve to preserve Soviet rule in north-east Estonia, but there was increasing confusion among Moscow-loyalists as demands for sovereignty begin mounting in the Russian Federation itself. According to a poll conducted in the spring, about one-third of the Russian-speaking population supported Estonian independence. But the election of Boris Yeltsin as the President of the Russian Federation and his commitment to setting Russian laws above those of the Soviet Union promised to incline the attitude of some Russians towards independence. Although the requests from the Estonian government for negotiations with Moscow about independence met with consistent rebuffs, preparations for economic independence and steps towards a market economy move slowly forward. The new government under the premiership of Edgar Savisaar plans to introduce the convertible Estonian kroon by the beginning of 1991. Close economic ties are being set up with Finland and Sweden.

Latvia

The Latvians are members of the Baltic group of Indo-European peoples. The territory was invaded in the twelfth century by the Germans and later by the Poles and Swedes, and in 1795 it became a part of the Russian Empire. In the interwar years Latvia already had a high percentage of ethnic minorities (24.5% in 1935). Under the Soviet occupation the Latvians' share has decreased to 51.8% (1989), which gives the nationalist issue a special urgency.

Latvia fared worse than Lithuania and Estonia during the 1960s and 1970s because of the Latvian purge of 1959–61 by Khrushchev, who accused the Latvian leadership of pursuing a policy of Latvianization. Some 2000 party and government officials were expelled, and were replaced by Russians and the *latovichi* (Soviet-born people with nominal Latvian lineage who came to Latvia after 1945). Since then, Latvians have been in the minority in the Communist Party of Latvia. The worst policies of Russification were carried out by two *latovichi*, Arvids Pelše and Augusts Voss, who favoured extensive immigration. During the postwar period over 700,000 immigrants have settled in Latvia. The political purge of 1959 also changed the cultural atmosphere of the republic. As late as 1967, an ex-Stalinist critic considered the stagnation in Latvian literature to be worse than under Stalin. Even folklore groups were prohibited. But Latvians, like Estonians and Lithuanians, learned to channel their national feelings into their culture. The young poets, Ojars Vacietis, Imants Ziedonis, Maris Caklais and Janis Peters, were popular in the 1960s because their poems were the only means of telling the truth about the past and the present. The revival of folklore groups at the end of the 1970s also became part of the Latvian struggle for self-esteem. They told the people that the continuity of the generations had been kept alive through folk songs and folk wisdom and that this link could not be broken.

LATVIA

Official name	Latvian Soviet Socialist Republic (4 May 1990 Republic of Latvia declared)
Area	63,700 sq. km (24,590 sq. miles)
Population	2,681,000 (1989)
Capital	Riga
Language	Latvian, Russian
Religion	Lutheran
Currency	rouble

During the 1980s groups of young people started restoring derelict churches and architectural monuments. All this activity helped to raise the Latvian national consciousness which the authorities had tried to suppress. These groups later joined the Environmental Protection Club (EPC) in the spring of 1986.

In July 1986 five people in Liepaja founded Helsinki 86 to monitor Soviet compliance with the 1975 Helsinki accords. These were people who had consciously remained outside the establishment, and although their work was manual, their background was often intellectual. Their *samizdat* bulletin *Tevija* (Fatherland) informed people about the activities of the KGB and human rights campaigns at a time when the republican press kept silent on such issues. They were also the first to organize mass demonstrations on 14 June and 23 August. Both were disrupted by the police. The group had no desire to become a mass-membership organization, but they tested the ground for the coming mass movements.

In October 1986 a campaign was launched to stop construction work of the Daugavpils Hydro-Electric Station on the Daugava River. An important role in the upsurge in public protest was played by an article by Dainis Ivans and Arturs Snips in the newspaper, *Literatura un Maksla*. On 6 November it was announced that the Soviet government had discontinued the project. For the first time in 50 years, Latvian public opinion had gained a victory.

In 1988 the leadership was taken over by the Latvian intelligentsia and other reformers within the establishment. A demonstration held in Bralu Kapi cemetery on 25 March to commemorate the deportation of 43,000 Latvians in 1949 was organized by the Creative Unions, and was the first peaceful demonstration without police interference in the postwar period.

On 27 April the Environmental Protection Club (EPC) organized a demonstration against the planned construction of the Riga Metro. They argued that this would lower the water table, affect the fragile foundations of old historical buildings and bring in thousands of immigrant workers. The EPC made it possible to hold an alternative point of view, and was especially popular among young people, who saw environmentalism as an expression of spiritual values.

The Latvian Writers' Union convened a plenum for representatives from all the Unions of creative workers on 1 June, which was a turning-point in the events of 1988. The speeches showed a degree of political expression and openness not hitherto seen at an official gathering in Soviet Latvia. The plenum adopted a resolution demanding the recognition of Latvia as a sovereign national state within a Soviet Federation with diplomatic representation. This helped to form an alliance between seventeen leading intellectuals, human rights activists from Helsinki 86, and clergy, who formed an organizing committee with the aim of founding a Popular Front (PF). But in order not to be too confrontational, the human rights activists were excluded from the committee, and the PF became more closely affiliated with the Latvian intelligentsia. Like the Estonian Popular Front, the Latvian PF became an umbrella organization, accommodating different movements.

In June 1988 the National Independence Movement of Latvia (NIML) was established under the leadership of Eduards Berklavs among others (purged in 1959). The existence of NIML and its openly pro-independence programme was instrumental in forcing the PF to adopt a similar stance later. In many cases, the NIML has taken credit for parts of the Popular Front (PF) programme. The main point of difference between the NIML and PF is in tactics. While the PF seeks to achieve independence through 'step-by-step' parliamentarian means (working with the present Soviet Latvian government), the NIML views the existing Latvian government as illegal and has taken a more confrontational approach.

In July in the procession of a folklore festival, 'Baltica', folklorists were among the first to bring out the Latvian national flag. They had proved themselves to be, in a real sense, the flag-bearers of Latvia's heritage.

The founding congress of the Popular Front took place on 8 October. One-third of the 1000 delegates were Communists. A Governing Council with 100 representatives was elected and after the congress this body elected a 13-member board, with Dainis Ivans as president. From the start, the PF has promoted pluralism and has included representatives from the NIML, the Environmental Protection Club, Helsinki 86 and the Lutheran Movement for Rebirth and Renewal. In October the PF began publishing a weekly newspaper, *Atmoda* (Awakening), which has become the most widely read weekly in Latvia. At its inception, the PF adopted a programme calling for Latvia's sovereignty within the USSR.

As a reaction to the congress, the Latvian International Working People's Front (or Interfront) was formed mainly by Russian speakers. Claiming the support of 48% of Russian speakers, it held its founding congress on 7 January 1989. Latvians view Interfront as a group of neo-Stalinists.

The significance of 1988 was that it saw the eclipse of the previous atmosphere of fear and hopelessness by a new enthusiasm and optimism. The following year was one of large-scale demonstrations and the foundation of new political organizations.

On 18 and 19 February 1989 the National Independence Movement of Latvia (NIML) held its first congress in Ogre. Many NIML members were also members of the Popular Front. The Presidium of the Latvian Supreme Soviet declared the programme, statutes and resolutions of the NIML to be in conflict with the Latvian SSR Constitution, and the Communist Party of Latvia publicly denounced the NIML as unconstitutional. Following government threats to ban the organization, the NIML organized an extraordinary congress on 28 May. The congress, however, further consolidated its demands for total economic and political independence.

On 26 March about 70% of the population voted in the National

Congress of the USSR elections. Candidates endorsed by the PF won 26 out of 34 seats. The Communist Party of Latvia's First Secretary, Janis Vagris, won barely 51% of votes in his district, largely due to the 'offshore' vote of the Baltic merchant marine fleet, which was conveyed by telegram from ships at sea at the last minute.

A political opposition party, the Latvian National Rebirth Party was formed in Riga on 2 April.

A delegation of 24 Popular Front leaders went on a one-month tour of Canada and the USA to legalize, within Latvia, the western Latvian emigré organizations such as the American Latvian Association. A symposium with over 100 West Latvian social and business leaders took place in Gananoque, Canada.

On 10 April a co-ordinating body for the registration of all citizens of the Latvian Republic and their descendants, the Latvian Citizenship Committee (LCC), was formed, sponsored by four informal organizations – the NIML, Helsinki 86, EPC and the Riga Chapter of Helsinki 86. The goal of the LCC was to convene a Congress of Latvian Citizens which would serve as the legal representative of the citizens of the Republic of Latvia. The PF expressed support for the concept of the Citizens' Committees, but the support of the Executive Board was lukewarm, although the local chapters were actively involved in the registration process. Registration started in June.

Inspired by the National Independence Movement congress, the Executive Board of the Popular Front proposed a referendum on 'total political and economic independence' for Latvia on 31 May. It was declared that 'the goal of the PF is to achieve national Latvian independence'. This appeal marked a major departure from the previously stated goal of a 'sovereign' Latvia within the framework of a federation of Soviet states.

In July a new party, the Christian Democratic Party, was formed by a pastor, Oskars Bogdanovs. The leadership of the Latvian Lutheran Church disassociated itself from the new party. The oldest Latvian political party, the Latvian Social Democratic Workers Party (LSDWP), resumed its activities under the leadership of Valdis Steins but subsequently split into two parties.

The proclamation of sovereignty and economic independence on 28 July 1989 was not as bold as the similar declarations adopted by the Estonian and Lithuanian Supreme Soviets. The Latvian legislature chose to follow in the footsteps of its neighbours rather than initiating something new, a course of action that illustrates the inherent cautiousness of the Latvian leadership.

On 7–8 October the Second Congress of the Popular Front adopted a programme with an open call for total political and economic independence, outside the USSR. It also supported a free market and a multi-party system.

Candidates supported by the Popular Front won some 70% of the seats at the election to the local councils in December. This was a major victory, which demonstrated that non-Latvians take less interest in political changes.

A multi-party system was introduced in Latvia on 11 January 1990. After that, a number of new parties were established (the Latvian Green Party, the Latvian Social Democratic Party, the Liberal Party and the Democratic Party).

Elections to the Latvian SSR Supreme Soviet on 18 March were real multi-party elections. The PF, the NIML and other democratic parties and movements formed a Democratic Bloc (the largest); influential Communist Party members and leading intellectuals formed a fringe coalition 'For the Latvian State, For a Free People' and farmers formed an independent Latvian Farmers Union. The candidates of the Interfront stood in opposition. The nationalist parties and movements won over two-thirds of the total of 201 seats.

The Latvian Citizenship Committee was formed on the example of a similar movement in Estonia in April 1989 (see above). By May, around 900,000 people had registered as citizens of Latvia. The Congress of Latvia took place on 1–2 May and elected the Committee of Latvia with Aigars Jirgens as chairman.

The newly-elected Supreme Soviet held its first session on 3–4 May and elected Anatolijs Gorbunovs as President and Ivars Godmanis as the Prime Minister. On 4 May the Supreme Soviet renamed the country the 'Republic of Latvia' and annulled the annexation of Latvia by the USSR. No co-operation has yet developed between the new Supreme Soviet and the Committee of Latvia.

Lithuania

The Lithuanians are members of the Baltic branch of the Indo-European peoples. Unlike Estonia and Latvia, Lithuania can look back on a period when it was itself 'a great power'. United dynastically and later constitutionally with Poland, Polish–Lithuanian Union was the greatest force in Eastern Europe, extending from the Baltic to the Black Sea, in the fifteenth and sixteenth centuries. The Lithuanian territories fell under Russian rule in 1795, and the policy of Russification also included suppression of the Roman Catholic Church. As a result, the close identification of Catholicism with nationalism has persisted to the present day.

The establishment of independence was more complicated than in Latvia and Estonia because of the dispute with Poland over Lithuania's historic capital, Vilnius. Lithuania was unable to prevent Poland from occupying Vilnius in 1920 and was forced to nominate a temporary capital in Kaunas. The 1939 Molotov–Ribbentrop Pact assigned Lithuania to the German sphere of interest, but after September 1939, when the USSR invaded East Poland and occupied Vilnius, Hitler was obliged to consign

LITHUANIA

Official name	Lithuanian Soviet Socialist Republic (11 March 1990 Republic of Lithuania declared)
Area	65,200 sq. km (25,165 sq. miles)
Population	3,690,000 (1989)
Capital	Vilnius
Language	Lithuanian, Russian
Religion	Roman Catholic, Lutheran minority
Currency	rouble

Lithuania to the Soviet sphere. After the Mutual Assistance Pact with the USSR on 10 October 1939, Soviet troops were stationed in Lithuania. In November the USSR restored Vilnius as the Lithuanian capital. Unlike Latvia and Estonia, Lithuania was a predominantly agrarian country.

Armed guerrilla resistance was maintained into the 1950s and a total of about 100,000 Lithuanians are estimated to have been involved.

After the war, religious dissent was the strongest manifestation of organized opposition to the Soviet regime. The main *samizdat* publication, *The Chronicle of the Lithuanian Catholic Church*, dates back to 1972. In 1978 (after the election of Pope John Paul II) five priests formed a Catholic Committee for the Defence of Believers' Rights, which became the unofficial spokesman for the Catholic Church in the USSR. In the 1970s and 1980s Lithuania produced more *samizdat* per capita than any other area of the USSR.

Mikhail Gorbachev's first campaign in the USSR was against alcoholism. This only followed that of the Lithuanian bishops, who had proclaimed 1980 to be 'The Year of Temperance'. The Lithuanian Supreme Soviet passed a similar decree, but that remained the only issue in which the Communist Party of Lithuania followed Gorbachev with any enthusiasm.

The anxiety about Chernobyl in April 1986 was higher in Lithuania than elsewhere in the USSR because people discovered the full scale of the disaster through Polish radio and television. The evasive official Soviet press reports were in sharp contrast to precautions taken in Poland, and left Lithuanians uneasy. Less than 80 miles from Vilnius at Ignalina, the first reactor of the world's largest nuclear power station was already operating with a Chernobyl-type reactor and the second was to go on-line in 1986. Some Lithuanians were aware of reports by Swedish experts in August of cases of increased radiation levels from Ignalina. The absence of any information about Ignalina in the local press until April 1988 prepared the ground for environmental protests, which led to demands for economic autonomy and to the formation of a movement for the support of *perestroika*.

At the beginning of 1987 several leading dissidents were released from prison. This helped to restore dissident groups, including the Lithuanian Freedom League (LFL). Since its foundation, the group had advocated full independence, and had been the first to test the credibility of democratization by organizing public demonstrations on 23 August 1987 and on 16 February and 22 May 1988 (the anniversary of the 1948 deportations). The League helped to raise national consciousness and, by uncompromisingly promoting independence, radicalized other movements.

The Lithuanian Restructuring Movement (commonly referred to as *Sajudis* or the Movement) was founded on 3 June 1988 by Party and non-Party intellectuals. Since *Sajudis* had been formed against the wishes of the Communist Party, its creation heralded a split within the Party itself.

During the summer *Sajudis* increased its support among the people by organizing mass demonstrations.

Of special importance was a demonstration by the Freedom League on 28 September, when a violent confrontation between police and demonstrators took place. *Sajudis* formed an alliance with the Freedom League by protesting against the violent action.

The policies of the Communist Party of Lithuania were criticized not only by *Sajudis* but also by the Communist Party of the Soviet Union. When a Politburo member, Aleksander Yakovlev, came to Lithuania in August 1988 he had pressed the Communist Party of Lithuania to be more active in directing change, to harness the 'national factor' as a force for reform, and not to lose its leading role (which it had already lost). After Yakovlev's visit the Lithuanian national flag and anthem were accorded equal status with the symbols of Communism. It was announced that further construction of the Ignalina nuclear power station would cease. Communist Party members could remain in *Sajudis*; and *Sajudis* would be allowed television coverage. After the Party order to suppress the September demonstration, Moscow decided to remove the inflexible leadership by promoting Algirdas Brazauskas as the Party's First Secretary a few days before the *Sajudis* congress.

The constituent congress of *Sajudis* on 22–23 October was a middle-class gathering, dominated by intellectuals. The congress elected a 220-member Assembly (*Seimas*) and a 35-member National Council. *Sajudis* acted as an informal organization, but, by public consent, it had deprived the Communist Party of Lithuania of its leading role.

The popularity of the Party increased with the introduction of Lithuanian as a state language. The co-operation of the Communists with *Sajudis* lasted until 18 November (a day after the Estonian Supreme Soviet had declared the sovereignty of Estonian law), when Algirdas Brazauskas managed to persuade the Lithuanian Supreme Soviet not to follow the Estonian example. That was the day when the Communist Party of Lithuania won in Parliament but lost in the country, and *Sajudis* lost in Parliament but won in the country. From its first defeat, *Sajudis* emerged as a much stronger organization by electing Vytautas Landsbergis as its president, and clarifying the criteria of membership. Despite the fact that the Communists had made further concessions (the release of political prisoners and the designation of Christmas and Independence Day as public holidays), by the time of the spring elections to the USSR Congress of People's Deputies in 1989, the Party had already lost control of the media, youth, higher education and part of its own membership.

Sajudis had another challenger in the Freedom League, the Christian Democratic Party (revived in February) and the Helsinki Group, all three of which boycotted the elections. Nevertheless, 82.5% of those eligible to vote took part in the March elections to the USSR Congress of People's Deputies. *Sajudis* won 36 of the 42 seats in the Congress. Algirdas

Brazauskas and his second secretary, Vladimiras Beriozovas, were elected because *Sajudis* did not contest their candidacies. A number of other top-level party officials were defeated.

On 18 May 1989 (exactly 6 months after the first rejection of sovereignty) the Lithuanian Supreme Soviet issued a declaration on state sovereignty and a law on economic sovereignty, asserting that all Lithuania's natural resources and all its territory, transportation, energy and communications enterprises were the property of the republic, and assuming its own right to veto legislation and legal acts by the USSR state government. It also established Lithuanian citizenship and control over immigration. The Communist Party of Lithuania had to accede to the demands of the voters and was forced to recognize that the movement for *perestroika* had become a national liberation movement against Soviet colonialism and Communism. It was at this time that the Party, in order not to be completely defeated, took the decision to become an independent Lithuanian Communist Party.

In such a political climate Lithuanian political leaders took steps to establish closer links with Lithuanian emigré communities in the West. Their meeting took place on the island of Gotland, Sweden, in August.

Since autumn 1989, Lithuania has acted in direct confrontation with Moscow. In September the Lithuanian Supreme Soviet passed laws on citizenship and referendums and amended Article 50 of the Constitution to give greater rights to believers.

On 6 December 1989 the Lithuanian Supreme Soviet decided to abolish the Communist Party's monopoly and establish the first multi-party system in the USSR. The Lithuanian Communist Party won much political capital by declaring its independence from Moscow on 20 December. The Party also benefited from the leadership of Lithuania's most popular politician, Algirdas Brazauskas. The independent Communist Party of Lithuania has a membership of 70,000. The continuing Communist Party of Lithuania, loyal to the CPSU, draws its support mainly from Russian-speaking Communists. The Lithuanian Christian Democratic Party, re-established in January 1990, could become an influential force. It was the largest party in pre-war Lithuania and has the backing of the Catholic Church.

The first test of the new multi-party system took place on 24 February, when *Sajudis* won 88 seats in the 141-seat Lithuanian Supreme Soviet. The newly elected Supreme Council proclaimed Lithuanian independence on 11 March 1990. Vytautas Landsbergis was elected as president, and Mrs Kazimiera Prunskiene became prime minister. The strategy of the Lithuanian government was to establish a legal basis for negotiations with Moscow founded on the presumption that Lithuania is already an independent state. Had this been acceptable to Moscow, they would have been prepared to be extremely flexible on the question of ownership of sections of the economy. In the event, the Supreme Soviet of the USSR declared

Lithuania's declaration of independence invalid, and Moscow's immediate response was to rule out negotiations. Shortly afterwards, Gorbachev declared himself in favour of a dialogue. Although Moscow had pledged not to use force, the military presence indicated that the Soviet government was determined to make a 'show of force' in the Baltic republic. Lithuania, however, responded to this provocation without any violence. On 16 April the central government imposed economic sanctions on the rebellious republic and despite a tour by Mrs Kazimiera Prunskiene to the Nordic countries, the USA, and the United Kingdom, by the middle of June, Lithuania had exhausted its reserves of energy. Despite lobbying by the Baltic communities in the West on behalf of their compatriots, Lithuania failed to become a major factor in the summit meeting of President Bush and President Gorbachev at the beginning of June, being eclipsed as a priority by the settlement of the German question. The Lithuanian people took comfort in the belief that by imposing sanctions against their nation, the government of the USSR had incidentally recognized the independent status of Lithuania. It is important to recognize that, under the Soviet centralized planning system, the economic blockade also affects other parts of the USSR. For this reason, both sides are interested in restoring normal relations, and Lithuania's ambition for self-determination may yet be fulfilled.

Conclusion

From the time of Gorbachev's accession to power in March 1985 the political aspirations of most of the people of the Baltic republics have evolved along with (and in certain cases determined) the general flow of *perestroika*. While the initial goal in 1986 was for greater cultural sovereignty, by 1987 it had come to include economic and, by late 1988, political sovereignty. The consensus by late 1989 and early 1990 was a clear desire for fully fledged independence. It remains to be seen which way brings the republics closer to their goal.

During the period 1987–9 it is possible to discern an interplay between three basic political forces. The first is represented by restorationist movements, the aim of which, from the very beginning, has been the restoration of the independent republics. The most significant are the National Independence Party of Estonia, the National Independence Movement of Latvia and the Lithuanian Freedom League. Their members are former political prisoners, human rights activists and people who have not co-operated with the political establishment. Their uncompromising confrontational tactics appeal to young people. This force has radicalized the centrists, who form the second force. Centrists comprise movements that work within the existing political structures (the Supreme Soviet, the Communist Party, Unions of Writers, Architects, Journalists, etc.) who prefer to work for change step by step. The intellectuals, technocrats and rank and file Communist Party members take up this position. Both the

Estonian and Latvian Popular Fronts and the Lithuanian *Sajudis* are numbered within this force. All of them had stood for the sovereignty of the Baltic republics within the Soviet confederation, but because of pressure from the restorationists they later came to support political independence. The third force, anti-reformist or conservative, includes Russian-speaking Party officials, the military, bureaucrats and immigrant workers who do not wish to lose their privileged status. None of them speak the local languages and all feel isolated from the present political movements. This force is represented by the Estonian and Latvian Interfronts and the Lithuanian *Yedinstvo*.

The co-operation of Lithuanians, Latvians and Estonians has been another key to their success. All the larger movements, both centrists and restorationists, have been organizing meetings to work out future tactics. The restorationists have tried to involve Ukrainians, Armenians, Georgians, Moldavians and others.

Of great importance in co-ordinating the work of the Popular Fronts and *Sajudis* has been the Baltic Council, founded at a 'Baltic Assembly' in May 1989 in Tallinn, which worked out a united programme for reform.

A Baltic parliamentary group formed by 90 of the deputies of the three republics in 1989 pressed for the creation of a commission of the USSR Supreme Soviet to investigate the MRP and for the acceptance of Moscow of Baltic economic autonomy. Before the fiftieth anniversary of the signing of the Molotov–Ribbentrop Pact on 23 August, 14 members of the USSR Supreme Soviet commission (but not its chairman, Aleksander Yakovlev, who maintained that the Pact had no connection with the incorporation of the Baltic states) concluded that the pact had infringed the rights of third countries, including the Baltic states. They recommended that the USSR Supreme Soviet should declare these protocols invalid. The Congress of People's Deputies adopted a watered-down version of the report on 24 December 1989.

The three popular fronts organized a 400-mile human chain on 23 August 1989, with nearly 2 million people commemorating the 50th anniversary of the Molotov–Ribbentrop pact. It was the largest anti-Soviet demonstration ever held on Soviet territory. After the CPSU Central Committee's condemnation of Baltic separatism, the Popular Fronts and *Sajudis* asked the United Nations to send a human rights commission to the Baltic republics, and requested a debate on the Baltic question at a UN General Assembly meeting.

Another Baltic joint action was to press the USSR Supreme Soviet to adopt a law on Baltic economic independence. Although the law was adopted on 27 November 1989 and was to go into force on 1 January 1990, the Moscow ministries have refused to hand over key elements of the economy to the Baltic authorities. Another blow came when the Estonian and Lithuanian branches of the USSR Foreign Trade Bank were closed in January. The provisions of economic autonomy are dictated by Moscow, and it has become increasingly clear that economic independence is impossible without political sovereignty.

Although in January 1990 Gorbachev had offered a new looser federation with great autonomy, and a mechanism by which a republic could secede, the Baltic deputies did not believe that such decrees were practicable. They further argued that the law of secession could not apply in their case. They did not voluntarily join the USSR, therefore secession was unnecessary. The inability to achieve greater sovereignty and economic independence through the decrees of the USSR People's Congress has been the main reason why the Estonian and (to a lesser degree) the Latvian Popular Fronts are pressing for confrontational measures. The political changes in Eastern Europe in 1989 (especially in East Germany) with the Soviet policy of non-intervention there gave the confrontational tactics more credibility.

All three republics have declared their countries' 'entry' into the USSR illegal and have sought to begin negotiations with Moscow on their independence. The economic blockade imposed by Moscow on Lithuania has brought the three Baltic republics closer together. Although Moscow has been trying to use a policy of 'divide and conquer' by offering Estonia and Latvia a special status, the Baltic unity was sealed with the renewal of a 1934 Treaty on Unity and Co-operation by the presidents of Estonia, Latvia and Lithuania on 12 May in Tallinn.

Liberalization and the achieving of real independence is a long-term process for two reasons; firstly, the countries are economically tied to the USSR and secondly, the USSR is interested in the region for strategic reasons and would seek to preserve at least part of its troops there, especially as it has to withdraw its troops from the countries of Eastern Europe.

For the Baltic States history is repeating itself. Once again world attention is concentrated on the fate of Germany and the dissolution of the Russian Empire. As in the period 1918–1920, when the Baltic peoples gained their independence, so, once again Lithuania, Latvia and Estonia must await the verdict of history on their powerful neighbours, before their own fate can be known.

12 BYELORUSSIA
Change on the way – but not yet

Population

Byelorussia is one of the fifteen constituent republics of the Soviet Union. As a founder member of the United Nations, it has full representation, alongside the USSR and Ukraine, both on that body and its dependent agencies.

The composition of the country's population reflects the complex and turbulent history of an area which for centuries had consisted of large landed estates – and therefore a mainly peasant population – and small, predominantly Jewish, towns. A breakdown into urban (65.5%) and rural (34.5%) population reveals the increasing rate of urbanization. The corresponding figures for the previous census of 1979 were 55% and 44.9%, respectively, and 7.9 million of the population declare themselves to be Byelorussians, of whom 80.2% regard Byelorussian as their first language, as against 83.5% in 1979. There are 1,342,000 Russians, of whom only 24.5% claim a fluent command of Byelorussian, a decrease from 29.4% in 1979. Some connection is discernible between the increase in numbers of Russians and the growth of the urban population. The number of people who regard themselves as Poles has increased (418,000 as compared with 403,000 in 1979), whereas the Jews continue to decline (112,000, down from 135,000 in 1979), largely as a result of emigration to Israel.

History

The earliest medieval Byelorussian state can be said to have developed around the city of Polotsk on the river Dvina. From the thirteenth century onwards Byelorussian lands were incorporated into the growing Grand Duchy of Lithuania. Despite its name, the Grand Duchy was a predominantly Slavonic state throughout its history, with a form of Byelorussian serving as its official language until 1696. As a result of union with Poland in 1569, the nobility became increasingly Polish in language and religion, switching from Orthodoxy to Roman Catholicism, and leaving the peasantry with no kind of leadership. The partitions of Poland at the end of the eighteenth century brought the Byelorussians into the Russian Empire. The growth of a new Byelorussian national consciousness can be traced to about the middle of the nineteenth century, largely as a result of the interest taken by ethnographers and folklorists in the inhabitants of the poorest and most backward part of European Russia. The first attempts

BYELORUSSIA

Official name	Byelorussian Soviet Socialist Republic
Area	208,000 sq. km (80,290 sq. miles)
Population	10,200,000 (1989)
Capital	Minsk
Language	Byelorussian, Russian
Religion	Roman Catholic, Russian Orthodox, with Baptist and Muslim minorities
Currency	rouble

were made to revive the language as a means of written communication, although they soon fell foul of the Tsarist censorship.

The national revival really commenced at the beginning of this century, and here, as elsewhere in east and central Europe, writers and intellectuals were in the vanguard. In 1914 the country once again became a battleground. The front line divided the country, and as a result national activities were split between Vilnia (Wilno, Vilnius) under German occupation and St Petersburg. The Bolshevik October Revolution of 1917 and the ensuing chaos gave what national leadership there was a chance to try to establish some form of autonomy or even an independent state. A Byelorussian National Republic was declared on 25 March 1918, but without armed forces of its own or international recognition it was doomed to fall prey to marauding Polish bands and German troops. Undoubtedly as the result of nationalist pressure, a Byelorussian Soviet Republic was declared in January 1919. The ensuing war between Soviet Russia and Poland led once again to the division of Byelorussia.

The Byelorussian Soviet Republic in the 1920s, based on little more than the province of Minsk, gave every appearance of developing into a truly national state. The language was encouraged, a national educated elite was in the process of formation. All this changed under Stalin. Writers and intellectuals were exiled; many of them were killed or died in Siberian labour camps. We now know, as a result of the discovery of the mass graves at Kurapaty near Minsk, that extermination was taking place on a grand scale in Byelorussia itself in the late 1930s. Language laws were promulgated to ensure that Byelorussian became more like Russian.

Life for Byelorussians under Polish rule was better, because they were at least spared the worst excesses of persecution. The Polish civil and religious authorities, however, did not tolerate too much cultural independence on the part of their Byelorussian minority, some 6% of the total population.

The Nazi–Soviet pact of 1939 is often viewed as paving the way for the division of Poland. It is equally valid to say that it led to the reunification of Byelorussia. The western frontier came to correspond more or less to the Polish-Soviet demarcation line that had been proposed by the British Foreign Minister, Lord Curzon, in 1920. The pact did not, of course, save Byelorussia from war and suffering during the German occupation in 1941–4. The present western frontier of Byelorussia was established by agreement with what was then the Polish People's Republic.

Politics

The political life of Byelorussia after the war has inevitably been dominated by the leading role of the Communist Party of the Soviet Union (the now notorious Article 6 of both the USSR and Byelorussian constitutions). Preoccupied with the need to rebuild the country's economy for which help from Moscow was absolutely essential, Byelorussia's political leaders seemed to follow a particularly subservient line. The one exception was P. M. Masherov, a popular First Secretary of the Byelorussian Communist Party, who died in a road accident in 1980. Rumours immediately began to circulate that he had been murdered by the KGB acting on instructions from Brezhnev himself. It now seems to have been a genuine accident, although facts are emerging about how Masherov refused to indulge Brezhnev's love of expensive presents. The current First Secretary, E. E. Sokolov, is regarded by many as a colourless *apparatchik*.

It is undeniable that what amounted to a deliberate policy of Russification was being pursued in the 1960s and 1970s. Fewer books in Byelorussian were produced, the print runs of Byelorussian newspapers were cut, the country's history was subjected to gross distortions, many writers were either completely banned or had selected works excised from their total output, the language was taught in an ever-decreasing number of schools. By the middle of the 1980s the situation had become so bad that there was not a single school in the capital city teaching its children in Byelorussian. As with the national revival earlier in the century, writers and intellectuals were the first to sound the alarm. Boldness inspired by *glasnost* has led to the publication of more and more previously banned works. A new and fresh look is being taken at Byelorussia's history with the aim of demonstrating that they are not simply Russians with a different name. A Byelorussian Language Association has been set up to foster the use of the language in all spheres. As in many other parts of the Soviet Union, there is also a Popular Front. It developed rather later than similar organizations in, for example, the Baltic republics, undoubtedly as a result of the weaker national self-awareness, but immediately encountered the implacable hostility of the authorities. The founding meeting on 24–25 June 1989 had to be held in Vilnius in accommodation provided by *Sajudis*, the Lithuanian Popular Front. It still does not have official permission to exist. The authorities refuse to register it on the grounds that several of its stated aims are 'unconstitutional', although nowhere does it state that it will seek to withdraw Byelorussia from the Soviet Union. In fact its aims centre on raising the status of the Byelorussian language and culture generally, on doing more to remedy the ecological disaster caused in a large area of Byelorussia by the Chernobyl accident, and on increasing Byelorussia's economic independence from the rest of the USSR.

The government has, to some extent, adopted the Front's policies on language in a watered-down form. Byelorussian was declared the official state language of the republic in the Law on Languages in the BSSR passed on 26 January 1990, and effective from 1 September. It is evident from the provisions of this law that Russian will continue to occupy a (cynical realists will probably say 'the') major place in the life of the state, and not only in its role as a 'means of interethnic communication'. A period of three years has been granted for Byelorussian to become the language of the media, but when it comes to education, including universities, the drafters of the law appear to believe that ten years will be necessary to make the switch from Russian. The law does not, of course, cover language use by armed forces, including frontier troops, stationed in Byelorussia.

As far as the aftermath of Chernobyl is concerned, the government is at last beginning to make information about radiation levels generally available in the press, although there is said to be considerable unease among the population which, at times and in certain areas, borders on panic. According to the permanent representative of the BSSR at the United Nations Organization, Lev Maksimov, 17 billion roubles (almost equivalent to two annual budgets for the republic) are required to undo the ecological damage caused in Byelorussia. Only a few days later I. Lishtvan, vice-president of the Byelorussian Academy of Sciences, mentioned a figure of 23 billion roubles. The affected area, with a population of 2,200,000 people (a detailed map was published in *Sovetskaia Belorussiia* on 7 March 1990), amounts to 70% of the total area of the European part of the USSR polluted by radioactive fallout. About 20% of Byelorussia's agricultural land and almost 15% of its forests have become unusable. A draft national programme has been drawn up, covering the years 1990–5, but still awaits confirmation from Moscow (presumably because of the resources involved). Provision is in the meantime being made for the resettlement of 7454 families in 1990 alone. Lishtvan gives a figure of about 120,000 people. (The Byelorussian Ecological Union is demanding the resettlement of over 300,000.) The Byelorussian Supreme Soviet has made an appeal for international aid, somewhat belatedly when one considers the claim made by a major government figure, A. T. Kichkailo, that information about radiation levels in Byelorussia was removed from the list of official secrets back in July 1988, before similar information was made available anywhere else in the Soviet Union. He is evidently seeking to counter the statements about inadequate government measures emanating from the Popular Front. Another senior member of the government, N. I. Dementei, Chairman of the Presidium of the Byelorussian Supreme Soviet, seeks to place the blame for the delay on 'almost four years of debate among scientists' as to the best course of action. Writing in the weekly newspaper of the Byelorussian Writers' Union on 16 March this year, academician R. Haretski states quite categorically that the delay was caused solely by the Party and Government.

The 1990 elections

Cultural and ecological matters were in the forefront of the electorate's attention during the period immediately before the elections to the Byelorussian Supreme Soviet on 4 March. The elections, in which 1427 candidates competed for 360 seats, were not held on a multi-party basis; the Popular Front, without official registration, was not permitted to put up its own candidates. The 'national ticket' was therefore frequently represented by candidates from organizations like the Byelorussian Language Association or the Byelorussian Ecological Union. There were accusations that even reached the press of local electoral committees' refusing to register certain candidates. Leaflets were widely circulated accusing the authorities of permitting Soviet troops stationed in Poland to participate in the Byelorussian elections. Clearly, such voters would have no knowledge of or interest in Byelorussian national affairs. The party and government bosses, E. E. Sokolov and N. I. Dementei, were so lacking in confidence that they would be elected if they stood in Minsk, they put themselves forward as candidates in rural districts of Brest province, where they were in fact duly returned. Despite a massive hostile press campaign, the leader of the Popular Front, Z. Pazniak, was elected. The Orthodox Metropolitan of Minsk and Grodno, Filaret, failed to gain sufficient votes in the first round of voting and accordingly had to submit himself to a second round of voting on 17–18 March, in which he was successful. The local government chief in Grodno, D. K. Artsimenia, was elected partially as the result of a campaign of support conducted by the Roman Catholic clergy of the area in the form of pulpit addresses and leaflets in Polish, this to ensure that a nationally minded Byelorussian candidate was not elected. This echoes a trend observed earlier in Lithuania, where the Polish minority provided support for the pro-Moscow Communist Party.

In the event, elections to about 280 of the 360 seats were held on 4 March. Further elections in most of the remaining constituencies took place on 22 April.

More details have emerged about the run-up to the elections on 4 March and the actual results. (The information comes from the first issue of a Byelorussian-language journal, *Svaboda*, published in April in Riga, in an article by V. Ivashkevich, chairman of the electoral commission of the Popular Front.)

On 10 February the Popular Front was instrumental in organizing an All-Byelorussian Democratic Forum, at which a Byelorussian Democratic Bloc was set up to fight the elections to the Byelorussian Supreme Soviet. Apart from the Popular Front, the Bloc comprised the Byelorussian Language Association, the Byelorussian Ecological Union, all the 'creative associations' (i.e. writers, artists, composers, cinema workers), the Byelorussian Workers' Association (a nascent free trade-union), the Byelorussian Peasants' Association and the Academy of Sciences. A public opinion poll carried out on behalf of the Byelorussian Communist Party revealed the following average figures for the whole of the country: 8% support for the Party, 14% support for the Popular Front, 78% undecided. In the large towns these figures changed to: 5% for and 48% against the Party, 40% for and 12% against the Popular Front, with about 50% undecided.

The Democratic Bloc was able to put up candidates in only 150 of the 360 constituencies (310 of these constituencies were organized on a territorial basis, the remaining 50 were allocated to the associations of the deaf, the blind, invalids and war veterans). Results obtained in the elections on 4 March were: 120 seats gained by the Party *nomenklatura* and its supporters, 60 gained by candidates supported by the Democratic Bloc and 50 by independents. The remaining seats were recontested in the new elections on 22 April. Of these, only nine results were initially declared; run-off elections had to be held in the other constituencies because of the lack of a clear majority.

Religion

The religious situation in Byelorussia has always been dire, and not only as a result of Soviet policies. In the nineteenth century, being Roman Catholic was equivalent to being Polish. Similarly, anyone professing Orthodoxy would automatically be regarded as Russian. The Greek-Catholic (Uniate) church, which is now clearly a force to be reckoned with in Ukraine, was abolished in 1839 in the Byelorussian territories. Attempts to develop Byelorussian national trends in the Catholic Church in Poland between the wars met stiff resistance from the Polish hierarchy. This situation still continues today, but with one significant change. The status of the Orthodox Church in Byelorussia has been raised to that of an exarchate, bringing it into line with the Church in Ukraine. This can be seen as a move to make the Church appear more aware of the development of national self-awareness. The status of the Roman Catholic Church in Byelorussia, essentially administered from Warsaw still, has also been enhanced by the appointment in 1989 of a parish priest from Grodno, Father Tadeusz Kondrusewicz, to the diocesan see of Minsk. This is unlikely to make an essentially Polish church more attractive to young Byelorussians, or indeed anyone of any nationality other than Polish. Information is beginning to emerge of Orthodox priests, together with their parishioners, wishing to adopt the Union and recognize the authority of the Pope. It is too early to give any details.

The first issue of an unofficial journal for Byelorussian Catholics (*Vera*) gives the following figures: in 1979 39.6% of people in rural areas and 20% in urban areas declared themselves to be believers. In western districts of the country these figures reach 60%. There are 370 Orthodox parishes with 383 priests. The monastery in Zhirovitsy has 33 nuns and 15 monks. There are 65 Catholic parishes and more than 1 million Catholics, 100 Baptist congregations, and a mosque for the dwindling community of Byelorussian Tatars in the small town of Iue (Grodno province).

The Orthodox seminary in Zhirovitsy has been re-opened for the training of priests. A Roman Catholic seminary is to be opened in Grodno, with teaching staff from Poland. Will the Polish Church hierarchy heed the clear statement of the Polish Foreign Minister, Krzysztof Skubiszewski (reported in *The Independent* on 11 May), that Poland has no claims on former territories east of the Bug River?

The economy

Byelorussia's main natural resources are its land, forests and water-courses. Oil and gas deposits are being worked on a small scale near Rechitsa on the Pripiat river. Peat extraction has been cut back sharply since 1974, and oil-shale deposits have been located.

Industry accounts for some 60% of GNP. Products include trucks, tractors and other agricultural machinery (Minsk, Mogilev), oil and oil products (Novopolotsk, Mozyr), fertilizers (Gomel, Grodno), personal computers (Minsk and Brest), refrigerators (Minsk), cameras (Vileisk), watches (Minsk), electronic components (two firms: 'Integral' and 'Planar'), radios and televisions (Minsk, Vitebsk) and clothing.

The year 1990 is the last of the twelfth five-year plan period, the expressed aim of which was to increase national income and industrial output by 26% and the average annual output of agriculture by 13.4%. The increase was to have been achieved by higher productivity, which would have freed labour for the service sector. Undoubtedly the greatest obstacle to attaining these goals will be the need to divert resources to clearing up the damage caused by Chernobyl, although the chaotic state of railway transportation, something that is admitted to be endemic throughout the USSR, will not help either. There are also instances of equipment, often bought for scarce foreign exchange, standing idle as the result of poor management.

1 January 1990 marked the changeover to self-management (*samoupravlenie*) and self-financing (*samofinansirovanie*) in Byelorussia, with the aim of bringing non-strategic industry and resources under the direct control of the Byelorussian authorities without reference to all-union ministries and departments in Moscow. This move is timed to coincide with the final year of the current five-year plan, so as to provide the necessary conditions for a transfer to full regional cost accounting (*regional'naia khozraschet*) at the start of the next plan period, and matches similar moves in the Baltic republics (i.e. the areas considered to be the most developed economically). Only Azerbaijan and Byelorussia have a positive balance of trade with other republics of the USSR – Azerbaijan because of oil, Byelorussia because of its industry and agriculture. Moreover, at least on the basis of the latest figures supplied by the republic's statistical committee (for 1988), Byelorussia has a budget surplus, unlike the Soviet Union as a whole.

The most immediate impact of this new policy will undoubtedly be felt in the area of social services. The money to provide them will have to come from local sources, i.e. taxes. New tax rates have been fixed (e.g. turnover tax ranging from 34.7% in Minsk city to 80.5% in Grodno province, income tax on blue-collar (*rabochie*) and white-collar (*sluzhashchie*) workers at 50%). The swingeing turnover tax levels fixed in certain areas may be the result of a continuing hostile policy to what are perceived as the excessive profits made by the co-operatives. It has also been decreed that, starting in 1991, all consumer goods produced over and above the figures for 1990 are to be at the disposal of the Byelorussian Council of Ministers in accordance with the best economic interests of the republic.

The removal of a central planning authority in Moscow that compels each republic to distribute a certain proportion of its manufactured goods and agricultural produce to other parts of the USSR will, it is hoped, go some way towards improving the present chronic shortage of consumer items, many of which are either rationed or virtually unobtainable. The supply situation is supposed to be better in Byelorussia (145 roubles' worth of goods available and an average monthly wage, in 1988, of 207.5 roubles) than elsewhere in the Union, but the shortfall is still massive. The general unavailability of goods to buy means that Byelorussian savers have amassed deposits of 13.5 billion roubles.

Much hope is clearly being placed in the potential of a restructured, less centrally controlled economy for encouraging foreign trade and attracting foreign investment. Some of the larger state enterprises have already created their own foreign trade sections (e.g. 'Veras', set up in 1987 by the production combine 'Atlant', whose Minsk factory produces refrigerators and has succeeded in selling some to Australia, France, Britain and Italy in the teeth of obstructive tactics by the USSR Trade Ministry). Altogether twelve enterprises in Byelorussia have been granted the right to enter into direct negotiations with foreign trade partners, seven of them based in Minsk. An organization called 'Belarus'mezhhandal' (in Russian: 'Belo-rusintorg') has been established as a fully self-financing body by the Byelorussian Council of Ministers to assist other firms which are too small to establish their own foreign trade departments. It has so far dealt in the export of consumer goods (pianos, furniture, china, skis), licences for inventions, fuels (chiefly wood and peat) and, in spite of Chernobyl, agricultural produce. It has been approached by ten co-operatives seeking to find a market for their products abroad, mainly jewellery and furniture but also some in the hi-tech area. Some sixteen joint ventures have been formed, and another twenty are at the negotiation stage. One such, called 'East–West Co-operation for the development of Mogilev province', is hoping to develop integrated co-operation at all levels of life in the province. On the Soviet side the partners are the artificial fibre combine 'Khimvolokno' and the meat and dairy products firm in Mogilev. The Western partner is a Dutch firm, Loorvink and Co. NV, which is seeking the participation of banks in America, Western Europe and Japan. Another joint venture, with the Delaware North Company Inc., is seeking to develop food outlets at the rail, bus and air terminals in Minsk.

In the Baltic republics, especially in Estonia, full regional cost account-ing has been linked to the introduction of a new currency. In Byelorussia such a development had been generally discounted until the Byelorussian Trade Minister, M. Petrushkevich, raised the possibility in an interview published in the Communist Party Byelorussian-language daily *Zviazda* on

24 February 1990. Later (1 April) the same newspaper, in answer to a reader's letter, informed the world that there would be a Byelorussian currency, to be called 'dukat', with plastic coins (to save metal) for one-quarter, one-half and one dukat, and banknotes for 2, 7, 150, 1,000 and 15,000 dukats (this latter mainly for the payment of wages in the co-operatives). One dukat is to be worth two roubles and 11 new Estonian crowns. It will be fully convertible against Western currencies. The date of publication is presumably significant.

Conclusion

It is most unlikely that the next few years will bring to Byelorussia the kind of separatist upheaval that we are now witnessing in the Baltic republics. On the other hand, there may well be major social unrest. The Party and Government are accused of lagging behind in the processes of *perestroika* and democratization. Health care, even without the additional burdens imposed by the Chernobyl disaster, is in a parlous condition. People are unlikely to be appeased by Sokolov's promise of a planned increase in the production of disposable syringes and needles. Young people are dis-affected, and as a result the Byelorussian Komsomol (Young Communist League) has almost ceased to exist as a viable organization. There are now bodies (e.g. the Byelorussian Popular Front and the Byelorussian Ecologi-cal Union) which have the makings of alternative political parties. Regional full cost accounting will lay bare the reliance that has in the past been placed on central subsidies. In the case of the antiquated sectors of industry, especially monoliths like the Minsk tractor plant, this could lead to the large-scale dismissal of workers. The potash mines near Soligorsk were the scene of unrest at much the same time as coal-miners came out on strike in Vorkuta and the Donbass, although in Byelorussia a strike was averted on this occasion.

Any moves towards full rouble convertibility, seen as essential by many Byelorussian economists if the reforms are to work, will also have serious social consequences. Without that convertibility, however, most of the planned or already-existing joint ventures are likely to remain paper companies.

For the foreseeable future, self-financing in Byelorussia will continue to be dependent on major economic decisions taken in Moscow. The initial enthusiasm for joint ventures seems to be on the wane among Gorbachev's economic advisers. It remains to be seen just how many of those planned or allegedly existing in Byelorussia will actually do anything. Politically, the status of the republic depends in large measure on the willingness of the USSR Supreme Soviet to countenance renegotiation of the treaty by which the union was established in the first place.

13 UKRAINE
The issue of national self-determination

Historical background

The Ukrainian Soviet Socialist Republic was established by the Bolsheviks after the 1917 Revolution and Civil War. It had a population of approximately 30 million people on a territory of 443,000 square kilometres, encompassing present-day Central and Eastern Ukraine. Western Ukraine came under control of the newly established states of Poland, Czechoslovakia and Romania. In December 1922 the Ukrainian SSR formally joined the USSR on the basis of the Treaty of Union. It was further enlarged during World War II with the annexation by the Soviet Army of Galicia and Volyn from Poland in 1939, northern Bukovyna and sections of Bessarabia from Romania in 1940, and Transcarpathia from Czechoslovakia in 1945. With the transfer of Crimea in 1954 from the Russian SFSR to the Ukrainian SSR, the republic further grew to its present size of 603,700 square kilometres.

With the collapse of Czarism in 1917, political control of the Ukrainian provinces of the Russian Empire was contested by the Provisional Government based in Petrograd, the Central Rada based in Kiev and the workers' parties (mainly Mensheviks and Bolsheviks) based in the urban soviets. The Rada emerged the strongest contender in October 1917. It took power with the overwhelming support of peasants on the land and in the army, and with a growing base among workers, especially in the northern provinces. In November the Rada declared the formation of the Ukrainian People's Republic.

Although the Bolsheviks entered the 1917 Revolution largely convinced that new nation states were an anachronism, their branches in Ukraine supported the Rada against the Provisional Government in October and then sought a place in the leadership of the Ukrainian People's Republic. Having failed to find agreement on their proportional representation, the Bolsheviks withdrew and established a competing Ukrainian People's Republic in December 1917, with headquarters in Kharkiv and based mainly on the urban soviets of the Donbas region in south-eastern Ukraine. The Kharkiv-based UPR became the Russian Bolsheviks' fig leaf for their military intervention against the Kiev-based UPR in January 1918, which led the latter to declare independence from Soviet Russia on 22 January 1918 and to seek military support from the Austro-German armies.

After three years of civil war, foreign interventions by Axis, Entente,

UKRAINE

Official name	Ukrainian Soviet Socialist Republic
Area	603,700 sq. km (233,030 sq. miles)
Population	51,704,000 (1989)
Capital	Kiev
Language	Ukrainian, Russian
Religion	Russian and Greek Orthodox, Roman Catholic, with Protestant, Jewish and Muslim minorities
Currency	rouble

White and Red armies, and no less than 14 separate governments, the Bolsheviks finally took power in Ukraine with the military and economic backing of Soviet Russia. They consolidated power here during the 1920s by conceding the New Economic Policy to the peasantry, which gave them a chance to prosper as individual producers, and by admitting left-wing sections of the patriotic intelligentsia to the Communist Party, to government office, the educational system, mass media and the trade unions. Through such institutions the Ukrainian intelligentsia set out in the 1920s to make Ukrainian the language of civil life, education and economic activity, and to strengthen the republic's rights *vis-à-vis* Moscow.

The first post-revolutionary decade is considered a golden era of national rebirth. The second decade leading up to World War II saw a brutal collectivization of agriculture, the death of approximately 7 million peasants in the genocidal famine of 1932–3, the extermination by Stalin's secret police of an entire generation of Ukraine's political, cultural, scientific and religious leaders, and the crash industrialization programme with which Stalin prepared his country for war.

World War II, which brought about the unification of practically all Ukrainian territories into the Ukrainian SSR, also cost the republic 6 million lives, or 30% of the USSR's total human losses, and the destruction of much housing, industry and communications, amounting to 47% of the USSR's material losses. These were compounded by the outbreak of famine in Ukraine in 1946–7, the continuing campaign by Soviet units in Western Ukraine against the guerrilla Ukrainian Insurgent Army and the mass deportations to Siberia and the Far East of this region's villagers on suspicion of nationalism and disloyalty to the Soviet regime. 'When the casualties of the civil war, collectivization, the purges and the Second World War are combined, more than half the male and a quarter of the female population perished' (Bohdan Krawchenko, *Social Change and National Consciousness in Twentieth-century Ukraine*, London: Macmillan, 1985, p. 171).

The *status quo* in Ukraine was challenged in the latter half of the 1950s and 1960s (the period of de-Stalinization throughout the USSR) by the opposition or dissident movement. Unlike its counterpart in Russia, the Ukrainian opposition movement was supported actively by workers, both in membership of its various organizations and participation in meetings, petitions, etc., particularly in its early years. This movement had as its primary objectives the restitution of civil rights and national self-determination for the republic. It gained support within the Communist Party of Ukraine and a number of key republican state institutions, in response to which the central Communist leadership under Leonid Brezhnev ordered the movement to be crushed. A wave of arrests of prominent oppositionists swept the republic in January 1972 and many were subsequently incarcerated to long terms in labour camps, psychiatric prison hospitals and internal exile. The Communist Party of Ukraine was purged of its patriotically inclined members and its First Secretary, Petro Shelest, was removed from office.

Volodymyr Shcherbytsky, Brezhnev's faithful ally, replaced Shelest in 1973. He ruled the republic until 1989, when he retired from office and died soon afterwards, in February 1990. By the end of his term in office Shcherbytsky had discredited himself publicly by his iron rule, subservience to Moscow and his cover-up of the immediate and long-term effects of the 1986 Chernobyl disaster. His failure to cope with the July 1989 miners' strike in Donbas or the emergence of the Popular Movement of Ukraine for Restructuring (Rukh) made him appear out of step with the times and a liability for the Party. In September 1989, after careful preparation in Moscow by the CPSU Politburo, a plenum of the CPU Central Committee in Kiev elected Volodymyr Ivashko as the Party's new republican First Secretary. At 57 years of age and a Party member since 1960, Ivashko was described by Mikhail Gorbachev as 'intelligent, cultured and simply very accessible' (Moscow Radio, 28 September 1989). His task was to steer the republic through an impending storm of political change, which was already blowing in adjacent Eastern Europe, and to keep the Party in office.

The political terrain

Three key political forces were evident in Ukraine at the beginning of 1990 – the Communist Party, Rukh and an array of independent workers' organizations, principally among the miners. Also, several new political parties were about to formally constitute themselves and seek office within a multi-party electoral system. The signal for such a system was given in February 1990 by the CPSU's declaration that it would give up its monopoly of power. The Ukrainian republican elections in March came too soon for a genuine multi-party contest here, but their outcome showed clearly that the CPU was destined to share power or to become a minor party in opposition.

The Communist Party of Ukraine claimed 3.3 million members at the beginning of 1989, one-sixth of the CPSU's total. However, it was losing both members and authority within society at large, because its leadership under Shcherbytsky was associated with the Brezhnev era. It was failing to improve the economic situation or to make any concessions to popular demands for change in linguistic and cultural policy, nuclear energy and environmental protection or political reform.

Through its control of electoral commissions, the Party prevented the nomination of all but a few Rukh candidates to stand in the first all-Union elections in March and April 1989 to the Congress of People's Deputies. The electorate responded with a boycott of many single-candidate constituency elections, thus defeating unpopular nominees of the CPU apparatus. On the other hand, reform-minded Communists in other constituencies who had publicly declared support for Rukh's programme were elected to the Congress.

Ivashko's first months in office saw the Party leadership steering several progressive pieces of legislation through the Ukrainian Supreme Soviet (parliament): on improving the status of the Ukrainian language in the republic; making its electoral law more democratic; and declaring the need to close the Chernobyl nuclear power station for good. Such measures were intended to improve the CPU's image, and to convince the population that Ivashko's elevation signalled a major turn to responsible and accountable government in the republic. But they did not arrest the flow of resignations from the Party. More alarming still, a wave of mass protest against oblast Party leaders on charges of corruption and patronage swept the republic in the first three months of 1990, forcing their resignation in five of the 25 oblasts. Ivashko acknowledged in March 1990 that it was no longer easy to attract professionals and people of standing in the community to the Party, and spoke of his previous career as a college lecturer as 'the better years of my life' (interview in Kiev with Marko Bojcun for HTV Wales, 1 March 1990).

Rukh has its origins in 1988 when attempts were made in various cities to launch popular-front organizations on the model of those in the Baltic states. The most active participants in such attempts were former political prisoners just released from labour camps and exile, radical students and members of the Ukrainian Writers' Union. Many of the last were also members of the Communist Party. However, all these attempts were crushed by the authorities until November 1988, when an initiative committee composed of prominent Kievan writers and other intellectuals was formed in Kiev. The committee wrote Rukh's draft programme, which was published in February 1989 in *Literaturna Ukraina*, the writers' union newspaper. Local Rukh branches sprang up in all 25 oblasts, the strongest centres being Kiev, Lviv and the towns of Central and Western Ukraine.

Despite intense pressure applied by the CPU leadership against its own members in Rukh, as well as a continuous campaign of slander and abuse against the organization in the state-controlled media, Rukh prepared and convened its first national congress in Kiev on 8–10 September 1989. Of the 1,158 delegates in attendance representing 280,000 Rukh members, almost a quarter were CPU members. Engineers, teachers, industrial and cultural workers were well represented. Ukrainians made up a majority of those in attendance, followed by Russians and Jews. Among the informal groups whose members were active also in Rukh, the Ukrainian Helsinki Union was the best organized and most prominent.

The founding congress adopted a new programme that deleted all previous acknowledgements of the 'leading role' of the Communist Party and declared 'humanism, democracy, openness, pluralism, social justice and internationalism' as its guiding principles. It elected Ivan Drach, a well-known writer, as its head and Mykhailo Horyn of the Ukrainian

Helsinki Union as chairman of its ten-member Secretariat. It declared its intention to issue a national newspaper, establish permanent headquarters in Kiev and run its candidates in future election campaigns.

The retirement of Shcherbytsky and his replacement by Ivashko soon after Rukh's first national congress was interpreted by many political observers as the Party's attempt to stem defections from its ranks to Rukh. Some in the CPU leadership like Leonid Krawchuk, Ideological Secretary in the Politburo and its emissary to the Rukh Congress, saw that a clear split in the CPU's ranks might result from the rapidly changing political conjuncture, and entertained the idea of a 'Hungarian evolution': a split between the old conservative wing and the younger reform Communists, but with the latter seeking to draw the more moderate and federalist wing of Rukh into a new formation with them.

As noted above, the CPU leadership also launched a number of legislative initiatives to improve its image. Finally, it skilfully dragged out negotiations with Rukh over the latter's access to printing facilities for a national newspaper and its legal registration. Both questions were critical to Rukh's participation in the March elections. In the end, Rukh was not registered until mid-February 1990, after nominations of election candidates were closed, and so its candidates were forced to seek nomination by other, registered organizations or on the basis of place of residence or occupation (as permitted in the new electoral law). Rukh managed to produce the first issue of *Narodna hazeta* (People's Newspaper) at the end of February, too late to have a significant impact on the first round of elections on 4 March. Yet it was still in the ascendant in the first months of 1990, with a membership surpassing half a million and an ability to organize, for example, a 300-mile human chain across the republic on 21 January to mark the anniversary of Ukrainian independence in 1918.

The third important political force to consider in Ukraine is the independent workers' movement, centred in 1989 and 1990 around Donbas mining communities. This movement was triggered by the July 1989 miners' strike, which spread from the Russian SFSR into Ukraine and encompassed all of Donbas and the Galician-Volynian coalfield. As in other parts of the Soviet Union, Ukrainian miners first established strike committees to lead them, negotiate with the government and maintain order in the towns. The strike committees evolved into workers' control committees in August, after negotiations were concluded, which were charged with monitoring implementation of the agreement. The control committees united into a regional organization in August and set out in September to found the Donbas Union of Workers, an independent union encompassing workers in all industries.

The workers' movement first emerged in Donbas for several reasons. Ukrainian miners have a long tradition of struggle, even in the most difficult years. The Association of Free Trade Unions, established in 1978 by Vladimir Klebanov and suppressed mainly by psychiatric abuse of its leading members, was based here. Problems of housing, food supply and working conditions became worse in the 1970s and 1980s as the central government shifted capital investment away from Donbas into Western Siberian open-cut mining. The accident rate soared. In 1987, in the midst of a spate of fatalities in the pits, the Ukrainian republic's coal ministry was abolished and control of the industry was recentralized in Moscow even more. By 1989 the situation here was clearly coming to a breaking point: in the first three months there were eleven strikes. A lull followed, and the twelfth strike on 17 July brought Donbas into the country-wide miners' strike.

The strikers did not limit themselves to economic demands, although these were clearly of paramount immediate importance. The miners wanted a form of enterprise autonomy and regional cost accounting that gave their own organizations control of capital investments, the wage fund, management appointments, domestic wholesale trade and a part in international trade of their coal as well. They demanded the removal of unpopular trade union, government and police officials; the Chervonohrad miners in Western Ukraine demanded Shcherbytsky's removal. Most important of all, strike committees in Ukraine, as in other parts of the Soviet Union, were the first to raise the demand for abolition of Article 6 of the Soviet Constitution that guaranteed political power to the Communist Party.

Further evidence of a rapid politicization of miners included: participation of their strike leaders (as observers) in the September Rukh congress; readiness to mount a general strike if the original CPU draft of the new republic election law was not withdrawn (the original draft reserved a number of uncontested seats for CPU-sponsored organizations); fielding candidates in the March elections; and the mounting of strikes and demonstrations in Donetsk oblast on the eve of the elections to force the oblast CPU leadership to resign.

The miners' strike and its aftermath had a lasting impact upon other groups of Ukrainian wage-earners. First, it demonstrated to them how the strike weapon could be applied effectively, without creating pretexts for a violent reaction from the authorities. This led to the formation of strike committees in numerous towns and cities that accepted the strike as a weapon of last resort in the pursuit of all manner of popular demands. Second, the miners impressed upon other workers the value of independent organization, which took form later in the Donbas Union of Workers, the Horlivka Workers' Union and Yednist (Unity), formed in February 1990 in Kharkov by workers' committees from 16 towns and cities across the republic.

The republican elections

All 450 seats in the Ukrainian Supreme Soviet, as well as those of municipal and oblast governments, were contested in the March 1990 elections. An average of six to seven candidates vied for each seat in the Supreme Soviet. Because Rukh was unable to field candidates in its own name, it entered into a Democratic Bloc with other registered and informal organizations that shared its programme, and had its candidates nominated by such registered organizations as the Taras Shevchenko Ukrainian Language Society, by work collectives or resident voters' meetings. In a number of constituencies protests were levelled against the Party-controlled electoral commissions for refusing to register Democratic Bloc, Green World (Zeleniy Svit – an ecological organization) and other candidates. Demonstrations against the commissions broke out in February in Vynnytsia, Kiev, Ternopil, Chernivtsi and Poltava.

The election campaign period was marred also by persistent rumours of impending pogroms against Jews and attacks by civilians on Soviet troops stationed in the republic. At rallies and in public appeals to soldiers and civilians, Rukh denounced these rumours as an attempt by conservatives in the Party leadership, KGB and military command to intimidate voters and strengthen their own nominees' chances in the elections.

In the end, 129 Democratic Bloc candidates and 72 independents supported by the Bloc stood in the elections. They were well represented in the western oblasts of Lviv, Ternopil and Ivano-Frankivsk, moderately so in the central oblasts, and poorly in the south and east, particularly Odessa, Crimea and Poltava, where they fielded no candidates at all. The Communist Party fielded its candidates in all 450 constituencies, but it was by no means clear that all those elected would remain loyal to the CPU leadership and not defect to the Democratic Bloc. A number of strike committees also managed to field candidates, mainly in the coal, steel and machine-building centres of south-eastern Ukraine. Many of them were supported by the Democratic Bloc.

In the first round of the elections 120 out of the 450 seats were filled by 71 Communist Party candidates, 36 Democratic Bloc candidates and 13 independents supported by the Bloc. In Western Ukraine, the Bloc did particularly well, taking a large majority of the available seats. In the remaining 330 constituencies, where no candidate had received 50% of the vote in the first round, and which had to go through to a second round runoff between the two leading contenders, the Democratic Bloc remained in the running in 103 constituencies. It secured another 72 seats in the second round, giving it a total of 108 deputies in the Ukrainian Supreme Soviet. Supported by independent deputies, the Democratic Bloc commanded up to 170 votes, against 280 behind the CPU leadership.

Such an outcome did not mean, however, that it would be simply consigned to opposition status for the coming five years. It became increasingly clear in the course of the election period and afterwards that the Communist Party of Ukraine was dividing into a reform wing that straddled both the Party and Rukh, and a conservative wing behind First Secretary Ivashko. Some of the most radical reformists were trying to mount a breakaway movement for an independent Ukrainian Communist Party on the Lithuanian model. Furthermore, many Rukh leaders belonging to the Communist Party, including Ivan Drach, Volodymyr Yavorivsky and Dmytro Pavlychko, publicly quit the Party after the elections, as did numerous groups of rank-and-file members, especially in the western oblasts. Therefore it was within the range of possibilities that the conservative wing of the CPU could be cast into opposition within the Supreme Soviet by an alliance of Rukh/Democratic Bloc, reform Communists and strike committee leaders.

The fragmentation of the CPU was fostered by the awareness that a multi-party system was only a matter of time. Similarly, while Rukh functioned well in this period as an umbrella organization of various democratic and patriotic political tendencies, the imminence of a multi-party system encouraged such tendencies to prepare for life as fully fledged parties. Thus in the first months of 1990 plans were put in motion to establish the following: a Ukrainian Democratic Party by reform Communists in Rukh; a Ukrainian Social Democratic Party by local groups in six cities; a Ukrainian Republican Party by the Ukrainian Helsinki Union; a Ukrainian National Party by a breakaway group from UHU; a Ukrainian Peasant Democratic Party by an initiative committee based in Lviv; and a Green Party by the Green World association.

Volodymyr Ivashko was elected chairman of the Ukrainian Supreme Soviet, and in June resigned as CPU First Secretary in the face of Democratic Bloc criticism that his occupation of these two posts was unconstitutional. Second Secretary Stanislaw Hurenko replaced Ivashko in the CPU leadership.

The issues

The major issues that shaped the election contest and will continue to dominate the political terrain in the future are: democratization, the economic crisis, the environment, and the complex and long-term question of national sovereignty.

In view of the Communist Party's declared readiness to relinquish its monopoly on power, the issue of democratization is now a question of *how* to end this monopoly and make the transition to a genuine multi-party system. The Communist Party is naturally concerned to retain some role in future governments and not be completely marginalized in the process. Rukh, on the other hand, faces the task of maintaining unity of all the groups under its wing in order to enforce this transition to a multi-party democracy, while at the same time allowing these groups to prepare themselves as competing political parties. A thoroughgoing process of democratization must also address the delicate issue of the KGB, the Soviet Army and other means of coercion available to the state authority. Without their subordination to a democratically elected government, the process will be incomplete.

Although its economic weight has declined since World War II in relation to the country as a whole, Ukraine remains a crucial economic region of the Soviet Union. Today it produces one-quarter of the USSR's food and one-fifth of its industrial goods. Donbas provides a quarter of the Soviet Union's annual coal output, while the republic's five nuclear power stations account for 40% of the USSR's nuclear generating capacity. Producer goods, which make up 70% of the republic's GNP, include rolled steel, diesel locomotives, coal mining and agricultural machinery.

The republic's economy is characterized by its intense use of fuels, raw materials and labour, both in the agricultural and industrial branches; by its relatively worn-out, technologically backward and ecologically harmful capital assets; and by grave disproportions between its base industries, manufacturing, social infrastructural and consumer goods sectors. Soviet Ukrainian economists estimate their economy is in a worse state than those of Russia, Byelorussia and the Baltic republics. Four years of *perestroika* have left it with a less desirable output structure than before (the consumer goods sector shrinking below 30% of GNP), in eleventh place in the average republican wages table, and below the Soviet average in provision of social services, trade turnover in consumer goods, per capita housing space and educational levels (*Radianskiy ekonomist*, 9 October 1989, pp. 2–3; and *Ekonomika Radianskoyi Ukrainy*, No. 4, 1989, p. 60).

The republic's leaders have been able to do very little until now to combat shortages, disproportions in output and other problems because economic decision making (investment allocations, wholesale and retail prices, tariffs, etc.) has been determined in Moscow and implemented by union ministries. The Ukrainian republic controls only 5% of the gross national product created on its territory. Enterprises run by union ministries control the rest, and these enterprises deposit into the republic's budget a mere 3.5% of their income as payment for labour and infrastructural costs (*Robitnycha hazeta*, 18 April 1989).

The terms on which Ukraine trades are disadvantageous to its own interests. Payments for its annual exports to other parts of the Soviet Union are 1 billion rubles less than the costs calculated to produce those exports. Its electricity exports to Central and Eastern Europe are sold at 1 kopek per kilowatt hour (*Izvestiya*, 9 September 1989). Although comprehensive analyses of the republic's trade are not yet available, the general feeling both in Rukh and the Communist Party is that Ukraine suffers a net outflow of wealth and has practically no say in the matter. Not surprisingly, insistent calls are now made to reclaim control of economic strategy, domestic production and trade from the central government and its agencies.

Five objectives, first articulated by Rukh but co-opted in large part by the Communist Party leadership, have been articulated: republican economic independence exercised by the Ukrainian Supreme Soviet and its Council of Ministers, with veto power over any centrally initiated project;

customs duty, banks, and other fiscal instruments under republican control; a new Treaty of Union laying down the division of powers between the union and republican government, with a radical increase in the powers of the latter; independent access to the world market; and the promotion of a mixed economy with personal, co-operative and state ownership enjoying equality before the law.

Serious differences do exist, however, between Rukh and the Communist Party in their interpretation of these objectives and the procedures needed to realize them. Fundamentally, the differences are as follows. The Party is seeking a new economic arrangement in a renewed Soviet federation, guaranteed and arbitrated by a powerful executive presidency, whereas Rukh seeks recognition of full republican economic independence first, to be followed by negotiations with Moscow and other republics about trade and co-operation. It is, nevertheless, important to stress that, as in the Baltic republics, Ukraine's entire political spectrum now wants a radical increase of its power over the economy.

Closely related to the economy, but an important issue in its own right, is the environment. The republic is facing a serious water shortage. Pollution has destroyed many sources of potable water. Irrigation systems covering more than 5 million hectares, various industrial processes and nuclear power stations all impose a heavy burden on available supplies.

Attempts to increase agricultural yields by irrigation and the intensive use of phosphate fertilizers have, over the years, exhausted and then poisoned Ukraine's once fertile black-earth zone, and contributed in turn to the further pollution of water. Industrial pollutants in the air, water and soil, particularly in the south-east, have pushed up the incidence of disease, genetic defects and infant mortality. A qualitatively new dimension was added by the 1986 Chernobyl disaster, which seriously contaminated 3.7 million hectares of land with its fall-out and damaged the health of still unknown numbers of people.

A growing awareness of the ecological situation, particularly after the Chernobyl disaster, has led to a widespread movement in defence of the environment, of which Green World is the main republic-wide organization. This movement has managed to block all further construction of nuclear power stations in Ukraine, including the abandonment of those close to completion. It will most likely force the complete closure and dismantling of the Chernobyl station, which has operated practically without interruption since the disaster there. The republic's leading scientists and economists are preparing a new energy strategy in the context of a decisive shift in economic strategy overall away from energy- and resource-intensive technologies and processes.

The question of national sovereignty in a renewed federation or outright independence is the overriding long-term political issue. Both Soviet and Western observers accept that without Ukraine the Soviet Union cannot be a superpower. It is conceivable that Moscow will let the Baltic republics go, but to lose even control of Ukraine would greatly accelerate the already-evident fragmentation of the Union and embolden all the non-Russian peoples seeking greater national self-determination.

What, then, will determine the outcome of this issue in the long term? The evidence so far suggests that a worsening Soviet economy will generate more urgent demands for political separation, an internal economic reorganization in the direction of self-sufficiency and proportionality within a single national/republican market, and the renegotiation of trade terms with other states. Similarly, the deepening political instability across the Soviet Union will strengthen separatist sentiment in Ukraine and weaken the central government's ability to combat it. Young men, for example, do not wish to serve in the Soviet Army if that means they will be sent to the Baltic republics, Transcaucasia or Soviet Central Asia to put down nationalist movements there. On the contrary, the mass demonstrations across Ukraine in late March and April in support for Lithuania's bid for independence showed that growing numbers of people support such movements elsewhere and the peaceful resolution of their demands.

These are negative features of the all-Union situation that are promoting the idea of Ukraine's separation. The positive feature is, above all, the re-awakening of national pride and dignity among the Ukrainians, which brings with it a confidence that their republic can stand alone if it wishes to and should determine its relations with other republics as equals with them. But the republic will stand alone only if the majority of its population becomes convinced that independence is needed to bring greater freedom, better living standards and greater security than they presently enjoy under Soviet rule.

There was a fairly strong desire within Rukh at the beginning of 1989 to renegotiate the terms of the Treaty of Union with Russia and the other republics. Only after that option had been tried and had proved unsatisfactory was independence going to be considered as a serious alternative. The CPSU leadership and central government in Moscow responded to such a desire (here, as in other republics) by drafting new proposals on the national question, on economic independence for the republics and, finally, mechanisms for negotiated disengagement from the Union. However, none of these proposals gave Rukh much hope in a new Treaty of Union. Their actual content showed that the central government was not interested in real concessions to the republics. The April 1989 Tbilisi massacre, the military intervention in Azerbaijan and Armenia, and Gorbachev's response to Lithuania reinforced such a view. Thus Rukh was forced to consider outright independence all the more urgently.

The main weakness of previous bids for Ukraine's independence – in 1917 and during World War II – lay in the historic division between Western Ukrainian nationalism and the Eastern Ukrainian proletariat. The former saw national unification and independence as a panacea, without considering fully the political and social-egalitarian aspirations of workers in such a movement for a new state. The latter, a multinational working class with a sizeable Russian component in the most industrialized part of Ukraine, was radical in social and political demands, but not quite sure whether its region should belong to Ukraine or to Russia. The conservative wing of the Communist Party of Ukraine is very much aware of this historic division, and has worked hard to re-create it, without much success, in the present situation. Of course, the size, location and composition of the working class has changed a great deal since World War II. By 1970 it accounted for more than a half of the total population; it was more evenly spread across the republic and three quarters of its members were Ukrainian. The important question, however, is what political outlook the just emerging workers' movement will take on the issue of national self-determination, and whether its leaders will look to Moscow or to Kiev as their political centre. This still largely unknown factor will have immense relevance for the future course of events in Ukraine.

14 MOLDAVIA
Reform and reunion

Historical background

The Moldavian Soviet Socialist Republic is an artificial republic created by the Soviet Union in 1940 from the region between the rivers Dniester and Prut, formerly known as Bessarabia, which had, and still has, a predominantly Romanian population. According to the 1979 census, the major peoples of the republic are Moldavians (Romanians) who number 2.5 millions and represent 64% of the population, Ukrainians 560,000 (14%), and Russians 500,000 (13%). Except for a period under Russian rule between 1812 and 1918, Bessarabia formed the eastern half of the Romanian principality of Moldavia and its population shared a common ancestry, language and, for the most part, history with the Romanian people. In March 1918 a national assembly of Bessarabian Romanians voted for the union of the province with Romania. The new Soviet government refused to recognize the union and, in order to formalize its opposition to Romania's annexation of the province and to offer a nucleus for a 'liberated' Bessarabia, created in 1924 the Autonomous Moldavian Republic (AMR) in the partly Romanian inhabited area of south-western Ukraine on the east bank of the Dniester. The Soviet interest in Bessarabia was conceded by Germany in a secret protocol to the Nazi–Soviet Pact of August 1939.

On 26 June 1940 the Romanian government received a Soviet ultimatum demanding the cession of Bessarabia and Northern Bukovina and, bereft of international support, decided to accede. From the union of most of Bessarabia with the western part of the AMR (the areas around Tiraspol, Dubossary and Rebnitsa) the Moldavian Soviet Socialist Republic was created on 2 August 1940. The greater, eastern, part of the AMR was returned to the Ukrainian Soviet Socialist Republic, thus revealing that its creation in 1924 was merely a political stratagem to give credibility to the Soviet claim to Bessarabia. By restoring most of the AMR's territory to the Ukrainian SSR the Soviet government admitted the fiction of 'Moldavian' in the autonomous republic's official name.

Immediately after the annexation of Bessarabia the Soviet authorities nationalized the land and private enterprises were taken over by the state. The process of sovietization was facilitated by the transfer of 13,000 specialists from Russia, the Ukraine and Byelorussia. Romanians were deported from the new republic to Central Asia in order to work in factories and collective farms as replacements for those drafted into the

MOLDAVIA

Official name	Moldavian Soviet Socialist Republic
Area	33,700 sq. km (13,010 sq. miles)
Population	4,341,000 (1989)
Capital	Kishinev (Chişinăv)
Language	Moldavian (Romanian), Russian
Religion	Russian Orthodox
Currency	rouble

army. Estimates of the total number of Romanians resettled in this way vary from 100,000 to half a million. The deportations were interrupted by the German attack of 22 June 1941 on the Soviet Union in which Romania, under General Ion Antonescu, participated in order to recover Bessarabia and Northern Bukovina. These lost provinces were regained by 27 July.

The reconquest of Bessarabia was accomplished by the Red Army on 20 August 1944, when the Soviet generals Malinovsky and Tolbukhin successfully launched a massive assault of almost one million troops and 1,500 tanks against the combined German and Romanian forces straddling the Prut. Most of Bessarabia was reincorporated into the Moldavian SSR in its August 1940 frontiers, the former southern Bessarabian districts of Ismail and Cetatea Albă being assimilated into the Ukrainian SSR. These territorial realignments were formalized in the Soviet–Romanian Armistice Convention of September 1944 and confirmed by the Peace Treaty of 1947 with Romania.

The fierce rearguard action fought by the German and Romanian armies in Bessarabia caused the virtual destruction of the towns in the province. The capital Chişinău (Kishinev) was reduced to ruins and the damage to roads, railways and bridges posed considerable supply problems for the Soviet authorities. The difficulties faced by the recreated Moldavian SSR, the economy of which was based almost entirely upon agriculture, were exacerbated by the severe droughts of 1946 and 1947, which created a widespread famine. Several thousand party activists were brought from the Ukraine and Russia to supervise the establishment of the republic's organizational infrastructure, thus diluting the Romanian element in the population, which was further weakened by mass deportations to the republics of Central Asia in the 1950s. Most of the Romanian schools were given over to teaching in Russian, for which teachers were imported from the other Soviet republics, while the ubiquity of Russian and Ukrainian activists in the republic's official apparatus provided the Soviet authorities with a justification for the priority given to the use of Russian in the official life of the republic. At the same time, the influx of Russians and Ukrainians acted as a check against potential nationalist agitation among the Romanians, who were now officially christened Moldavians.

Soviet difficulty in winning over the native Moldavians to the party was exemplified by the choice of First Secretaries of the Moldavian Communist Party (MCP), none of whom were of Romanian origin. The best-known was Leonid Brezhnev, who held the position between 1950 and 1952. Throughout the republic's postwar history the percentage of Moldavians who have been members of the MCP has been the lowest among any indigenous nationality in a Soviet republic.

Urbanization and migration

The process of russification in the Moldavian SSR was accelerated by enforced socio-economic changes, the most important of which were urbanization and migration. The urban growth rate in the republic since 1944 has been among the most rapid in the Soviet Union. Indeed, comparison of the 1959 and 1979 censuses showed that it was the highest of any republic during that period. When considering this development it should be borne in mind that before World War II, Moldavia (i.e. Bessarabia) was a predominantly agricultural province largely starved of Romanian investment. Its towns were mainly peopled by Russians, Ukrainians and Jews. The demographic changes registered between 1959 and 1979 reflect not only a period of intense urban development but also a shift in the balance between urban and rural populations. The rural population fell from 77.7% of the total in 1959 to 61% in 1979, while the urban population increased from 22.3% in 1959 to 39% in 1979.

A concomitant of Moldavia's urbanization was migration, both within the republic from rural to urban areas and from outside it. Of the migrants who came from outside Moldavia between 1968 and 1970 (the only years for which these figures are available), 46% came from the Russian Republic and 36% from the Ukraine. Between 1959 and 1979 the numbers of Russians in Moldavia increased considerably from 290,000 to over 500,000. This influx not only consolidated the use of Russian as the republic's official language but, more significantly for the position of the Moldavian language, led to an increase in the adoption of Russian as the native language among the other peoples of the republic. As language is considered by Moldavians to be the badge of national identity, their fears about assimilation by the Russians grew as more of their number became bilingual in Moldavian and Russian.

Economic and language reform

These trends, coupled with the fact that the number of Moldavian-language newspapers published in the republic had been surpassed in 1975 by Russian-language ones, and that the Moldavian percentage share of the number of books published had been declining steadily since 1960, were highlighted by *glasnost*, which brought to the surface previously repressed dissatisfaction among the Moldavian intelligentsia of the republic about the status of their language and provision for schooling in Moldavian. The authorities in the republic responded to such complaints by issuing a decree in May 1987 which increased provision for teaching Moldavian in schools and expanded air-time given to radio broadcasts in Moldavian. This concession could not remedy the fact, revealed at a Moldavian Communist Party meeting in September 1987, that in the republic's medical and agricultural institutes not a single subject was taught in Moldavian, and that in the town of Tiraspol, which included 25,000 Moldavians in its population, there was not one Moldavian school.

It was further disclosed at this same meeting that the 600,000 Ukrainians in the republic did not have a single school or newspaper.

The encouragement of *glasnost* prompted further demands from Moldavian intellectuals, which were encapsulated in the call on 1 September 1988 from the editors of *Literatura şi arta*, the principal Moldavian literary review, that immigration from the other republics be stopped immediately, that the Moldavian language become an official language, that textbooks containing the true history of Moldavia be written, and that the Latin alphabet be restored.

At the same time, the model of the Baltic states provided an example and precedent to the Moldavians as to how far they could press their demands. It was not without significance that *Glasul* (The Voice), the first newspaper to appear in Moldavian in the Latin alphabet since 1944, was printed in Latvia in March 1989 in 60,000 copies, which were sold out on the day of distribution in Chişinău on 13 March. Three months later a number of Moldavian journals renounced the Cyrillic for the Latin alphabet.

Pressure for economic and language reform continued to be exerted by a number of newly created groups, the most notable of which were the Moldavian Democratic Movement in Support of Perestroika and the Alexei Mateevici Cultural Club. Semyon Grossu, the Communist Party leader, not only refused to consider reform but also attempted to persuade the non-Moldavians in the republic to oppose the Moldavian demands. Denied access to the media and the possibility of legal registration, the unofficial Moldavian groups decided in May 1989 to join together to found the Popular Front of Moldavia. The Front set itself two objectives: to act as an umbrella organization for its constituent groups in any dialogue with the republican or Soviet authorities and to create links with other unofficial movements elsewhere in the Soviet Union, and second, to co-ordinate public actions in pursuit of common aims.

Two public demonstrations organized by the Popular Front in the following month demonstrated its rapidly growing influence and an embitterment of Moldavian opinion. On 25 June 1989 the Front held a mass rally in Chişinău to mourn the Soviet annexation of the territory of the republic on 26 June 1940. According to the organizers, about 70,000 people attended, making it the largest unofficial rally in the history of the republic. In contrast, the authorities' attempts to celebrate the anniversary of the entry on 28 June 1940 of Soviet troops into Bessarabia was foiled by a mass counterdemonstration in the capital. Profiting from the momentum gathered by these protests, the Front mobilized support for language demands in a series of demonstrations in Chişinău, which culminated in a rally attended by half a million people in the capital on 27 August, two days before the Moldavian Supreme Soviet was due to consider draft laws making Moldavian the official language of the republic. Opposition to the laws came from Russian-speakers in the republic, 100,000 of whom went on strike on 29 August 1989, demanding that Russian also be proclaimed a state language and the language of inter-ethnic communication. In Moldavia's second largest city, Tiraspol, which has a Russian-speaking majority, 30,000 protesters called for the withdrawal of two Moldavian books recently printed in the Latin alphabet from local bookshops. Faced with these conflicting pressures, the Moldavian Supreme Soviet approved on 1 September legislation which made Moldavian the state language of the republic, which reinstituted the use of the Latin alphabet, proscribed by Stalin following the annexation of Bessarabia, and which designated both Moldavian and Russian as languages of inter-ethnic communication.

Party leader Semyon Grossu's opposition to language reform and *perestroika* finally led to his sacking on 16 November. His dismissal was caused by disturbances which marred the 7 November Revolution Day celebrations in the capital Chişinău, and a riot three days later during which the headquarters of the Interior Ministry was set on fire. Grossu was replaced by Pyotr Luchinsky, aged 49, a man said to be more in tune with the ideas of Mikhail Gorbachev. Luchinsky, a native of Moldavia and, unlike his predecessor, a fluent speaker of Romanian, had previously served as Second Secretary in the Central Asian republic of Tajikistan. He immediately made a gesture of goodwill by organizing the withdrawal of 2,000 Soviet Interior Ministry troops who had been rushed to the republic to restore order after the riot. The Moldavian Popular Front responded by promising to avoid a confrontation in order to give the new leader a breathing space.

Reunion with Romania?

The Romanian revolution and the Lithuanian Communist Party's decision to break with Moscow led to calls from the Moldavian Popular Front for reunion with Romania. In this respect there is a different and (for the Soviet Union) more dangerous element to Moldavian nationalism. The Baltic states do not have a large sister sovereign state adjacent to them whereas Moldavia does. While independence is the limit to the demands of the Baltic states, Moldavian aspirations can go one step further. By reincorporation into Romania, Moldavia's loss to the Soviet Union will represent a neighbouring sovereign state's gain.

At a mass rally in Chişinău on 30 December there were calls from representatives of the Moldavian Popular Front for the republic to follow Lithuania's example and to establish an independent Communist Party, and for union with Romania. But at a later rally on the same day, Party Secretary Luchinsky was pressed by Russians in the republic to take strong action against Moldavian nationalists and opponents of Communist rule. The Russians and Ukrainians in Moldavia are extremely concerned that they will now lose their privileged positions in the republic, since the decision to make Moldavian a state language would relegate them to the status of second-class citizens, and that independence and union with

Romania would leave them exposed to the same kind of linguistic assimilation which formerly threatened Soviet Moldavians. To defend their interests, they have formed themselves into an association called the Yedinstvo, which is virtually a mirror-image of the Moldavian Popular Front.

Elections

Elections for a new Moldavian parliament were held on 25 February 1990. Although the Communist Party was the only party that was officially recognized, the most significant political forces in the elections were the Moldavian Popular Front and the Yedinstvo. Acting the role of a patriotic umbrella organization, the Popular Front's endorsement of Communists who profess to place Moldavian interests first weighed heavily with the voters, although the Front did not attempt to validate candidates in predominantly Russian- and Ukrainian-speaking constituencies. Some 83% of the electorate turned out as 1,892 candidates competed for 380 seats, and 140 of the seats were filled while a re-run was required in the remaining constituencies where none of the candidates received the requisite number of votes. The repeat ballots in 237 constituencies took place on 10 March. Of the 370 deputies elected to the parliament, 85% were Communists, 70% were Moldavians, with 112 deputies receiving the backing of the Moldavian Popular Front, 15% were Russians, and about 10% were Ukrainians.

The parliament opened its first session on 17 April and its deputies are due to consider bills proposing sovereignty for the republic and economic autonomy. Developments in Lithuania show that Moscow will not allow Moldavian independence for the time being, although a compromise answer to Popular Front demands would be to adopt the German model and open the border between the republic and Romania, thereby allowing free movement between a divided people.

Appendix 1 THE WARSAW PACT, 1955
(SIGNATORY STATES: ALBANIA, BULGARIA, CZECHOSLOVAKIA, GDR, HUNGARY, POLAND, ROMANIA, USSR)

Key statements include the following:

The Contracting Parties,

Reaffirming their desire to create a system of collective security in Europe based on the participation of all European States, irrespective of their social and political structure, whereby the said States may be enabled to combine their efforts in the interests of ensuring peace in Europe;

Taking into consideration, at the same time, the situation that has come about in Europe as a result of the ratification of the Paris Agreements, which provide for the constitution of a new military group in the form of a 'West European Union', with the participation of a remilitarized West Germany and its inclusion in the North Atlantic bloc, thereby increasing the danger of a new war and creating a threat to the national security of peace-loving States:

Being convinced that in these circumstances the peace-loving States of Europe must take the necessary steps to safeguard their security and to promote the maintenance of peace in Europe;

Being guided by the purposes and principles of the Charter of the United Nations;

In the interests of the further strengthening and development of friendship, co-operation and mutual assistance in accordance with the principles of respect for the independence and sovereignty of States and of non-intervention in their domestic affairs;

Article 1

The Contracting Parties undertake, in accordance with the Charter of the United Nations, to refrain in their international relations from the threat or use of force and to settle their international disputes by peaceful means in such a manner that international peace and security are not endangered.

Article 2

The Contracting Parties declare that they are prepared to participate, in a spirit of sincere co-operation, in all international action for ensuring international peace and security and shall endeavour to secure, in agreement with other States desiring to co-operate in this matter, the adoption of effective measures for the general reduction of armaments and the prohibition of atomic, hydrogen and other weapons of mass destruction.

Article 3

The Contracting Parties shall consult together on all important international questions involving their common interests, with a view to strengthening international peace and security.

Whenever any one of the Contracting Parties considers that a threat of armed attack on one or more of the States Parties to the Treaty has arisen, they shall consult together immediately with a view to providing for their joint defence and maintaining peace and security.

Article 4

In the event of an armed attack in Europe on one or more of the States Parties to the Treaty by any State or group of States, each State Party to the Treaty shall, in the exercise of the right of individual or collective self-defence, in accordance with Article 51 of the United Nations Charter, afford the State or States so attacked immediate assistance, individually and in agreement with the other States Parties to the Treaty, by all the means it considers necessary, including the use of armed force.

Article 5

The Contracting Parties have agreed to establish a United Command, to which certain elements of their armed forces shall be allocated by agreement between the Parties, and which shall act in accordance with jointly established principles. The Parties shall likewise take such other concerted action as may be necessary to reinforce their defensive strength, in order to defend the peaceful labour of their peoples, guarantee the inviolability of their frontiers and territories and afford protection against possible aggression.

Article 8

The Contracting Parties declare that they will act in a spirit of friendship and co-operation to promote the further development and strengthening of the economic and cultural ties among them, in accordance with the principles of respect for each other's independence and sovereignty and of non-intervention in each other's domestic affairs.

Article 9

The present Treaty shall be open for accession by other States, irrespective of their social and political structure, which express their readiness, by participating in the present Treaty, to help in combining the efforts of the peace-loving States to ensure the peace and security of the peoples.

Article 11

The present Treaty shall remain in force for twenty years. For Contracting Parties which do not, one year before the expiration of that term, give notice of termination of the Treaty to the Government of the Polish People's Republic, the Treaty shall remain in force for a further ten years.

In the event of the establishment of a system of collective security in Europe and the conclusion for that purpose of a General European Treaty concerning collective security, a goal which the Contracting Parties shall steadfastly strive to achieve, the present Treaty shall cease to have effect as from the date on which the General European Treaty comes into force.

Appendix 2 CHARTER OF THE COUNCIL FOR MUTUAL ECONOMIC ASSISTANCE (COMECON), 1959
(*SIGNATORY STATES:* ALBANIA, BULGARIA, CZECHOSLOVAKIA, GDR, HUNGARY, POLAND, ROMANIA, USSR)

Purposes and principles

1. The purpose of the Council for Mutual Economic Assistance is to promote, by uniting and co-ordinating the efforts of the member countries of the Council, *the further deepening and perfecting of cooperation and the development of socialist economic integration*, the planned development of the national economies and the acceleration of the economic and technical progress of those countries, the raising of the level of industrialization of the countries with a less-developed industry, a continual growth in the productivity, *the gradual approximation and equalization of the levels of economic development*, together with a steady increase in the well-being of the peoples, of the member countries of the Council.

2. The Council for Mutual Economic Assistance is based on the principle of the sovereign equality of all the member countries of the Council.

Economic and scientific-technical co-operation between the member countries of the Council shall take place in accordance with the principles of *socialist internationalism, on the basis of respect for state sovereignty, independence and national interest, non-interference in the internal affairs of countries*, complete equality of rights, mutual advantage and friendly mutual aid.

Appendix 3   POSTWAR SUMMIT MEETINGS

Since the last of the Great Power conferences took place at Potsdam following the end of World War II, the following meetings have taken place between US and Soviet leaders:

1955 (July) *Geneva*

Eisenhower and Khrushchev met, together with British and French leaders (Eden and Fauré). They gave instructions to their foreign ministers to draw up proposals on European security and Germany, disarmament and East–West contacts. Nothing came of it.

1959 (September) *Camp David, Washington*

Eisenhower and Khrushchev agreed to reopen negotiations on Berlin. No progress was made on disarmament or German reunification.

1960 (May) *Paris*

Eisenhower, Khrushchev, Macmillan and de Gaulle met. Khrushchev walked out after U2 spy plane piloted by Gary Powers was shot down over Soviet territory.

1961 (June) *Vienna*

Kennedy and Khrushchev met. No progress made.

1967 (June) *Glassboro, New Jersey*

Johnson and Kosygin met, but the Soviet offer to act as an intermediary in the Vietnam War was rejected.

1972 (May) *Moscow*

Nixon and Brezhnev signed ABM (anti-ballistic missile) and SALT-1 (strategic arms limitation) treaties.

1973 (June) *Washington*

Nixon and Brezhnev signed agreements on the prevention of nuclear war and the principles of a further SALT pact.

1973 (July) *Helsinki* – see Appendix 4

1974 (June–July) *Moscow*

Nixon and Brezhnev signed protocol strengthening ABM treaty and a treaty limiting underground nuclear tests. The latter remained unratified.

1974 (November) *Vladivostok*

Brezhnev and Ford reached outline agreement on SALT-2.

1975 (July–August) *Helsinki*

Brezhnev and Ford met twice; no progress made.

1979 (June) *Vienna*

Brezhnev and Carter signed SALT-2, but it was never ratified.

1985 (November) *Geneva*

Gorbachev and Reagan pledged to speed up arms talks.

1986 (October) *Rejkjavik*

Gorbachev and Reagan narrowed their differences on an INF treaty and agreed limits for a new strategic arms reduction (START) pact. The plan to abolish ballistic missiles fell through owing to the American determination to go ahead with the 'Star Wars' programme.

1987 (December) *Washington*

Gorbachev and Reagan signed INF treaty abolishing land-based medium-range missiles; progress was made on START.

1988 (May–June) *Moscow*

Gorbachev and Reagan exchanged instruments of ratification for the INF treaty, but failed to bring the START treaty within reach. They signed agreements on ballistic missile testing, nuclear test monitoring, space research and cultural exchanges.

1988 (December) *New York*

Reagan made promise to Gorbachev that existing US policies would continue under incoming President Bush, who also attended the meeting.

1989 (December) *Malta*

Bush and Gorbachev reached agreement on pursuing START talks in time for a further summit in the US in June. Some progress was made on chemical weapons. There was agreement that neither side should interfere with the liberal reforms in Eastern Europe. The US proposed moves to integrate the USSR into the Western economic system.

1990 (May–June) *Washington*

Bush and Gorbachev agreed to stop producing chemical weapons and halve existing stocks by the year 2000. They signed a START treaty providing for a 30% reduction in long-range nuclear missiles. There was provisional agreement on increasing trade links, but no consensus on the future strategic alignment of a united Germany.

Appendix 4   THE HELSINKI CONFERENCE, 1973–75

The Helsinki Conference or, to give it its full title, the Conference on Security and Co-operation in Europe (CSCE), was originally proposed by the Soviets. No general peace conference had ever taken place following World War II (although the Great Powers had met), and the Soviet Union saw such an assembly as a means to consolidate, or 'legitimize', the favourable strategic position it had attained in Europe as a result of the war. That is, it sought not only recognition for postwar boundaries (including the division of Germany) but also for the political order imposed in much of the region. Although Moscow had established Communist rule in its satellites and had stationed tens of thousands of troops there, it remained nervous about the prospects for 'socialist rule' given continuing evidence of popular discontent. The advent of *détente*, coming on the heels of Brandt's *Ostpolitik*, made the atmosphere favourable to such talks.

Preliminary negotiations began in 1972. Eventually on 3 July 1973 the representatives of 35 nations (all the European states – except Albania – with the USA and Canada) sat down for talks in the Finnish capital. Far from being a speedy 'summit' though, the talks dragged on and on. As Vojtech Mastny has written '. . . the conference that Brezhnev has hoped to finish quickly and climax in a glittering summit, with himself as the superstar, turned into a two-year diplomatic marathon instead'. The Final Helsinki Document was not signed until 1 August 1975.

While the Soviet Union wanted the Conference to concentrate on security matters, and was prepared for some general statements on economic and cultural co-operation, the West wanted a broader overall programme for the improvement of pan-European relations. Western nations felt that for real *détente* to be achieved, the rights of individuals would have to be secured. This meant:
i) a minimum consensus on the development of human rights.
ii) liberalization as regards exchanges of people and ideas.
The Soviet side was hostile to the thrust of Western moves. The Western emphasis upon the freedom of the individual in relation to the state contrasted with the notion that had developed in state socialist societies that such freedoms as the individual possessed were inextricably linked – and even conditional upon the individual's duties and obligations to state and community. According to the latter precepts, socialist régimes arrogated to themselves the right to prescribe the limits of acceptable behaviour of their citizens. Moreover they refused to countenance intervention in defence of their citizens' rights, branding it 'unwarranted interference' in the internal affairs of the given state.

Eventually, however, Soviet resistance to discussion on human rights was overcome by Western persistence. There was agreement to consider humanitarian and cultural questions on the conference agenda as a separate item. The Swiss delegation had proposed the idea of dividing the agenda into more manageable units – 'baskets'. So it was that the concerns of the conference became divided into three 'baskets'; the first dealing with security in Europe, the second dealing with economic matters, and the third dealing with human rights. The main link was between the first and third baskets. The Soviets were forced to recognize that the security and stability they so earnestly desired could not be guaranteed by weapons or inter-governmental treaties alone. It was dependent also upon their willingness to take the aspirations of individual citizens into account. Furthermore the Western nations made clear that they were not prepared to talk about peace and security without reference to human rights.

The Helsinki Final Act (or Helsinki Accord, as it is sometimes called) is not an international treaty. The participating states at the conference had made clear that they did not want one. The Act had limited legal significance, therefore, although the participant states declared their resolve to pay due regard to, and to implement, its provisions. But the Final Act did contain clauses with reminders of the legal obligations which participating states had assumed previously (for example, by ratifying the European Convention on Human Rights, or the UN Covenant on Political Rights). It therefore strengthened the principles underlying these earlier treaties. Moreover, the Soviet Union adopted the principles of the Final Act into its 1976 Constitution, thereby strengthening their universal validity regarding standards of international conduct.

Finally, it should be emphasized that the Final Act established a basis for continuing dialogue on the matters dealt with. It initiated a process for seeking information and exchanging views on the issues raised by the conference, as well as monitoring compliance. Subsequently, Helsinki 'follow-up' conferences (such as those at Belgrade (1977), Madrid (1979), Stockholm (1984–5) and Vienna (1986)) were held to review the working of the agreement.

Extracts from the Helsinki Accord
Questions Relating to Security in Europe (Basket 1)
The 'Declaration on Principles Guiding Relations between Participating States' bound the signatories to:

I Respect each other's sovereign equality and individuality, as well as all the rights inherent and encompassed by its sovereignty . . .

II Refrain from the threat or use of force . . .

III Regard as inviolable all one another's frontiers as well as the frontiers of all States in Europe . . .

IV Respect the territorial integrity of each of the participating States . . .

V Settle disputes among them by peaceful means in such a manner as not to endanger international peace and security and justice . . .

VI Refrain from any intervention, direct or indirect, individual or collective, in the internal or external affairs falling within the domestic jurisdiction of another participating State, regardless of their mutual relations . . .

VII Respect human rights and fundamental freedoms, including the freedom of thought, conscience, religion or belief, for all without distinction as to race, sex, language or religion . . .

VIII Respect the equal rights of peoples and their rights to self-determination, acting at all times in conformity with the purposes and principles of the Charter of the United Nations and with the relevant norms of international law, including those relating to the territorial integrity of States . . .

IX Develop their co-operation with one another and with all States in all fields in accordance with the purposes and principles of the Charter of the United Nations . . .

X Fulfil in good faith their obligations under international law, both those obligations arising from generally recognized principles and rules of international law, and those obligations arising from treaties or other agreements, in conformity with international law, to which they are parties . . .

This section dealing with the first 'basket' contained two further sections. The first set out matters 'related to giving effect to certain of the above principles'; the second was a 'Document on confidence-building measures and certain aspects of security and disarmament'. The latter carried provisions for the prior notification of military manoeuvres and exchange of observers in the event of manoeuvres being held.

Co-operation in the Field of Economics, of Science and Technology and of the Environment (Basket 2)

I Commercial exchanges

The participating States resolved to promote the expansion of trade and to ensure conditions favourable to such development by:

a) improving business contacts,

b) promoting the publication of economic and commercial information

c) encouraging organizations, enterprises and firms connected with foreign trade to develop further the knowledge and techniques required for effective marketing

II Industrial co-operation and projects of common interest

The participating States resolved to encourage industrial co-operation between their countries, and to encourage major projects of common interest (in the fields, for example of energy exchange, research for new energy sources, transportation).

III Provisions concerning trade and industrial co-operation

The participating States:

a) reaffirmed their interest to achieve the widest possible international harmonization of standards and technical regulations

b) recommend, where appropriate, to organizations, enterprises and firms in their countries to include arbitration clauses in commercial contracts and industrial co-operation contracts, or in special agreements

c) would consider favourably the conclusion, in appropriate cases of specific bilateral agreements concerning various problems of mutual interest in the fields of commercial exchanges and industrial co-operation (e.g. with a view to avoiding double taxation; to facilitating the transfer of profits).

IV Science and technology

The participating States expressed their awareness of the need to develop scientific and technological co-operation, and affirmed that such co-operation could be developed and implemented bilaterally and multilaterally at the governmental and non-governmental levels.

V Environment

The participating States agreed to the following aims:

a) to study those environmental problems which, by their nature, are of a multilateral, bilateral, regional or sub-regional dimension.

b) to increase the effectiveness of national and international measures for the protection of the environment.

c) to take the necessary measures to bring environmental policies closer together and, where appropriate, to harmonize them.

d) to encourage efforts by interested organizations, enterprises, and firms to develop, produce and improve equipment designed to monitor, protect, and enhance the environment.

VI Co-operation in other areas

The participating States considered it desirable to encourage, promote and safeguard:
a) the development of transport
b) the promotion of tourism
c) the economic and social aspects of migrant labour
d) the training of personnel

Co-operation in Humanitarian and Other Fields (Basket 3)

I Human Contacts

The participating States expressed their aim to facilitate freer movement and contacts, individually and collectively, whether privately or officially, among persons, institutions or organizations of the participating States and to contribute to the solution of the humanitarian problems that arise in that connection. They expressed their intention to facilitate movement arising from the following situations:
a) contacts and Regular Meetings on the Basis of Family Ties
b) reunification of Families
c) marriage between Citizens of Different States
d) travel for Personal or Professional Reasons
e) improvement of Conditions for Tourism on an Individual or Collective Basis
f) meetings among Young People
g) sport
h) expansion of Contacts

II Information

The participating States express their intention in particular to improve:
a) Circulation of, Access to, and Exchange of Information
b) Co-operation in the Field of Information
c) Working Conditions for Journalists

III Co-operation and Exchanges in the field of Culture

The participating States set themselves the following objectives:
a) to develop the mutual exchange of information with a view to a better knowledge of respective cultural achievements.
b) to improve the facilities for the exchange and dissemination of cultural property.
c) to promote access by all to respective cultural achievements.
d) to develop contacts and co-operation among persons active in the field of culture.
e) to seek new fields and forms of cultural co-operation.

IV Co-operation and Exchanges in the Field of Education

The participating States sought to strengthen the links among educational and scientific establishments and to encourage their co-operation in sectors of common interest by:
a) concluding co-operation agreements in education and science
b) facilitating and intensifying exchanges between educational, scientific and cultural institutions
c) increasing the exchange and dissemination of scientific documentation
d) encouraging the study of foreign languages and civilizations as an important means of expanding communication among peoples, and for the strengthening of international co-operation.
e) promoting the exchange of teaching methods at all levels of education as well as the use of teaching materials.

Sources: *Conference on Security and Co-operation in Europe. Final Act.* HMSO Cmnd.6198.

V. Mastny, *Helsinki Human Rights and European Security. Analysis and Documentation.* Duke University Press. Durham, 1986.

T. Buergethal (ed), *Human Rights, International Law and the Helsinki Accord.* Allanheld, Osman, New Jersey, 1977.

Appendix 5   ECONOMIC STATISTICS

i) External Trade with OECD countries, 1988 (in $US million)

	Exports	Imports	Balance
Albania	n/a	n/a	
Bulgaria	780	2436	−1656
Czechoslovakia	3804	3588	−316
East Germany	2748	2976	−228
Hungary	3804	4008	−204
Poland	5652	4968	684
Romania	4056	1284	2772
Yugoslavia	7386	6483	−903
USSR	23652	24804	−1152

Sources: OECD data; Economist Intelligence Unit country reports, 1989/90.

ii) Estimated convertible currency debt (1988–89) (billion US$)

	1988		1989	
	Gross	Net*	Gross	Net*
Bulgaria	7.7	5.9	9.0	7.7
Czechoslovakia	5.2	3.5	5.1	3.1
East Germany	20.2	10.7	20.6	11.0
Hungary	19.6	18.2	20.6	19.5
Poland	39.2	35.6	39.9	36.5
Romania	3.1	2.3	1.4	−0.1
Eastern Europe	95.0	76.3	96.5	77.7
Soviet Union	41.7	26.5	48.3	34.1
E. Europe +				
Soviet Union	136.8	102.7	144.8	111.8

*The net figure represents gross debt minus assets held with Western banks – those reporting to the Bank of International Settlements. The data do not take into account indebtedness to countries outside the BIS area (e.g. developing market economies).

Source: Norman Scott, 'East–West Trade on the Threshold of the 1990s: Current State and Prospects' (Nato Economics Directorate, Brussels)

iii) United Kingdom Trade with Selected Countries, 1988*

	UK Exports	UK Imports	UK Balance
Bulgaria	161	45	116
Czechoslovakia	269	263	6
East Germany	202	272	−70
Hungary	234	175	59
Poland	313	532	−219
Romania	89	163	−74
USSR	1009	1178	−169

*(in millions of US$, annual totals)

Source: The Economist Intelligence Unit country reports, 1989

iv) Estimated annual* per capita income (in US$)

Albania	860
Bulgaria	3200
Czechoslovakia	6000
East Germany	5400
Hungary	1722
Poland	1900
Romania	2687
Yugoslavia	1850
USSR	4200
UK	7156

*for 1985

Source: *The World in Figures* (Economist Publications, London 1987)

v) Possession of luxury items (per 'ooo of the population)

	Telephones*	Radios	TVs	Cars
Albania	n/a	167	83	1.6
Bulgaria	200	221	189	115
Czechoslovakia	226	256	285	171
East Germany	212	663	754	199
Hungary	134	586	402	135
Poland	105	289	263	98
Romania	67	288	173	11
Yugoslavia	132	235	209	125
USSR	98	685	310	40
UK	523	1145	434	292

*1984/5. All other figures for 1987.

Sources: UNESCO Statistical Yearbook, 1989; The World in Figures (Economist Publications, 1987)

Appendix 6   EASTERN EUROPE AFTER THE FIRST WORLD WAR

The peace treaties of 1919, following the end of World War I, created as many problems as they tried to solve. Some were solved by plebiscites under League of Nations auspices. Others were the result of unilateral action (Teschen, Fiume, Vilnius, see below). Some national groups achieved independence or autonomy, only to lose it by force to those whose temporary weakness had made their emergence possible (particularly true of the Byelorussian, Ukrainian and Caucasian republics). Nevertheless, the most significant achievement of the peace treaties was the creation of a belt of central European states from the buffer zones of the pre-war German, Austro-Hungarian and Russian empires. Their true independence proved short-lived; within two decades the expansion of Nazi Germany and the Soviet Union had erased their autonomy, if not their actual independence.

Areas of dispute
Aland Is: disputed between Sweden and Finland. Granted to Finland (1921) and neutralized
Memel: Allied occupation 1920–23, annexed by Lithuania 1923, autonomous 1924
Vilnius: annexed by Poland 1920, plebiscite for Poland 1922
Marienwerder and Allenstein: Plebiscite to join E. Prussia (Germany) 1920
Polish Corridor: Continuing German demands for access to E. Prussia
Poznan: disputed between Germany and Poland. Reverted to Poland 1918
Upper Silesia: divided between Germany and Poland by plebiscite 1921
Teschen: partitioned between Czechoslovakia and Poland 1920
Sopron: granted to Austria in 1918, reverted to Hungary after plebiscite 1921
Fiume: disputed between Italy and Yugoslavia. Free state established 1920. Italian Fascist coup 1922. Partitioned 1924
Macedonia: Greek–Bulgarian conflict 1925
Western Thrace: ceded to Greece from Bulgaria 1919
Adrianople: occupied by Greece 1920–22
Corfu: Union with Crotia-Slovenia proclaimed 1917. Disputed between Italy and Greece 1923–24.

Appendix 7 EUROPEAN ECONOMIC AND DEFENSIVE BLOCS

ECONOMIC BLOCS, WITH DATES OF MEMBERSHIP
★ European Community (EC)
▲ Benelux Customs Union, 1947
▼ Council for Mutual Economic Assistance (CMEA/COMECON)
● European Free Trade Association (EFTA)

MILITARY PARTITION, WITH DATES OF MEMBERSHIP
■ North Atlantic Treaty Organization (NATO)
○ Brussels Pact, 1948
□ Warsaw Pact Organization

The Twelve		FDR (W. GERMANY)	★ 1957 ■ 1955	ITALY	★ 1957 ■ 1949	PORTUGAL	★ 1986 ■ 1949
BELGIUM	★ 1957 ▲ ■ 1949 ○	FRANCE	★ 1957 ■ 1949 ○	LUXEMBOURG	★ 1957 ▲ ■ 1949 ○	SPAIN	★ 1986 ■ 1982
DENMARK	★ 1973 ▲ 1960–72 ■ 1949	GREECE	★ 1981 ■ 1952	THE NETHERLANDS	★ 1957 ▲ ■ 1949 ○	UNITED KINGDOM	★ 1973 ● 1960–72 ■ 1949 ○
		IRISH REPUBLIC	★ 1973 ● 1970–72				

AUSTRIA	● 1961	TURKEY	★ applied for EC membership 1987 ■ 1952	ALBANIA	▼ 1949–61 □ 1955–68	ROMANIA	▼ 1949 □ 1955
FINLAND	● (ass. member 1961–85)			BULGARIA	▼ 1949 □ 1955	USSR	▼ 1949 □ 1955
ICELAND	● 1970 ■ 1949			CZECHO-SLOVAKIA	▼ 1949 □ 1955	YUGO-SLAVIA	▼ limited involvement from 1964
NORWAY	● 1960 ■ 1949			GDR (E. GERMANY)	▼ 1950 □ 1955		
SWEDEN	● 1960			HUNGARY	▼ 1949 □ 1955		
SWITZER-LAND	● 1960			POLAND	▼ 1949 □ 1955		

Appendix 8   NATIONS AND LANGUAGES OF EASTERN EUROPE

ETHNIC GROUPS

Albanians	Italians	Slovaks
Bulgarians	Macedonians	Slovenes
Czechs	Poles	Turks
Germans	Romanians	Ukrainians and Byelorussians
Hungarians	Serbs and Croats	

Appendix 9   NATIONALITIES IN THE USSR

Appendix 10   POLLUTION IN EUROPE

Sulphur dioxide emissions*

	1980		1987
	A.	B.	
Albania	n/a	39	n/a
Bulgaria	517	508	570
Czechoslovakia	1550	1832	1450
East Germany	2500	2415	2500
Hungary	817	813	710
Poland	2050	1741	2270
Romania	100	757	100
Yugoslavia	588	837	588
USSR**	6400	8588	5100
UK	2335	2342	1840

Statistics listed in column A, and those underlined in the 1987 column, are provided by governments. Those under 'B' are independent estimates.
*Figures refer to thousands of tons.
**The European part only.

Source: *Environment*, vol. 30, no. 2 (March 1988)
Acid Rain, no. 8, September 1989.

Appendix 11   1990 ELECTION RESULTS

Albania
No elections held.

Bulgaria
10 and 17 June 1990

Seats in the Grand National Assembly (Total: 400)
200 seats were be decided by direct election and 200 by proportional representation.

Bulgarian Socialist Party	211	(45.6% of the vote)
Union of Democratic Forces	144	(36.6%)
Movement for Rights and Freedoms	23	(5.8%)
Bulgarian Agrarian Party	16	(7.8%)
Fatherland Union	2	
Independent	2	
Social Democratic Party	1	

Czechoslovakia
8 June 1990

Seats in the Federal Assembly (Total: 300)

Civic Forum/Public Against Violence	164
Communist Party	40
Christian Democrats	35
Society for Moravia and Silesia	16
Slovak National Party	11
Co-Existence	10

The Czechoslovak electoral system is made simpler by the stipulation that parties must achieve 5% support in order to receive representation. However, percentage voting returns are calculated on the basis of elections to two chambers, and are also divided according to whether they are from the Czech lands or from Slovakia. Consequently, it is extremely difficult to give an overall figure for percentage support.

The German Democratic Republic (East Germany)
18 March 1990

Seats in the East German Volkskammer (Total: 400)

Alliance for Germany	193	(48% of the vote)
of which, Christian Democrats	164	(41%)
German Social Union	25	(6%)
Democratic Awakening	4	(1%)
Social Democrats (SPD)	87	(22%)
Party of Democratic Socialism (PDS) (former Communists)	65	(16%)
Free Democrats	21	(5%)
Alliance 90	12	(3%)
Democratic Peasants' Party	9	(2%)
Greens + Independent Women's League	8	(2%)
Others	5	(1%)

Hungary
25 March and 8 April 1990

Seats in the Hungarian parliament (Total: 386)

Democratic Forum	164 seats	(42.49% of the votes)
Alliance of Free Democrats	92	(23.83%)
Independent Smallholders	43	(11.4%)
Socialist Party	33	(8.55%)
Christian Democrats	21	(5.44%)
Alliance of Young Democrats	21	(5.44%)
Independents	6	(1.55%)
Agrarian Alliance	1	(0.26%)
Joint Party Candidates	4	(1.04%)

Poland
4 and 18 June 1989

Seats in the Polish Sejm (Total: 460)

Polish United Workers' Party (Communists)	173	(37.5%)
United Peasant Party	76	(16.5%)
Democratic Party	27	(6%)
PAX (pro-regime Catholics)	10	(2.2%)
Christian Social Union	5	(1.1%)
Solidarity	161	(35%)

Solidarity-sponsored candidates for the Sejm won all 161 seats for which the opposition was allowed to compete. Solidarity also won 99 out of 100 seats in the upper chamber (the Senate), and together, therefore, 260 out of the 261 parliamentary seats for which it was eligible to compete.

The Council of State determined the proportional arrangement of forces within the ruling coalition; each seat was allocated to a single party, to be decided by competition among its members alone.

Romania
20 May 1990

Seats in the Romanian Chamber of Deputies (Total: 387)

National Salvation Front	263	(66.3% of the vote)
Hungarian Democratic Union	29	(7.2%)
National Liberal Party	29	(7.1%)
Christian Democratic National Peasants Party	12	(2.5%)
Ecological Movement	12	(2.45%)
Romanian Unity Alliance – AUR	9	(2.15%)
Agrarian Democratic Party	9	(1.59%)
Romanian Ecological Party	8	(1.38%)
Socialist Democratic Party	5	(1.11%)

A further 7 political parties gained less than 1% of the vote each and between them 9 seats in the Assembly.

Yugoslavia
Election results not complete at the time of going to press.

Appendix 12   USEFUL ADDRESSES

Diplomatic and Consular*

Bulgarian Embassy,
188 Queen's Gate,
London SW7
071-584 9400

Czechoslovak Embassy,
25 Kensington Palace Gdns.,
London W8
071-229 1255

Embassy of the German
Democratic Republic,
34 Belgrave Square,
London SW1
071-235 9941

Hungarian Embassy,
35 Eaton Place,
London SW1
071-235 4048

Polish Embassy,
47 Portland Place,
London W1
071-580 4324

Polish Consulate,
2 Kenya Road,
Edinburgh EH3 5PE
031-552 0301

Romanian Embassy,
4 Palace Gdns.,
London W8
071-937 9666

Soviet Embassy,
10 Kensington Palace Gdns.,
London W8
071-727 6888

Soviet Consulate,
5 Kensington Palace Gdns.,
London W8
071-229 3215

Yugoslav Embassy,
5 Lexham Gardens,
London W8
071-370 6105

Banking and Trade

Anglo-Romanian Bank Ltd.,
42 Moorgate,
London EC2
071-588 4150

Anglo-Yugoslav Bank Ltd.,
11 St Mary at Hill,
London EC3
071-283 6111

Bank Handlowy w Warszawie
(Polish),
4 Coleman St.,
London EC2
071-606 7181

British–Soviet Chamber of
Commerce,
2 Lowndes St.,
London SW1
071-235 6477

Bulgarian Foreign Trade
Bank,
1 Gracechurch St.,
London EC3
071-626 1888

Department of Trade and
Industry,
Overseas Trade Division 3/5,
1–19 Victoria St.,
London SW1
071-215 5265 (USSR)
071-215 5152 (Czechoslovakia,
E. Germany, Romania,
Yugoslavia)
071-215 4735 (Albania,
Bulgaria, Hungary, Poland)

East European Department,
Confederation of British
Industry,
Centre Point,
New Oxford St.,
London WC1
071-379 7400

East European Trade Council,
25 Victoria St.,
London SW5
071-222 7622

Hungarian International
Bank,
95 Gresham St.,
London EC2
071-606 0237

London Chamber of
Commerce and industry,
69 Cannon St.,
London EC4
071-248 4444

Moscow Narodny Bank Ltd.,
81 King William St.,
London EC4
071-623 2066
071-623 2500

Yugoslav Economic
Chambers,
Trade Promotions Office,
143 Regent St.,
London W1
071-437 2870
071-734 2581

Yugoslav Trade Agencies
Ltd.,
58a West Heath Drive,
London NW11
081-458 1001

Zivnostenska Bank
(Czechoslovakia)
104–106 Leadenhall St.,
London EC3
071-623 3201

Further points:
The embassies of the
respective country will have a
Commercial Counsellor who
should be contacted for more
information about trading.
As moves are made to
open up the economies and
to encourage trade with the
West, more trade offices with
responsibility for particular
industries will be opening up.
Information on these can be
obtained from the
Department of Trade and
Industry.
Most of the major banks,
including the big four clearers
(Barclays, Lloyds, Midland
and NatWest) have
departments dealing with
east and east-central Europe.

Travel and Tourism

Aeroflot Soviet Airlines,
70 Piccadilly,
London W1
071-493 7436

Balkan and Bulgarian
Airlines,
322 Regent St.,
London W1
071-637 7637

*At the time of writing Britain has no diplomatic relations with Albania.

Balkan Holidays (Bulgaria, Romania, Yugoslavia)
19 Conduit St.,
London W1
071-491 4499
071-493 8612

Berolina Travel (East Germany),
22a Conduit St.,
London W1
071-629 1664

Bulgarian Tourist Office,
18 Princes St.,
London W1
071-499 6988

Czechoslovak Airlines,
17 Old Bond St.,
London W1
071-499 6445
(reservations 071-499 6442)

Czechoslovak Travel Bureau (CEDOK) Ltd.,
17 Old Bond St.,
London W1
071-629 6058

Danube Travel,
6 Conduit St.,
London W1
071-493 0263

Fregata, Polish Travel Bureau,
100 Dean St.,
London W1
071-734 5101

Hungarian Airtours,
3 Heddon St.,
London W1
071-437 1622

Intourist Moscow Ltd.,
Soviet Tour Operator,
292 Regent St.,
London W1
071-631 1252/071-580 4974

Malev Hungarian Airlines,
10 Vigo St.,
London W1
071-439 0577

Polish Airlines (LOT),
313 Regent St.,
London W1
071-580 5037

Polorbis Travel,
82 Mortimer St.,
London W1
071-636 2217 (five other numbers listed)

Romanian Tourist Office,
29 Thurloe Place,
London SW7
071-584 8090

Romania Airlines,
29 Thurloe Place,
London SW7
071-584 7955

Tazab, Polish Travel Agency,
273 Old Brompton Road,
London SW5
071-373 1186

Travellines,
154 Cromwell Road,
London SW7
071-370 6133

Yugoslav National Tourist Office,
143 Regent Street,
London W1
071-734 5243/071-734 8714/071-439 0399

Yugoslav Airlines,
37 Maddox St.,
London W1
(Fare Quotations 071-409 1544)
(Flight reservations 071-493 9399)

Cultural and Educational

British–Bulgarian Friendship Society,
69 Upper St.,
London N1
071-359 0507

British–Soviet Friendship Society,
36 St John's Square,
London EC1
071-253 4161

British–Yugoslav Society,
121 Marsham St.,
London SW1
071-828 2762

Collett's International Bookshop,
129 Charing Cross Road,
London WC2
071-734 0782

Czechoslovak News Agency,
59 Kensington Pl.,
London W8
071-727 7354

Polish Cultural Institute,
34 Portland Place,
London W1
071-636 6032

Polonez (Polish Book and Gift Shop)
129 Shepherds Bush Centre,
Shepherds Bush Green,
London W12
071-749 3097

School of Slavonic and East European Studies,
University of London,
Senate House,
Malet St.,
London WC1
071-637 4934/38

INDEX

A

Abalkin, Leonid 173
Abkhazian and Ossetian minorities 177
Adamec, Premier 64–5
Afghanistan 198
  Soviet invasion of 26–7
Agreement, Helsinki 62, 113
  Moscow 56
  Munich 125
  Percentage 11, 127
  Yalta 112
Albania 8, 13, 35–42
  aid for 39
  and Moscow, tension between 40
  China's aid for 40
  Communist Party in 38
  economic and industrial decline of 40
  founding of Communist Party in 36
  German army invasion of 36
  history of 36
  population of 9
  post-Hoxha leadership of 41
  reforms in 41–2
  Yugoslavia's ambition to annex 38
Alexandrov, Choudomir 45
Alia, Ramiz 41–2
alliance, Big Three Powers' wartime 11, 15
Alliance, North Atlantic 19
Allied Control Commission (ACC) 73
Allies, Western 11–12
Alma Ata 178
Antall, Jozsef 107
Antonescu, General Ion 127, 141, 239
Aral Sea, ecological disaster in the 179
Armenia, conflict in 176
Armenian earthquake 177–8
  economy, the 177
  national movement 178
Armenians, Turkey's massacres of 178
artel 187
Artsimenia, D.K. 219
Asia 176
  Communist states in Central 10
  the economy of Central 179
  Turkic peoples of Central 178
Asian republics, nationalist feeling in the Central 178
Astafer, Viktor 187
Atanasov, Georgi 49
Azerbaijan and Armenia, conflict between 177, 179
  inter-ethnic violence in 177
  oil production in 178
  Popular Front in 177–8

B

Babiuch, Prime Minister 114
Baku 177
Balcerowicz, Leszek 120, 122
Baltic States, the 8–12, 193–212
  States Council 210
  deportations, mass 195
  economic independence 212
  emigration to the West 195
  entry to the League of Nations 193
  model, the 177
  national liberation 195
  nationalist feelings in the 176
  Pacts and Mutual Defence and Assistance 194
  political forces in the 211
  popular fronts in the 180
  republics, pro-independence in the 180
  Russian minorities in the 180
  Soviet demonstration, anti- 212
  Treaty on Unity and Co-operation 213
'behaviourist' policy, the West's 30
Bartoszcze, Roman 123
Belene 51
Benes, Eduard 55–8
Berghofer, Mayor Wolfgang 80–1, 87
Beriozovas, Vladimiras 210
Berklaus, Eduards 204
Berlin 16–17
  air lift 17, 73
  blockade 17, 73
  reunited, East and West 71
  Wall, the 7, 24, 28, 76
    breaching of the 84
    building of the 75
    opening of the 86
Bessarabia 12
Beszelo 102
Bilak, Vasil 63
Black Sea, the 8
Blandiana, Ana 133
Blyukher 168
Bobu, Emil 132
Bogdanovs, Oskars 205
Bogomolov, Oleg 173
Bohemia, German protectorate of 55
Böhme, Ibrahim 88
Bolshevik Party, the 167
Bolsheviks, the 9
Borba 159
Boris of Bulgaria, King 43
Brandt, Willy 25, 88
Brazauskas, Algirdas 209–10
Breslav (Wrocław) 12
Brezhnev Doctrine 28, 60, 119
  Leonid 26, 59–60, 63, 77, 171–2, 226, 239
brigady 187
Brucan, Silviu 133
Bucharest, fall of 13
Bukharin, N. I. 168
Bukowina 12
Bulgaria 9, 13, 43–52
  aid from Arab World to 47
  and the Axis 43
  Alternative Socialist Organization of 49
  Article One of 1971 Constitution of 48
  BANU party of 43, 48–9
  BCP/BSP party of 50
  Central Committee of 49

Bulgaria – *cont.*
change in 45–6
Committee for the Defence of Religious Rights
in 46
Communist rule in 7
-Agrarian coalition of 45
control of Macedonia by 43
creation of 43
Democratic Forum of 49
Discussion Club for the Support of *Perestroika*
and *Glasnost* of 46
Econglasnost of 46
end of era in 47–8
Extraordinary Congress of (14th) 49
Fatherland Front of 43
Green Party of 47
Independent Association for the Defence of
Human Rights of 46
Jews in 43
'July concept' of 45
June (1990) elections in 30, 50
Labour Code of 1986 in 45
Macedonians in 51
Movement for Democratic Socialism of 49
Nikola Petkov Agrarians in 47, 49
opposition groups in 46
Podkrepa group of 46
reforms in 43
Road to Europe Platform of 49, 51
Soviet interest in 11
sovietization of 45
Turkish issue in 45–8, 51
Union of Democratic Forces (UDF) in 47–8
Bulgarian Agrarian Nation Union (BANU) 43
Communist Party 45, 48–9
Revolution, turning point of 47
Social Council 48
Socialist Party (BSP) of 49
Bush, President George 131, 211
Byelorussia 9, 214–223
aid for 218
Chernobyl and 217–18, 222–3
economic independence of 217
economy of 221–2
elections in 218–19
history of 214, 216
nationalist feelings in 176
politics of 216
Popular Front in 217
population of 214
religion in 220
Russification of 217
separatist upheaval in 223

C

Caklais, Maris 201
Čalfa, Marian 66
Carl Zeiss Jena 76
Carol II, King 125
Caucasus Mountains, the 8, 177
Ceauşescu, Elena 132
Ceauşescu, Nicolae 29, 101, 105, 119, 128–43
Charter 77 (see Czechoslovakia)
Chernobyl 172 (*see also effects in individual countries*)
China, Hoxha's support of 40
Churchill, Winston 11–12, 15
Clementis, Vlado 58

COCOM restrictions, relaxation of 31
Cold War, the 7, 33, 73, 161
the onset of the 15–16, 20, 26, 28
CMEA (*see Comecon*)
Comecon (Commission for Mutual Economic Aid,
CMEA) 18–19, 119, 121, 128
Cominform, founding session of 15–16
Comintern 145, 148, 161
Communism, goal of 171
Communist age, dawning of the 9
economic systems, failure of 22
Information Bureau (*see Cominform*)
Party Central Committee, plenum of the 172
excommunication of members of 17
Party's monopoly of powers, threats to 41
regimes 8
characteristics of 20–3
toppling of 30
repression, symbol of 24
rule, collapse of 32, 36
consolidation of 17
dismantling of 8
east-central Europeans' dislike of 24
nature of 20
Russia 10
states 7, 10
utopianism 173
Communists, Chinese 27
Community development funds, channelling of 31
Conference, Ecoforum (1989) 46
Helsinki CSCE 26
Final Act 26
Madrid (1983) 26
of Communist parties (1960) 40
on Security and Co-operation in Europe (CSCE)
25, 46
Potsdam (1945) 7, 16, 73
Strasbourg (1989) 28
Teheran (1943) 11, 111
Versailles 7, 10, 14
Vienna (1986–9) 26
Yalta (1945) 7, 11–13, 26, 111–12
conferences, Great Powers' 7, 11, 26
Congress debates, the 172
Communist Party's (1990) 180
of People's Deputies 172, 181
Soviet Party's Twentieth 24, 168
Constitution (1923) 10
Cornea, Doina 133
Cruise missiles, Soviet campaign to prevent
dispersal of 27
Czarnogursky, Jan 66
Czechoslovakia 9, 12–14, 17–18, 53–70
Agrarian Party of 56
anniversary of Soviet invasion of 64
Carpathian Ruthenia in 55–6
Charter 77 (Czechoslovakia) 26, 62–3
Christian Democrats of 70
Civic Forum of 65, 69–70
Comecon in 58
Communist Party (CPC) in 24, 57, 59
regime in 56, 65
rule in 7, 58
Constitution of 59
cultural and political purges in 58
Depression in 55
economic failures of 64
reform in 68

Czechoslovakia – *cont.*
  economy of 61
  elections in 14, 30, 69–70
  Federal Assembly 67
  German rule in 55
  Government of National Unity 66
  Husák regime in 61, 63
  industry 61, 69
  invasion of 20, 60
  investment interest in 31
  liberation of 56
  massacre of Lidice in 55
  morality in 67
  Munich and after 55
  National Council 60
    Front Party of 55, 57
  People's Party 65
  Pětka party of 53
  Pope's visit to 70
  postwar elections in 56–8
  'Prague Spring' in 25, 59–60, 62–3
  Public Against Violence 65, 69
  Red Army troops in 56–7, 60, 68
  religious belief in 63
  restoration of democracy in 67
  Slovak minority of 55
    National Council in 60
    Populist Party of 56
  Social Democrats in 59
  Socialist Party of 65
  Soviet liberalization in 63
  Stalinist orthodoxy in 59
  Statni Bezpecnost (St. B) 69
  Sudety region of 55
  under Masaryk 53
  'velvet revolution' of 63, 69
  Warsaw Pact neighbours of 59

D

Debrecen 13
Dej, Gheorge Gheorghiu- 128
Dementei, N. I. 217–18
Democratic Front, the 42
Deng, Xiao-ping 131
détente, East-West 25
deutschmark, introduction of the 73
Dienstbier, Jiri 63, 66
Djilas, Milovan 12
Drach, Ivan 228, 232
Dubček, Alexander 24, 59–61, 64–5, 67
Duma 49, 186
Dushanbe 179
Dzierzynski, Feliks 120
Dziewanowski, M. K. 56

E

East-West dialogue, need for 26
  -West relations, developments in 25
  transformation in 23
Ebeling, Pastor Hans-Wilhelm 88
Economist, The 120
Ekmecic, Milorad 161
Eppelmann, Pastor Rainer 80, 88
Estonia 8–9, 194–201
  CPE (Communist Party of Estonia) 196, 198
  Congress of 200

dissent in 196
Declaration of Sovereignty in 199
EGM (Estonian Green Movement) in 198–9
EHS (Estonian Heritage Society) in 198–9
elections in 199–200
ENIP (Estonian National Independence Party)
  198–9
environmental protests in 196
IMF (Economic Self-Management) proposal for
  196
Internationalist Front in 198
MRP-AEG (Estonian Group for Publication of
  the Molotov-Ribbentrop Pact) in 196, 198
Nature Protection Act in 196
PF (Popular Front) in 198, 200
'Singing Revolution' in 198
Europe, changes in Eastern 8
  collapse of regimes in central 29, 32
  Declaration on Liberated 12
  division of 15
  export restrictions to central 31
  funds for East and central 31
  future political character of central 33
  geography of Eastern 8
  peoples of east-central 7
  political map of 7
  post-cold war 33
    -Versailles 33
    -war division of 24
    stability of Western 34
  reform Communists in Eastern 180
  regimes in East-central 20
  role of superpowers in 33
  Soviet policy towards central 25
  withdrawal of American troops from 19
Europe's postwar frontiers, recognition of 26
European Bank for Economic Reconstruction 31
  Community 8, 31
    membership of the 32
  Recovery Programme 16
  Security System, pan- 33
  states, aid for central 31
  Union, West 19

F

Far East, Communist states in 10
Ferdinand of Bulgaria, Prince 43
Fergana Valley, the Uzbek population in the 178
Fischer, Oskar 86
Forck, Bishop Gottfried 81
Ford, President Gerald 129

G

Gagarin, Yuri 24
Gazeta Wyborcza (Election Gazette) 118–19
GDR (German Democratic Republic) 17, 71–91
  Alliance 90 89
    for Germany 88, 90
    of Free Democrats 89
  1989 anniversary celebrations 76, 79
  Central Committee Plenum 86
  Christian Democrats (CDU) 73, 88
  churches in the 80
  coalition government 90
  Communist Party 73
  Demise of 71, 75–6

GDR – *cont.*
Democratic Awakening (DA) 88
Demokratischer Aufbruch 82
demonstrations in the 80–3
economy of the 75
elections in the 30, 90
emigration from the 78–9
end of era in the 90–1
free speech in the 79
German Social Union (DSU) 88
Gorbachev's influence on the 77–9
historical background of the 71
isolation of the 78
Liberal Democrats (LDP) 73, 81, 86
march of hope 82
National Democratic Party 73
Democrats 86
Front 73
Neues Forum 80, 83–5, 88
Office for National Security 86, 89
Peasants' Party 73, 86, 89
people-power in the 79
political, economic and social decline of the 76–7
refugees from the 75, 78, 83
religion in the 80
reunification opinion polls 89–90
Round Table, composition of the 89
SED 75–6, 81
Congress 87
destruction of 83–4
failure of 91
-PDS 87–8
plenum of the 85
politburo 85
renewal of 86
turmoil within 87
Social Democrats (SPD) 73
socialism in the 77–8
Socialist Unity Party 71
Stasi 84–5
dissolution of the 86
statistics of the 76
Volkskammer 86–7, 89
Genscher, Hans-Dietrich 89
Geremek 124
Gërö, Erno 92
Georgia 8, 177–9
nationalist feeling in 176
pro-independence in 179
tourist industry in 177
German economic strength 20
Federal Republic 19
military growth, restrictions on 32
power 20
-Soviet co-operation 10
unity 76
Germany, Communist rule in East 7
defeat of Nazi 11, 16
division of 16
investment interest in East 31
mass demonstrations in East 29
rearmed 19
reunification of 32, 88
upheaval in East 24
West 171
Gidaspov, Boris 190
Gierek, Edward 22, 25, 112–13, 115

glasnost 30, 41, 75, 77, 131, 152, 172, 177–8, 181, 187, 195, 217, 240–41
Glasul (The Voice) 241
Glemp, Cardinal 117
Godmanis, Ivars 206
Gomulka, Władysław 24–5, 112
Göncz, Arpad 107
Gorbachev, Mikhail 19, 23, 28, 41, 63, 68, 75–8, 85–6, 105, 119, 130, 171–3, 175–7, 179–81, 196, 208, 211–12, 223, 227, 235
Gorbunovs, Antatolijs 206
Gosagroprom 71
Gospriyomka 171
Gottwald, Klement 57–8
governments, provisional and coalition 13
Great Patriotic War 11
Greece 11–12, 36
Grossu, Semyon 241–2
Grósz, Károly 104–5
Groza, Petru 128
Gysi, Grego 87–8

H

Hager, Kurt 78, 86
Hahn, Mayor Heinz 82
Haretski, R. 218
Havel, President Václav 22, 33, 62–8, 70
Helsinki Watch 142
Hempel, Bishop Johannes 81–2
Herger, Wolfgang 86
Herrman, Joachim 85
Heydrich, assassination of Reinhard 55
Heym, Stefan 82
Hitler, Adolf 10–11
-Stalin Pact 8
Holzer, Professor 116
Honecker, Erich 28, 75–82, 84–5, 87, 91, 131
Höpcke, Klaus 82
Horthy, Miklos 92
Horyn, Mikhailo 228
Hosking, Professor Geoffrey 187
Hoxha, Enver 38–40
death of 41
Hungary 12–14, 92–108
aid for 31
Alliance of Free Democrats in 103, 105
central planning in 98–9
change in 27
Christian Democracy in 107
coalition in 107
Communist Party in 92–5, 97–8, 102, 106–8
rule in 7, 105, 107
demonstrations in 94
depoliticizing society in 95–6
elections in 14–15, 30, 94, 102, 107
Factory Guard 107
foreign debt in 99
Free Democrats in 107
intellectuals and intelligentsia in 96–8
investment interest in 31
Kádár regime in 92–7, 100–1
the fall of 104–6
legitimacy in 98–9
Marxist-Leninist orthodoxy in 99
-Leninist party in 98
media in 101
New Economic Mechanism in (NEM) 98–102

Hungary – *cont.*
  one-party pluralism 102
  opposition rivalries in 103–4
  Party Reformers in 102–3
  People's Front for Independence in 94
  populists in 102
  Red Army in 92, 94
  Rising in 24
  size of 9
  Smallholders and Social Democrats in 105
    Party (KGP) 94
  Social Contract 102–3
  Soviet interest in 11
    Union's relationship with 97
  Stalinist elements in 94–5
  Turning-point and Reform 101
  uprising (1956) 20
  Workers' Councils in 95
  Writers' Union Congress in 101
Hungarian Democratic Forum 102, 105, 107
  Socialist Party 107
Husak, Gustav 61, 63, 66, 69

I

Iliescu, President Ion 133–6, 142
IMF, membership of 32
Iron curtain, descent of the 15
Islam, identification with 179
Ivans, Dainis 203–4
Ivashkevich, V. 219
Ivashko, Volodymyr 227–9, 231

J

Jakeš, Milos 63–4, 66
Janicki, Czeslaw 121
Japan, war against 11
Jaruzelski, General Wojcich 27, 114–16, 118–19, 124
John Paul II, election of 113
Jurgens, Aigars 206

K

Kádár, Janos 27, 84, 92, 94, 100, 102, 104–6
Kállai, Gyula 92
Kania, Stanislaw 114
Karabakh Committee 177
Kazakh Party, the 178
Kazakhstan 178
Kelam, Tunne 200
Kennan, George 55
Khrushchev, Nikita 22, 24, 39, 40, 112, 167, 170, 201
Kichkailo, A. T. 218
Kiesinger, Chancellor Kurt 25
Kirgizia 178
Kiszcsak, General Czeslaw 117, 119
Klaus, Vaclav 69
Klebanov, Vladimir 229
Klímová, Rita 66
Kohl, Chancellor Helmut 90, 122
Kohout, Pavel 61
Komárek, Valtr 68
Kondrusewicz, Father Tadeusz 220
KOR (Poland) 26
Kostov, Trajcho 18

Kozlodui 51
Krack, Mayor Erhard 81
Krawchuk, Leonid 229
Kremikovtsi 51
Kremlin leadership, radical policy changes by 23
Krenz, Egon 28–9, 81–2, 85–6, 87, 89, 91
Kronstadt Naval base, revolt in the 167
Kulaks 186–7, 189
Kun, Bela 9, 92
Kuron, Kacek 113
Kursk, victory of 11
Kustar 187

L

Lada cars 174
Landsbergis, Vytautas 209, 211
Lange, Bernd Lutz 80
Lassig, Jochen 83
latovichi 201
Latvia 8–9, 194, 201–7
  Communist Party of 201
  demonstrations in 203
  elections in 204, 206
  EPC (Environmental Protection Club) 201, 203
  Helsinki Accords 201
  multi-party system in 206
  NIML (National Independence Movement of Latvia) 203–4
  PF (Popular Front) in 203–6
  Russification of 201
  Writers' Union in 203
Latvian Association, American 204
Lederer, Jiří 63
Leich, Bishop Walter 81, 85
Leipziger Volkszeitung 83
Lenin, V. I. U. 9
Leninist model of socialism 167
Ligachev, Yegor 172
Lilov, Alexandur 49
Lishtvan, I. 218
Literetura un Maksla 204
Literatura si arta 241
Lithuania 8, 194, 208–11
  Chernobyl anxiety in 208
  Communist Party of 209–10
  constitutional amendment in 210
  economic blockade of 211, 213
  Gorbachev's visit to 179
  LFL (Lithuanian Freedom League) 208
  multi-party system in 210
  religious dissent in 208
  Sajudis 209–12
Lloyd-Roberts, Sue 42
Loukanov, Andrei 49
Lubeck 8
Luchinsky, Pyotr 242
Luxembourg, Rosa 122
Lwow 12

M

Maizière, Lothar de 88, 90
Malinsky, General 239
Mandelshtam 168
Manescu, Manea 132
Maniu 127
Mao Tse-tung, 'Cultural Revolution' of 40

Maksimov, Lev 218
Markov, Georgi 23
Marković, Ante 156, 162
Marshall Plan, the 16, 18
Marx, Karl 9
Marxian idea of the future 97
Marxism 20–1
 -Leninism 20, 59, 97, 146, 179
Marxist ideology, collapse in belief in 30
 -Leninist dogma 80
  ideology 190, 192
  social and economic revolution 167
  socialism 97
Masherov, P. M. 217
Masur, Kurt 80, 82–3
Masaryk, Jan 58
Masaryk, Tomas 53, 55, 67
Mazilu, Dumitru 133, 134
Mazowiecki, Tadeusz 119, 121–4
Meskhetian Turks, the 178
Messner, Zbigniew 117
Meyerhold 168
Michael, King 127–8, 141
Michnik, Adam 21, 113, 118–19
Middle East, the 176
Mielke, Erich 86
Mikolajczyk, Stanislaw 112, 123
Militaru, General Nicolae 134
Milošević, Slobodan 152, 153, 163
Mindszenty, Cardinal 17
mir 187
Mittag, Gunter 76, 85
Mladenov, Petur 29, 47, 49
Mlynář, Zdenek 61
Modrow, Hans 77, 86–9
Moldavia 237–43
 AMR (Autonomous Moldavian Republic)
  237
 demostrations in 242
 economic reform in 240–42
 elections in 243
 historical background of 237, 239
 language reform in 240
 MCP (Moldavian Communist Party) 239–40
 migration within and outside 240
 nationalist feelings in 176
 Popular Front in 241–3
 reunion with Romania 242–3
 Russian minorities in 180
 Russification of 240
 Soviet Socialist Republic of 237, 239
 urbanization of 240
 Yedinstvo 243
Mongolian People's Republic 10
Moravia, German Protecterate of 55
Moscow 172, 180
 Agreement 56
 and Albania, tension between 40
  Yugoslavia, reconcilliation between 39
 Armenian's attitude to 178
 authority of 177
 pressure from 7
 propaganda by 19
 relaxation of control from 176
 rule 9
Munteanu, Aurel Dragos 134
Muslim Azerbaidjans 178
 religion 178

Turks 178
Mussolini, Benito, annexation of Italy by
 36

N

Nagornyi-Karabakh, Armenian enclave of 177–8
Nagy, Imre 20, 24, 92, 94–5, 104, 106
Najder, Zdzislaw 23
Narodna hazeta 229
Nasă Reč 155
NATO 19
 birth of 73
 united Germany remaining in 32
Nazi coalition, anti- 11
Nazism, defeat of 11
Němec, Jiří 61
NEP 167, 173
Neues Deutschland 77, 81, 89
Nixon, President Richard 129
NKVD forces 13
nomenklatura 22–3, 41, 49, 123, 152, 219
Non-Aligned Movement 160
Novotny, Antonin 59

O

Odessa 174
OECD, membership of 32
Opletal, Jan 65
Orthodox Church, campaign against the 171
Ostpolitik 25

P

Pact, Atlantic 17
 Balkan 20
 Hungary's withdrawal from 24
 Molotov-Ribbentrop (MRP) 194, 196, 208, 212
 Mutual Assistance 208
 Nazi-Soviet 10, 12, 109, 111, 216, 237
 troops in Czechoslovakia, Warsaw 24
 Warsaw 17, 19–20, 27, 32, 64, 94, 100, 119, 121,
  131
Pacts, creation of Eastern bloc 20
Palach, Jan 60, 64
Palffy, Attila 138
Pamyat 166, 180, 190
Pavlychko, Dymtro 232
Pazniak, Z. 219
Pelse, Arvids 200
perestroika 41, 75, 77, 86, 131, 159, 171–2, 181,
 187–8, 190, 195, 198, 208, 210–11, 223, 233, 242
Peters, Janis 201
Petkov, Nikola 45
Petrograd, revolt of sailors and workers in 167
Pflugbeil, Sebastian 88
Pisudski, Marshall Jozef 109
Poland 12–13, 17, 109–124, 180
 aid for 31
 change in 27
 Citizens' Committee 117
 Communist regime in 7, 25, 111–12
 consultations begin in 117–18
 constitution of 120, 124
 deferment of debts in 122
 economic failure of 113
  prospects of 122

Poland – *cont.*
  reform in 115
  sanctions on 114–15
  elections in 14–15, 118–19, 123
  foreign relations in 121
  future of 122
  Gdansk 113–14
  Greens in 123
  Hitler's attack on 10
  IMF loans to 120
  International relations in 121
  Lublin Committee 111
  martial law in 25
  Military Council of National Salvation (WRON) 115
  Monarchists in 123
  National Assembly 118
  Party Plenum (1979) 113
  Peasant Party (PSL) 123
  plebiscite in Soviet-occupied 12
  political transformation in 109
  population of 9
  postwar 111
  prewar 109–11
  Provisional Government of National Unity 112
  Red Army in 111
  reforms in 120–21
  religion in 111
  Rzeczpospolita polska 120
  SD 118–19
  SDU 122
  Sejm 117–18
  Solidarity 113–19, 123–4
  Stalin's policies in 111–12
  unification of peasant factions in 123
  Warsaw rising 12, 109, 111
  Workers' Defence Committee (KOR) 113
  ZLP 118
  ZSL 119
Polish Baltic Coast, unrest along 25
  Censor, Black Book of the 23
  Communist Party 111
  Home Army 12
  October uprising (1956) 24
  Republic, Social Democratic Party of the 122
  United Workers Party (PUWP) 111, 118–19, 122
Politburo, the 23, 28, 171
Polityka 116–7
Pope, attempted murder of the 45
Popieluszko, Father Jerry 115
Popov, Gavriil 172
'Potemkin villages', the twentieth century 167
Pozsgay, Imre 27, 103, 105
propaganda and terror, use of 13
Prunskiene, Mrs K. 210–11
Pyjas, Stanilaw 113

R

Rabotnichesko Delo 45, 49
radio stations, jamming of 23
Rakowski, Matyas 92, 94
Rákowsi, Mieczyslaw 117, 120
Rajk, Laszlo 18, 92
Rasputin, Valentin 187
Rauchfuss, Wolfgang 86
Reagan, President Ronald 26
Red Army, the 9–10, 12–13, 127, 168

Reich, Jens 88
Reiche, Steffan 88
Renner, Hans 58
Revolution, bicentenary celebrations of French 7
  'October' 9
  Russian 175
revolutions, aftermath of 30
  (1989) 7
Roberts, Sir Frank 15
Roman, Petre 133, 134–5
Romania 9–10, 12, 125–143
  Allied (Soviet) Control Commission in 127
  Ceauşescu's legacy in 135–8
  Common Market trading status in 129
  Communist rule in 7
  Council of the Front 133
  demonstrations in 29, 130–3, 138
  economic decline in 129
    problems of 135–8
    self-reliance in 128
  elections in 30, 128, 135–6, 142
  ethnic differences in 138–9
  food shortages in 137
  foreign debt in 129
    relations in 128–9
  Front for National Salvation (NSF) 132–5, 140
  -GATT membership 129
  Hungarian Democratic Union 140–1
  -IMF membership 129
  instability in 141
  involvement with Germany 125–6
  National Front in 142–3
    Liberal Party of 140–1
    Peasant Party of 140–2
  nationalism in 138–43
  -Paris Peace Settlement 125
  Party Congress 131
  political problems of 135
  postwar period in 128–9
  private enterprise in 137
  Provisional Council for National Unity (PCNU) 133–4
  reforms in 130
  revolution against Ceauşescu 131–2
  Russians in 127
  Soviet interest in 11
  Stalinist policies in 130
  systemization policy in 131, 136
  Vatra Românească 139–40
  -World Bank membership 129
Romanian People's Republic 128
  Workers' Party 128
Roosevelt, President T. 11
Rousé, poisoning of Bulgarian city of 45
RSFSR (Russian Soviet Federated Socialist Republic) *see Russia*
Rudé Právo 58, 64
Russia, attacks on Jews in 180
  Bolsheviks in 184, 192
  budget deficit in 189
  Communist Party in 190
    rule in 187
  co-operatives in 189
  Democratic 191
  DS (Democratic Union) 191
  economic reform in 188–9
    strength of 184
  elections in 190

Russia – *cont.*
geography and economy in 182–6
historical view of 186–8
Inter-Regional Group in 191
national identity of 186–8
nationalism in 192
New Economic Policy (NEP) 184, 189
OFT (United Front of Workers) in 190
organizations in 189–92
political choices in 189–92
culture in 187
religion in 187
Siberian rivers project in 187
Soviet Federated Socialist Republic (RSFSR) 8, 182, 187–8, 190–1
Russian Empire, the 176
history 167
Ryzhkov, Nikolai 175

S

Sacher, Richard 68–9
Sakharov, Andrei 191
samizdat literature 190
Savisaar, Edgar 190, 201
Schabowski, Gunter 71, 81–2, 88
Schalck-Golodkowski, Alexander 77
Schnur, Wolfgang 88, 90
Schürer, Gerhard 86
Schwanitz, Wolfgang 86
SDI programme 171–2
Seidel, Mayor Bernd 81–2
self-determination, calls for 8
Shabashniki 187
Shcherbytsky, Volodymyr 227, 229
Shelest, Petro 227
Shkodër, disturbances in 42
Sigurimi 38–9
Skubiszewski, Krzysztof 220
Slánský, Rudolph 58, 66
Snips, Arturs 203
Sokolov, E. E. 217, 219, 223
Solidarity 25, 27, 62–3
Solzhenitsyn, A. 168
Soviet agricultural workforce 173
-Albanian alliance 40
-Armenia 178
army, the 179
bloc, Communist states of the 7
nations, military alliance of 19
regimes, toppling of 65
borders, Communist regimes outside 8
Central Committee plenum (the January 1990) 175
-Chinese ideological dispute 40
citizens, conditions of ordinary 181
diplomacy 171
East European satellites, the 172
economic reform 175
economy, the 173
exports 174
GNP 170, 174
leadership, break-up of the 23
policy, characterizing principles of 27
propaganda 168
-Romanian armistice 127
Russia's links with Germany 10
states established after World War II 8

tourism 175
trade with Britain 174
with West Germany 174
Union, the 11–12
1978 amendments to the constitution of the 179
— an anachronism? 167
Christian and Islamic cultures in the 175
economic system in the 176
economy of the 168
European republics of the 8
export restrictions, lifting of 31
food supply in the 175
foreign trade and the 174
future of the 181, 186
inter-ethnic conflict in the 180
international reputation of the 172
market economy in the 180
nationalities question in the 176
private enterprise in the 175
reform in the 179
World War II casualties of the 11
Stalin, Josef 10–12, 14–15, 17, 38–9, 71, 167–8, 171–2, 179
death of 24, 39, 94, 167, 173
Khrushchev's denunciation of 24, 40
Stalin's legacy, continuing 35
Stalingrad, victory of 11
Stalinism, intellectuals and intelligentsia under 97
Stalinist revolution, the 73
Stamboliiski, Alexander 43
Stanculescu, Colonel-General Victor 136
'Stars Wars' programme, America's 27, 171
Steins, Valdis 205
Stepan, Miroslav 66
Stettin (Szczecin) 12, 15
Stolypin, Pyotr 184
Stoph, Willi 86
Subranie 48–9, 51
subversion, intrigue and bribery, use of 14
Sumgait, murder of Armenians in 177
Summit Meetings, Geneva (1955) 19
35-nation 33
Washington 32
Suto, Andras 141
Svoboda, General 60
Szalasi, Ferenc 92

T

Tadzhikistan 178
tanzimat 159
Tbilisi 176
terror, 1947 campaign of 15
Tevija 201
Tiananmen-style solution 176
Times, The 7, 29
Tisch, Harry 77, 86
Tito, J. P. 13, 17, 38, 40, 112, 145–6, 149, 152–5, 160–1
Tolbukhin, General 239
Tokes, Pastor Laszlo 131
Transcaucasia 8, 176–7
Treaty, Berlin (1878) 43
Bulgaria 25
Comecon 32
Czechoslovakia 25
East German 25

Treaty – *cont.*
  Hungary 25
  Trianon (1920) 92
  Versailles 10
  Warsaw (1970) 25
Treaties, Soviet bloc 32
Trieste 8, 15
Trotsky, Leon 168
Trud 85
Truman Doctrine, the 15–16
Tsarist regime, the 167
Tsars, multinational empire of the 10
Tudjman, General 163
Tukhachevskii, Marshal M. N. 168
Turkey 178–9
Turkmenia 178

U

Ulbricht, Walter 73, 75, 87
Ullman, Wolfgang 89
Ukraine, the 8–9, 224–6
  Chernobyl disaster in the 227, 234
  CPU (Communist Party of the Ukraine) 227–9,
    231–3, 235
  Democratic bloc in the 231–2
  Donbas Union of Workers in the 229–30
  economic crisis in the 232–6
  elections in the 227, 230, 232
  environment in the 232–6
  history of the 223, 226–7
  Horlivka Workers' Union 230
  independence in the 235
  independent workers' movement 229
  major issues in the 232–6
  nationalist feelings in the 176
  political forces in the 227–30
  Rukh (Popular Movement of Ukraine for
    Restructuring) 227–35
  sovereignty of the 234–6
  Treaty of Union 233, 235
  Yednist (Unity) in the 230
Ukrainian Helsinki Union 228
  SSR, population of the 9
UN Economic Commission for Europe 31
Urbanek, Karel 66
USSR (Union of Soviet Socialist Republics) 10
Uzbec Popular Front (Birlik) 178
Uzebekistan 178–9

V

Vacietis, Ojars 201
Vagris, Janis 204
Valjas, Vaino 198–9
Vassiliev, Dmitrii 191
Vienna Award 127
Vladivostok 9
Volkskammer 88
Voss, Augusts 201

W

Wałesa, Lech 25, 113–19, 123–4
Warsaw Treaty Organization (*see* Pact, *Warsaw*)

Wilczek, Mieczyslaw 117
Wilno (Vilnius) 12
Wojtyla, Cardinal (*see John Paul II*)
Wolf, Christa 82
Wyszynski, Cardinal 17

X

Xoxe, Koci 38–9

Y

Yakovlev, Aleksander 105, 211–12
Yao Yilin 81
Yavorivsky, Volodymyr 231
Yeltsin, Boris 171, 191, 201
Yugoslav federation 38
Yugoslavia 8, 144, 164
  aid from the West to 160
  Axis 147, 151, 161
  Balkanization of 144, 150, 161–2
  Communist ideology, demise of 157,
    163
    Party of 144–5, 147–8, 160
    regime in 161–2
  Communists in 152–4, 156
  confederation of territories 149
  Congress, Fourteenth 158–61
  constitution of 149–51, 155
  Democratic Alliance of Kosovo 158
    Alternative 155
  economy of 155–7
  elections in 30, 162–4
  ethnic-religions communities in 9, 161
  federalism and nationalism in 148
  financial market, integrated 155, 159
  Kosovo, situation in 153
  Marxist-Leninist groups in 158
  Mikulic government, resignation of 152
  multi-party system in 157–8
  People's Liberation Struggle in 144–6
  Postscript: an open question 162–4
  postwar 146–7
  self-determination in 162
  Serbs and Croats in 146–7, 150, 152
  SKJ (League of Communists) 144, 149, 151,
    157–9
  Socialism, road to 155
  Socialist Alliance in 158–9
    Federal Republic of 161
  Soviet interest in 11
  Stalinist system in 150
  Tito's legacy in 150–5
  United Democratic Initiative in 158

Z

zemstva 186
Zhdanov Doctrine 16
Zhivkov, Todor 29, 45–6, 49
Ziedonis, Imants 201
Zimmermann, Pastor Peter 80
Zinoviev, G. 168
Zog, King (*see Zogu, Ahmet*)
Zogu, Ahmet 36